Clowns in the Burying Ground

STUDIES IN THE GRATEFUL DEAD
A series edited by Nicholas G. Meriwether

Clowns in the Burying Ground

THE GRATEFUL DEAD,
LITERATURE, *and*
THE LIMITS *of* PHILOSOPHY

Christopher K. Coffman

DUKE UNIVERSITY PRESS
Durham and London 2026

© 2026 DUKE UNIVERSITY PRESS. All rights reserved
Project Editor: Lisa Lawley
Designed by Courtney Leigh Richardson
Typeset in Warnock Pro and Queens Compressed by
Westchester Publishing Services

Library of Congress Cataloging-in-Publication Data
Names: Coffman, Christopher K., author.
Title: Clowns in the burying ground : the Grateful Dead, literature, and the limits of philosophy / Christopher K. Coffman.
Other titles: Studies in the Grateful Dead (Duke University Press)
Description: Durham : Duke University Press, 2026. | Series: Studies in the Grateful Dead | Includes bibliographical references and index.
Identifiers: LCCN 2025024299 (print)
LCCN 2025024300 (ebook)
ISBN 9781478033202 (paperback)
ISBN 9781478029748 (hardcover)
ISBN 9781478061939 (ebook)
Subjects: LCSH: Grateful Dead (Musical group) | Rock music—History and criticism. |
Modernism (Literature)—Influence. | Rock music—Texts.
Classification: LCC ML3534.3 .C64 2026 (print) | LCC ML3534.3 (ebook)
LC record available at https://lccn.loc.gov/2025024299
LC ebook record available at https://lccn.loc.gov/2025024300

Cover art: Composite adapted from Adobe Stock contributors erkan, ascrea, and valyalkin.

For Kathleen

And for Beckett, Dashiell, and Sidney

If I had the world to give...

Let the words be yours

Contents

	NOTE ON SOURCES	ix
	INTRODUCTION: Beyond Description Art at the Limit	1
1	THAT'S WHEN IT ALL BEGAN Beat Literature, Future-Founding Poetry, and the Grateful Dead	35
2	JUST LIKE MARY SHELLEY The Gothic Tradition, the American Past, and the Grateful Dead	64
3	PERCHANCE TO DREAM Ovid, William Shakespeare, and the Grateful Dead	97
4	ON THE HEELS OF RIMBAUD Bob Dylan, the Grateful Dead, and the Nature of the Literary	121
5	LIKE AN ANGEL James Joyce, Rainer Maria Rilke, and Robert Hunter's Modernist Inheritance	155
	CONCLUSION: All That's Still Unsung	197

ACKNOWLEDGMENTS	211
NOTES	213
BIBLIOGRAPHY	229
INDEX	243

Note on Sources

I follow, throughout this book, the titles and lyrics of Grateful Dead songs as presented in Alan Trist and David Dodd's *The Complete Annotated Grateful Dead Lyrics*. Rather than cite each lyric individually, I rely on their collection as the authoritative source. Fans of the Grateful Dead will know that there are some variations between sung lyrics and published lyrics, and also between the Trist and Dodd collection and other reliable sources for lyrics such as Robert Hunter's *A Box of Rain*. I believe Trist and Dodd provide a consistency and authority that strikes the best balance among competing versions of the lyrics and titles.

Dates, locations, and setlists of most Grateful Dead concerts are generally well documented. Nevertheless, the records of some performances, especially in the band's early years, are more obscure and not infrequently incomplete. I have relied on *DeadBase 50*, compiled and edited by John W. Scott, Stuart Nixon, and Michael Dolgushkin, for all information of this sort.

Bob Dylan's career is much entangled with that of the Grateful Dead. He changes the lyrics to many of his songs, sometimes substantially, in performance. In the interest of achieving some level of consistency, and rather than cite each of his lyrics individually, I rely on Dylan's official website (https://www.bobdylan.com/songs/) as the authoritative source for his song lyrics.

Introduction
BEYOND DESCRIPTION:
ART AT THE LIMIT

A central contention of this book is that the Grateful Dead engaged the literary tradition to a degree that is woefully underrecognized. A corollary argument is that the literary tradition provided the band with terms to articulate, and to interrogate, the concerns and challenges it faced at various points in its career. The band's participation in this tradition took many forms. In terms of social history, the band was friendly, and sometimes shared the stage, with a number of contemporary poets and novelists. Too, individual band members frequently expressed interest in particular texts and authors. Likewise, many notable authors wrote about the band, with a greater or lesser degree of appreciation, not infrequently acknowledging the inspiration the Grateful Dead's music and lyrics provided. Perhaps more important than these personal ties and predilections are the many intertextual connections between the literary canon and Grateful Dead song lyrics. At one fairly superficial level, these connections were expressed via allusion—the lyrics of the songs adopted images, motifs, and expressions from a wide array of texts. Yet, more complex varieties of intertextuality are evident in the lyrics as well, including the inflections of particular genres and modes of literary expression and the perspectives and conventions defined by the governing assumptions of one or another literary movement or era. While all the aforementioned aspects of the Grateful Dead's literary identity will be treated more extensively in the following chapters, this introduction considers an even more fundamental connection between the Grateful Dead and literature: the degree to which its lyrics engage certain problems in philosophical aesthetics that have been central to the Western tradition for almost the entirety of the modern era.

Courting the Fragment

An entrance to the Grateful Dead's engagement with some of the foundational problems of philosophical aesthetics can be found in remarks by band members themselves on the lyrical and musical elements of their compositions. Guitarist Jerry Garcia often remarked on his fondness for fragmentary song lyrics—ones that fall somewhere short of exhaustive conceptual completion or narrative conclusion. In a 1987 interview, for example, Garcia reflected on the contrast between lyricist Robert Hunter's original version of "Terrapin Station" and the one recorded and performed by the Grateful Dead: "He's got one version [that] has a beautiful conclusion, where everything comes together finally in the end. I prefer the open—you don't know what happened, we don't know what happened. . . . It's like the storyteller makes no choice—and neither do we. And neither do you, and neither does anybody else. I prefer that."[1] More than a decade earlier, Garcia articulated the point in more general terms:

> Personally, I have this hang-up about songs, I'm fascinated by fragments. I'm fascinated by fragments because of my involvement in traditional music, there's a lot of things around that are fragments of songs, old traditional songs, and there'll be like this tantalizing glimpse of two or three verses of what was originally a thirty-verse extravaganza, and there'll be like two or three remaining stanzas left in the tradition, that you read them or hear them and they're just utterly mysterious and evocative, for odd reasons. . . . I like for a song to be speaking to the mysterious. . . . I like songs that are more evocative than, say, thought-provoking or obvious.[2]

It is worth noting that Garcia does not display any desire to reach for the complete traditional song of which only a part still exists. His point is, instead, that while a few lines or verses of an old song may have first been merely part of a whole, the independent presentations of those lines or verses have, over time, taken on new value. Furthermore, the significance that the surviving part of an earlier composition had in its original context seems less remarkable, to Garcia, than the "fragments" that have persisted and consequently become "utterly mysterious and evocative." Similar assessments of the appeal to the Grateful Dead of a song that enjoys a fullness and coherence in its incompletion and narrative disjunction appear in a number of Garcia's and Hunter's other remarks.[3] Intriguingly, Garcia's assertions that the fragmentary nature of those songs of which he is fondest provides their power are more than somewhat reminiscent of his and other band members' remarks on the nature of the musical compositions that accompany such lyrics.

Of the Grateful Dead's many compositions, "Dark Star" is viewed by both musicians and fans as particularly notable. The special acclaim reserved for this piece is succinctly expressed in David Shenk and Steve Silberman's *Skeleton Key*: "'Dark Star' is considered ... the ultimate ... song, but the word 'song' doesn't do it justice. [It] is more an approach, a platform for exploration, a gate swinging open to THE ZONE."[4] As these sentences assert, "Dark Star" is regarded as the Grateful Dead piece most open to musical adventurousness and most likely to deliver the magical, transformative experience that so many listeners sought when attending shows.[5] Yet, it would be a misunderstanding to hear the song as being so entirely different from other Grateful Dead compositions as to be in its own category—not because it is not necessarily exceptional in itself, but because it bleeds into performances of all the band's material. Garcia once made exactly this point, saying, "'Dark Star' is a little of everything we do, all the time. ... I mean, our whole second half is 'Dark Star,' you could say."[6] The "second half" to which Garcia here refers is the second set of the standard-format Grateful Dead concert, during which the band tended to pursue the more innovative and outré improvisational possibilities in its music.

While Garcia makes significant claims about what we might call the metaphysical dimensions of music, in asserting that "Dark Star" is everywhere, in "everything," and "all the time," Grateful Dead keyboardist Tom Constanten poses the notion in a sense that is perhaps even more profound, arguing, "'Dark Star' is going on all the time. It's going on right now. You don't begin it so much as enter it. You don't end it so much as leave it."[7] Bassist Phil Lesh made a similar point about the band's music in general, describing the phenomenon that occurs when everything is unfolding particularly well on stage as an opening to "the eternal moment ... where music really lives." He adds, "Music is about bringing eternity to time."[8] Lesh's perspective on the Grateful Dead's music, and Constanten's perspective on "Dark Star" in particular, frame its work as a receptiveness to a wellspring of musical possibility that exists outside the band. This understanding allows one to consider any performance of "Dark Star" (or any other Grateful Dead piece) as a portion of a much larger whole—a whole that resides in a seemingly eternal space to which the band has access, but which can only be partially exposed by individual performances. Together, Constanten's, Lesh's, and Garcia's comments propose that the Grateful Dead's music is situated within a framework that transcends and contextualizes the music played by the band on a given night. From this perspective, each performance by the band is the result of the musicians' exploration of the limits of this framework and provides musicians and listeners alike with glimpses of the transformation of the potential into the actual. Celebrating "Dark Star" as the composition that most strongly foregrounds the idea that a given performance is only an evocative fragment of a piece that exists on a grander scale is remarkably like Garcia's comments about the power of the lyric fragment. In the cases of both lyrics and musical compositions, the Grateful Dead's performances would seem to derive some of their power from the suggestion of truths that resist total incorporation or expression within the bounds of a single piece, as offered on a given night.

Furthermore, one could approach the band's performances, beyond the specific nature of the lyrics sung or the music played, in terms of a similar model of parts evoking a greater whole. Whatever their individual strengths or shortcomings, on one night or across their careers, band members often described the Grateful Dead as much greater than the sum of its parts. One articulation of this dimension of the band's identity comes from Lesh, who points to the vision of "group mind" provided in Theodore Sturgeon's 1953 novel *More Than Human*. In that text, as Lesh explains, "the protagonists each have a single paranormal talent . . . and are joined by a quadruple paraplegic who acts as a central processing unit. The process by which they become one is called 'bleshing,' from a combination of *mesh* and *blend*."[9] In a 1991 interview, Garcia makes a similar point, speaking of the individual members being subsumed by a "larger consciousness" when the band is at its best.[10]

That live performances by the Grateful Dead evoke something greater than the sum of individual contributions was sensed not only by the group, but by listeners as well. Bill Walker, who provided the cover art for the band's 1968 album *Anthem of the Sun*, writes:

> I recall back in the late 60s or early 70s that the "entity" which sometimes manifested itself at a Dead show, when the Band and the audience seemed to achieve a transcendent state of rapport and unity, was affectionately referred to as The Beast. This was believed to be a manifestation of the sum total of energies of the Band, the audience and the location. The music was the breath and pulse, the audience its life and animation and the place gave its form (i.e., if the show was inside it had a different form than if was happening outside). There was no individual identity, one was just another part of the breathing, dancing, singing organism—like just another cell in the organism contributing

your energy to its life, and the organism in turn nourished and animated you.[11]

What Walker calls "The Beast" would seem to be akin to what others call the "X-Factor" or "The Zone," a special component of the very best Grateful Dead performances that resists easy description. While the vagueness of some of the terms used to describe this ineffable phenomenon point to mystery and the importance of place in its realization and shaping, Walker's metaphor remains notable for its compatibility with the idea that whatever it is that emerges from the best Grateful Dead performances exists on a level that synthesizes and transcends setting, band, and audience. Others follow Walker in describing the power of the band's best nights as animate. Drummer Mickey Hart "has said 'the wolf walked' after certain sets," and famed mythographer Joseph Campbell regarded the synergy and ecstasy he observed at a Grateful Dead show as "Dionysus talking."[12] While the terminology and conception change somewhat from commentator to commentator, such remarks demonstrate that many in and around the band regard even the very best performances as only a portion of a much greater whole—one that, at least metaphorically, has a life of its own.

Garcia's comments on the evocative power of the lyric fragment, Constanten's, Lesh's, and Garcia's assertions that the performance of an individual Grateful Dead piece articulates only part of a whole composition that eludes coherent expression, and the band's and fans' conclusions that the performances by individual musicians are but one element in a much grander and more complex process together highlight the degree to which many central aspects of the Grateful Dead, as conceived abstractly and as realized in performance, are shaped by an evocative encounter signaled by varieties of incompletion. In recognizing the centrality of evocative incompletion to the Grateful Dead's work, one uncovers an important point at which its music intersects with a central concern of modern continental aesthetics—a concern that is fundamentally literary: the function of the fragment in expressing the limits of philosophy.

A Genealogy of the Literary-Philosophical Fragment

Few thinkers have done as much as Jean-Luc Nancy to articulate the import of the fragment for modern philosophy, and for this reason, some familiarity with his thought on this front is helpful. While Nancy has approached the philosophical value of the fragment from many perspectives across his career, his most important consideration may be that undertaken with Philippe Lacoue-Labarthe in their *The Literary Absolute*. An attempt to understand better Lacoue-Labarthe and Nancy's discussion of the fragment may be aided by a reminder regarding its philosophical genealogy, which arguably begins with the disruptive implications for the philosophical subject of Immanuel Kant's transcendental philosophy.[13] Prior to the eighteenth century, the subject was generally viewed as unitary and self-affirming—as, for example, in the Cartesian cogito. While the unsettling of the assumptions undergirding the pre-eighteenth-century subject was not among Kant's explicit intentions, it did grow out of his attempts to provide a more secure foundation for philosophical thought.[14] Kant's overturning of traditional understandings of the subject is tied to his arguments regarding the multiple faculties involved in the process of forming knowledge about the world—faculties he describes across the first part of the *Critique of Pure Reason* roughly as follows: Humans apprehend things in the world at a "sensible," or sensory, level (an "aesthetic" activity); the sensible is understood via a schematic judgment or evaluation of its content; and reason generates inferences based on these judgments (a "logical" activity). As this very brief summary suggests, Kant believes reason operates in the realm of Ideas, which are formed prior to, and thus remain independent of, the subject's experience of the sensible world. Consequently, Ideas cannot in themselves be represented sensibly, and the reasoning mind cannot consider things in the world directly, or at all, unless and until the sensible has been schematized by the imaginative work that makes them available to reason's conceptual and categorical principles.[15] So, our knowledge of the world is therefore of "phenomena," which is to say, of our representations of things; furthermore, while things in the world—or "noumena"—do exist, they are never knowable in themselves, but only as they have been subjected to those mental processes of representation that allow us to reason about them.[16] In short, Kant's philosophy proposes a gap between our knowledge of things in the world and the things themselves; while this gap can be bridged by certain perceptual and intellectual faculties, it can never be closed.

Kant further proposes that the subject, in order to consider itself, submits itself to a similar process of representation. It is made an object of intellectual attention by representing itself to itself, in a fashion akin to that process of representation that transforms noumena into phenomena. Too, like noumena, the subject as it is in itself remains finally unknowable to itself. So, in place of immanent self-knowledge, Kant's conception of the subject is that of one that encounters itself as a representation; that is to say, the understanding of the subject is eminently an aesthetic one. In conceiving the process of knowing the self on the same terms as the process of knowing the world, Kant sidesteps David Hume's proposal that the subject is little more than an epiphenomenon of empirical experience, while issuing a provocative challenge to pre-eighteenth-century conceptions of the subject. Lacoue-Labarthe and Nancy succinctly describe this challenge as a "hiatus introduced at the heart of the subject."[17] The limit to self-knowledge Kant's transcendental philosophy proposes has many implications, three of which are most worth mention. First, the Kantian subject is not unitary, but something more like an empty form. Second, the Kantian subject is not self-affirming, but rather serves as an indication of a profound uncertainty. Because reason encounters an approximation behind which the actual self remains unknown, one must acknowledge the impossibility of achieving the sort of complete understanding of the self on which an authoritative system of knowledge could be based. Finally, Kant's argument leaves somewhat unaddressed the intriguing problems of whence the material that the self employs in its self-representation comes and why the self is compelled to reflect on itself in the first place.

There are several possible responses to the problems that Kant's arguments seem to produce. One influential option is that of German Idealism, as realized in the writings of Friedrich Wilhelm Joseph von Schelling and G. W. F. Hegel, via Friedrich von Schiller and Johann Gottlieb Fichte, the latter of whom proceeds by turning away from those things in themselves that Kant suggests lie behind or beyond the phenomenal. In terms of the subject, Fichte articulates a position that is in some senses more Kantian than Kant's own arguments, defending the idea of a self-positing "I" that generates itself in an ongoing process of free invention.[18] Hegel later follows a similar course of argument in his *Science of Logic*.[19]

Another path forward, more pertinent here, is pointed out by early German Romanticism, which partially takes shape within and thus overlaps with Idealism, although it diverges from it in some important regards. Philosophical Romanticism, beyond the work of Johann Wolfgang von Goethe and Friedrich Schiller, reached its maturity in a circle that formed in Jena and produced the short-lived *Athenaeum*, a journal that ran to six issues between 1798 and 1800. The Schlegels—August Wilhelm, Caroline, Friedrich, and Dorothea— were at the center of this concern, but several other major poets and thinkers were brought into its orbit. The group thus also includes, among others, Novalis, Friedrich Hölderlin, Friedrich Schleiermacher, and, to a somewhat lesser degree, Fichte and Schelling. While significant differences could be observed between the position of the Romantics and the Idealism of Fichte, Schelling, and Hegel, the most germane here is the Romantic willingness to accept the possibility—indeed, the productive necessity—of incompletion: of a paradoxically unsystematic system that suggests the completion of philosophy outside of philosophy, or, perhaps more accurately, of the dissolution of the boundary between philosophy and a non-philosophical absolute (which is, for these thinkers, literature), that achieves something philosophy cannot. This conception of the absolute presents itself in the fragment, a form Lacoue-Labarthe and Nancy declare to be "the romantic genre *par excellence*."[20]

A central terminological point must be emphasized before unpacking more fully how the fragment performs the sort of extra-philosophical work the Romantics ascribe to it, for Lacoue-Labarthe and Nancy use "fragment" in a specific fashion. They take pains to establish that the Romantic fragment with which they are concerned is distinct from a *Bruchstück*. The latter, German term describes the residue of an irrecoverable ensemble, and therefore primarily highlights the act of breaking. For example, *Bruchstück* could be used to describe a shard of pottery that provokes us to mourn the destruction of the decorated vase of which it was a part, or a verse from a now-lost song that calls us to think about the failures of sense resulting from the gaps in the lyrical text. While the Romantic fragment is not, they continue, a *Bruchstück*, they also want to remind readers that it is not complete. It is not the pensée or maxim, instances of which are like fragments in their brevity, but unlike them because their concision promises an exhaustive and self-contained entirety of a sort that the fragment avoids. So, the Romantic fragment is neither a partial remainder of a lost whole nor a unitary artifact. Instead, it is "a determinate and deliberate statement" that both elides the "dispersion or the shattering" of a work (unlike the *Bruchstück*) and "involves an essential incompletion" (unlike the pensée or maxim).[21] Thus, the accidental or involuntary nature of fragmentation stages a "plurality" that is "the exergue of the total, infinite work."[22] The Romantic fragment therefore falls short of achieving entire unity, but gestures toward the inexhaustible processes that underlie creative powers in general. The significance of the literary and philosophical implications of this position demands a more developed articulation of Lacoue-Labarthe and Nancy's thought.

Nancy and Lacoue-Labarthe on the Literary-Philosophical Fragment

Nancy arrives at his interest in the Jena Romantics and his specific formulation of the nature of the literary-philosophical fragment due to a line of thought that challenges the validity of Kant's claims regarding the intellectual purity of philosophical inquiry. Nancy explains in *Logodaedalus* that Kant wants to secure the space of philosophical discourse by following the example of the conceptual purity of mathematics, which can offer its insights with remarkable precision.[23] In this way, Kant aligns philosophical language with the eminently rigorous presentation of mathematics, and he also relegates all non-philosophical uses of language to the inferior position of mere "literature." Yet, Nancy argues, Kant here makes an unsupported claim because the idea that the language of philosophy is somehow purer than the alternative implies the possibility of standing outside philosophical language to compare it to other kinds of writing—something one cannot do without hypocritically sacrificing the very position of philosophical purity one seeks to preserve. In this sense, the desire for philosophical precision reveals that what lies outside of philosophy is architectonic to and inaccessible within philosophy. Consequently, Nancy regards Kant's assertion that philosophical language enjoys an exceptional conceptual clarity as problematic, insofar as philosophical invention is, from the first, entangled with literary invention in general; while a philosophical rigor may be conceptually maintained within certain bounds, the explanation of that rigorous philosophy requires presentation in language that is not philosophical in itself. To put this even more succinctly, as soon as thought presents itself, it becomes something other than philosophical thought. Nancy concludes that the literary exists in balance with philosophy, for the legitimacy of Kant's attempt to articulate the autoproduction of philosophy has revealed its dependence on literature.

While Nancy's observation regarding the inconsistency of Kant's position is provocative, he was not the first to propose the interdependence of philosophy and literature: Lacoue-Labarthe and Nancy find agreeable predecessors (via the intermediaries of Maurice Blanchot and Friedrich Nietzsche) in the Jena Romantics. These thinkers certainly recognize those relations between philosophy and literature toward which Nancy's own thought leads. As Friedrich Schlegel concisely asserts in his critical fragment 115, "Poetry and philosophy should be made one."[24] For Lacoue-Labarthe and Nancy, this sort of claim declares a comfort with, and recognizes the importance of, exchanges between philosophical and non-philosophical expressions—as Kant's arguments did not. The claim also highlights the power of the literary as conceived by the Romantics, for whom "romanticism is neither mere 'literature' . . . nor simply a 'theory of literature.' . . . Rather, it is *theory itself as literature* or, in other words, literature producing itself as its own theory"; they continue, "The literary absolute is also, and perhaps above all, this absolute *literary operation*."[25] Lacoue-Labarthe and Nancy's point is that literature properly understood is both individual texts that unfold within certain bounds and also a set of tacit arguments about the nature of literature, the use of language, and the value of artistic expression in general. Literature is consequently an "absolute" because its individual works constantly engage questions about the nature of literature at a level that surpasses and contextualizes the nature of those individual works; just as, according to Nancy, literature surpasses and frames the language of philosophy. This absolute, then, is the point at which literary practice brushes up against philosophical thought. Here, literature is both philosophy and the limit of philosophy. It houses those intellectual spaces against which the narrowly philosophical defines itself by contrast, even as it operates via a more fundamental or encompassing authority.

Furthermore, the Jena Romantics' conception of literature as an "operation" positions the literary absolute not as a rigid border, but as a context responsive to that which it contains. Neither a static nor a stagnant entity, true literature is a productive, fluctuant, and adaptive process rather than a completed task. Friedrich Schlegel declares, in *Athenaeum* fragment 116, that the "particular essence" of poetry is "that it should forever be becoming and never be perfected."[26] Consequently, Lacoue-Labarthe and Nancy express philosophy and literature via the following formula: "*Work in progress* henceforth becomes the infinite truth of the work."[27] According to Lacoue-Labarthe and Nancy, this early Romantic prioritization of production, in contrast to product, indicates an attraction to "the essence of poiesy, in which the literary thing produces the truth of production itself, and thus ... the truth of the production *of itself*."[28] This shift away from an exclusive concern with the nature of the literary work as understood entirely within its own bounds favors expansion over contraction and creation over inanition. For Lacoue-Labarthe and Nancy, the "literary absolute" unites the finite and signals an unpresentable infinite. Literature is therefore a kind of production that tacitly articulates the terms of its own production, enacting what philosophical understanding cannot.

A final point that makes the Jena Romantics attractive to Nancy is their conception of the nature of the productive activity that characterizes literature. As Blanchot asserts, "literature" signals for the Romantics "the totality of forms of expression," and the term therefore includes not only the sort of obviously constructive activities one might expect to find when considering creative activity, but also the various related "forces of dissolution."[29] The Romantics thus make space for incompletion and discontinuity to be regarded as principles of form, rather than only as unproductive or disruptive forces.[30]

Blanchot's arguments find their predecessors in Friedrich Schlegel's writings, which recognize the necessity of an interchange between order and disorder that demands one rethink the distinction between creation and destruction. In fragment 1048, for instance, he proposes, "When the end is reached, it should start again from the beginning, alternating between chaos and system, chaos preparing for the system and then a new chaos."[31] Likewise, in his *On the Study of Greek Poetry*, he writes that the poetry of his era is marked by the inclusion of a certain kind of chaos: "a chaos of everything sublime, beautiful, and charming . . . like the Chaos of old out of which, according to legend, the world emerged."[32] Such are the ideas that lead Lacoue-Labarthe and Nancy to declare "chaos . . . the locus of possible generations, of potential production."[33] From this perspective, the creative work "is at once part and whole, in keeping with the fragmentary logic itself," as it "never ceases to assemble and disperse itself."[34]

The idea of destruction as an act of creation is hardly new. Mikhail Bakunin, not the first to make the point, might have articulated it most forcefully when he introduced it into the political sphere in 1842, declaring, "The passion for destruction is a creative passion, too!"[35] Yet, the Jena Romantics differ from Bakunin not only in their primary areas of intellectual interest, but also in the degree to which they emphasize the mystical role of the agent of creative destruction. Friedrich Schlegel, in his idea 131, writes, "To become an artist means nothing other than to consecrate oneself to the gods of the underworld. In the enthusiasm of annihilation, the meaning of divine creation is revealed for the first time." These sentences not only bridge the space between the death of the self and the emergence of truth but also precede, in Schlegel's text, a clause that anticipates the Grateful Dead's skull-and-lightning-bolt insignia, known to fans as a "Stealie": "Only in the midst of death does the lightning bolt of eternal life explode."[36]

In this way, the Jena Romantics, and Lacoue-Labarthe and Nancy after them, find in the fragment a means to move from a consideration of the limits of philosophy to meditations on the power of literature, and from reflections on creative activity to interrogations of the nature of the artist. They also move from these topics to a response to Kant's reformulation of the subject. Following the Romantics, Lacoue-Labarthe and Nancy describe the creative act as a process that proceeds from the artist's dedication of the self to death—the event via which the terms of creation are discovered. These terms are likewise those they ascribe to the subject in general, which does not find itself so much as it creates itself by means of a dance between dissolution and ambiguity on the one hand (with Lacoue-Labarthe and Nancy's model found in Novalis) and between shaping and systematization on the other (following a "Schlegelian path").[37] From their perspective, in other words, one's efforts to think about the nature of artistic activity are of a piece with thinking about other creative activities, including the creation of the self. As they write, "We ourselves are implicated in all that determines . . . literature as auto-critique and criticism as literature. Our own image comes back to us from the mirror of the literary absolute."[38]

The productive exchanges between creation and destruction that Nancy and the Jena Romantics discuss in relation to the subject are, in fact, anticipated somewhat in Kant, who adds yet another dimension to the point when he claims that the imagination works according to the terms of freedom.[39] One aspect of the subject's constituent freedom is a productive freedom-from, the security that celebrates nothingness as a space allowing presence; the other is a freedom-to, a liberty to organize experience into comprehensible representations. Hegel, too, affirms this understanding of the connection between freedom and the interplay of nothingness and creation, writing, "In its highest form . . . nothingness would be freedom. . . . This highest form is negativity insofar as it inwardly deepens itself to its highest intensity; and in this way it is itself affirmation."[40] Here, nothingness is a foundation of existence. Neither absent nor present, it is the necessary condition of creation, for it stages a playful tension out of which emerges that which exists. For Nancy, this necessity of freedom for thought is found at the shifting limit between the understood and the mysterious: "Every thinking is . . . a thinking about freedom at the same time that it thinks by freedom and thinks in freedom. It is no longer exactly a question here of the limit between the comprehensible and the incomprehensible. Or rather, what happens here in the free arising of thought, happens precisely on this limit, as the play or very operation of this limit. The limit of comprehending defines thinking. Thus thinking is always thinking about the incomprehensible—about this incomprehensible that 'belongs' to every comprehending, as its own limit."[41]

For these reasons, to produce a fragment—in Nancy's sense of the literary-philosophical fragment—is to court central mysteries that take shape in writing, at the limit of philosophy. The fragment is not only itself, but also a statement of the terms of its creation and the terms of creation in general. It figures artistic activity as well as the nature of the active subject, recalling the interplay between creation and destruction, and the freedom on which that exchange relies and from which it emerges.

Three Varieties of Incompletion: The Literary-Philosophical Fragment and the Lyrics of the Grateful Dead

As the preceding section of this introduction explains, the celebration of the fragment by Nancy and many of his predecessors in the Western philosophical tradition derives from their recognition that the fragment's incompletion signals something much grander than itself: the fundamental mysteries of creation—mysteries that stand at the limits of rational comprehension and define artistic activity and the self in terms of the interplay of destructive and productive forces. While each of the various forms of incompletion that characterize the concept of the Grateful Dead as a platform for creative exercise—including its appreciation of the evocative power of the lyrical fragment; the understanding that any one performance of a composition reveals only a part of its whole; and the sense that the contributions of one participant in a performance are relatively minor in comparison to the collective event engendered at the intersection of audience, musicians, and setting—lends itself to consideration in light of the literary-philosophical fragment, this book's interest in the literary valences of the Grateful Dead directs attention primarily to the manner in which its lyrics exemplify the several ways that it serves as a conduit for the creative and destructive energies at productive and endless play in the "eternal moment" to which the band and many listeners felt the ensemble offered access.

The chapters that follow this introduction explore the band's lyrics in relation to specific literary texts and contexts at key points across the Grateful Dead's career. In this section of the introduction, I undertake three preliminary interpretations in the interest of illustrating the viability of the approach used throughout. Each case touches on, in one or more senses, three arguments that will return in different forms throughout the succeeding chapters: first, that the lyrics of the most powerful Grateful Dead songs, in addition to doing whatever else they do, are always engaged in the ongoing critical project of teaching us how to listen to Grateful Dead songs; second, that the controlling idea of the band's best lyrics is found in "Terrapin Station," particularly Hunter's claim that a true storyteller's "job is to shed light / and not to master"; and, third, that Nancy's discussion of the literary-philosophical fragment provides an interpretive guide that can help us to understand better how Grateful Dead songs open themselves to self-reflection and productive inconclusions. These broad similarities aside, each of the following three readings foregrounds a different aspect of the evocative power of the fragment. The first, a reading of "Dupree's Diamond Blues," considers how the complex narrative form of that piece transforms sources transmitted by the folk music tradition into a critical commentary on the processes of that transmission. The second reading, which addresses "Let It Grow," focuses more explicitly on the literary tradition, particularly on how the songwriters have drawn on an ancient poetic genre to present the interplay between destruction and production that characterizes creation in general. The final interpretation below, of "Saint of Circumstance," approaches that song as a reflection on the sort of playful indeterminacy that, Nancy argues, reveals a vision of the self as born out of a meditation on freedom undertaken at the limit of thought.

"Dupree's Diamond Blues" allows listeners to see the degree to which Grateful Dead lyrics reshape traditional folk materials, both honoring their conventions and offering commentary on their reception and reinterpretation. The song also, especially in its handling of narrative form, calls listeners to engage in critical interpretation themselves. In other words, as much as the song reshapes a well-known folk story, it also acknowledges the complexity of that act, inviting listeners to consider its implications through metalyrical reflection. While this is a fair amount of work to accomplish within the bounds of a relatively short composition, Hunter and Garcia are helped by the strength of the piece's traditional origins. The song draws on the conventions of murder ballads, and particularly examples of the "bad man" subgenre written about the murderer Frank DuPre. The first of these compositions was recorded in 1925, only a few years after DuPre's death, and several others soon followed. The audio recordings were joined, as early as 1926, by print transcriptions of unrecorded folk pieces on the same topic. Several such songs, notably versions by such relatively well-regarded performers as Brownie McGhee (1955), Dave Van Ronk (1959), Harry Belafonte (1962), and Peter, Paul, and Mary (1965), appeared on records in the decade or so before the Grateful Dead offered its own versions.[42] In every case, the narrative follows the course of events in the last year or two of the killer's life. Those familiar with "Dupree's Diamond Blues" will recognize the skeleton of the historical tale. To secure the affection of Betty Andrews, DuPre undertook a desperate armed robbery of a jewelry store in Atlanta in 1921. In the process, he killed one man and badly wounded another. After a manhunt that spanned several states and garnered significant media attention, he was apprehended, tried, and sentenced to death by hanging, a punishment carried out in late 1922.[43]

"Dupree's Diamond Blues" was not the Grateful Dead's first engagement with the story of DuPre and its presentation in popular song. The band played a traditional piece devoted to the topic, "Betty and Dupree," at least twice in 1966. The first known performance of that song by the Grateful Dead is from a rehearsal session on March 2. The second known version is live, from the December 1 show at the Matrix in San Francisco. Furthermore, Nicholas Meriwether asserts that two of Garcia's pre–Grateful Dead folk music outfits, the Wildwood Boys and the Black Mountain Boys, featured the song in their coffeehouse-era performances.[44]

While the 1966 performances of "Betty and Dupree" are strong for the era, the DuPre piece that the Grateful Dead offered a few years later, "Dupree's Diamond Blues," persisted much longer as part of the band's repertoire. At least one account places the debut of this song in late 1968, but more likely contenders for the debut are January 20, 1969, during a studio session at Pacific Recording in San Mateo, and January 23, 1969, live at the Avalon Ballroom in San Francisco. A studio recording was released on the album *Aoxomoxoa* later that year. Following the first half of 1969, "Dupree's Diamond Blues" had an uneven performance history. It disappeared entirely for more than half a decade, reemerging with a handful of airings in 1977 and 1978, before winning a regular place in the rotation throughout most of the 1980s, and ultimately returning for two performances in the 1990s. Songs about DuPre were therefore in setlists from the very start, and they remained—particularly as "Dupree's Diamond Blues"—a somewhat inconsistent presence throughout the band's career.

An appreciation of the degree to which the Grateful Dead's "Dupree's Diamond Blues" both participates in the folk tradition and turns an acutely self-aware and critical eye on naive engagements with that tradition requires some consideration of its narrative structure. The arrangement of the song's lyrics is fairly simple. With one exception, the verses and chorus each have four lines, with end rhymes in a rough AABB pattern. The first three verses are followed by a chorus, that sequence is repeated, and the whole is capped by a final verse. What is more intriguing about "Dupree's Diamond Blues" than the structure of its verses and chorus are the shifting temporality and voicings of its narrative events. Consider some alternative approaches to the one Hunter uses. One option for the author of a popular song is to tell the tale entirely through a single diegetic or extradiegetic narrator.[45] An example of the former would be Ma Rainey's mid-1920s version of a Stagger Lee song, "Stack O' Lee Blues," which is told entirely from the perspective of the titular killer's girlfriend. Another song telling the Stagger Lee story, such as "Stackerlee," the 1947 Alan Lomax field recording of a singer named Bama at Parchman Farm, is slightly more complex. Primarily an instance of extradiegetic narration, it contains several passages that directly introduce the voices of Stackerlee and his victim, Billy Lyon. This inclusion of characters' voices provides a sense of immediacy and temporarily shifts the feel of the narrative in the direction of a first-person account, even though the song as a whole holds itself aloof from any single perspective in the world of the story.

Unlike many folk songs, those composed about DuPre were from the first more like Bama's approach to composing a Stagger Lee song, as is evident from examples included in Howard W. Odum and Guy B. Johnson's 1926 collection *Negro Workaday Songs*. One version transcribed therein, simply titled "Dupree," begins in the third person ("Dupree was a bandit . . .") but offers a number of verses largely given over to first-person voices, always introduced directly with a similar formula, as in "Betty tol' Dupree," "Dupree tol' the Lawyer," "The judge tol' Dupree," and so forth.[46] Another DuPre song Odum and Johnson include foregrounds the act of telling in its very title, "Dupree Tol' Betty." In this case, listeners encounter the voices of the characters involved from the song's start, and the third-person narrative voice vanishes almost entirely, having been reduced to a formulaic mechanism for the direct introduction of characters' speech.[47] These tendencies demonstrate that, unlike many other folk songs—even examples of the "bad man" genre, such as those about Stagger Lee—songs about DuPre (and Betty) were composed from the beginning with an impressive variety of voices, one of which was often that of a narrator. This is true as well of the first DuPre song played by the Grateful Dead, "Betty and Dupree," which introduces the voices of both titular characters and a narrator.

"Dupree's Diamond Blues," however, moves more quickly between a greater variety of narrative perspectives, voices, and time frames than we encounter in even the most complex of its predecessors in the folk tradition. The ambiguities engendered by that complexity cause the listener to experience something of the disorientation felt by the characters in the song, but they also foreground the degree to which the Grateful Dead resist offering merely another reiteration of the DuPre legend. Instead, the band injects a strong dose of uncertainty into its interpretation and, in doing so, maintains that inconclusion that Nancy regards as central to the nature of the fragment as a productive force. An appreciation of this inconclusion is evident in the complications of agency and action signaled by the third verse:

> Down to the jewelry store packing a gun,
> says, "Wrap it up, I think I'll take this one."
> "A thousand dollars, please," the jewelry man said
> Dupree, he said, "I'll pay this one off to you in lead."

Several noteworthy elements are evident here. One is the narrator's failure to introduce immediately the agents of the verse's initial actions. While the jewelry man is identified as speaking in line 3, it is not until the final line that listeners can confidently attribute the verse's other speech to Dupree.[48] Likewise, whoever serves as the subject for "down"—presumably a colloquialism for "went down," "goes down," or "is going down"—is obscure. The lack of initial identification of the actors and speakers in the verse creates temporary uncertainty in the listener, who is forced to suspend understanding on the point for at least a few bars.

A similar uncertainty in the identification of speakers and their actions obtains at the level of the song as whole. The song's narrator, introduced simply as "I" in the first line, begins the tale not by immersing the listener in it, but also by establishing several kinds of distance. One of these is the distance between the narration of the song in the present and the narrator's presentation of himself in his early youth (the song's initial line immediately returns listeners to the narrator's personal past, with "When I was just a little young boy"). The second distancing occurs when the speaker hands over the verse to the directly introduced voice of his "Papa," who offers the advice "Son, you'll never get far." The temporal distance between the narrator-in-present and the narrator-as-child, as well as the provisional handing over of authority to the narrator's "Papa," result in some confusion about the speaker of the second verse, which begins, "Well, baby, baby wants a gold diamond ring." Who speaks these words, and in what time frame are they being articulated? The father seems to have fallen silent, but, as the above remarks on the third verse make evident, we cannot be certain we have encountered the voice of Dupree. Consequently, the second verse possibly presents the thoughts of the song's initial, first-person narrator. So, while a listener familiar with the historical DuPre narrative may be inclined to conclude that the first voice in the song is the same as that of the second verse, and that both verses are being told from Dupree's perspective, the third verse's direct introduction of Dupree's speech suggests instead that the narrated thoughts of the second verse, which conclude, "When I get those jelly roll blues / . . . I'd go and get anything in this world for you," are, in fact, those of the song's initial speaker, who, like Dupree, is experiencing the powerful disorientation that comes with desire, and perhaps also contemplating the theft of a ring that could be used to secure his own Betty's affection.

Furthermore, the temporal confusion is reinforced by the third verse. Beyond the ambiguous tense of the colloquial verb form "down," listeners may register quick movements between present- and past-tense narration, from "says" in line 2 to "said" in line 4. Hunter has done something quite striking. The action described—Dupree stealing the ring from the jeweler—would transpire in moments, but the signals of narrative time for that action slide sharply between "then" and "now." That later verses consistently present the Dupree narrative in the past tense suggests that the "down" and "says" at the start of the third verse may have been actions of the narrator, and that the action of the song transitions into the Dupree narrative only in the middle of the third verse. Wherever one draws the line between narrator and Dupree, and between past and present, the verse's slippery narrative temporality creates a sense that time frames are collapsing, emphasizing the parallels between the narrator's situation and Dupree's.

These complexities extend across the remainder of the piece, preserving and reinforcing the sort of uncertainties that make fragments so productive. The chorus begins without any introduction of a speaker, but the formulaic opening "Well, you know, son . . ." recalls the address of "Papa" to the primary narrator at the start of the song, "Son, you'll never get far." The first verse and third verses after the initial chorus offer a return of Dupree's voice and are largely given over to his conversation with the "Judge," as introduced with the conventional syntax of "Judge said . . ." and "Dupree said . . ." The fifth verse stands out because it narrates events about Betty in a somewhat different form. The fourth line of the verse comprises only four short syllables, "then go on out," a strong contrast to the final line, which, like the closing lines of several other verses, requires that the singer rapidly deliver a lot of words (thirteen syllables' worth, in this instance). Thus, the contrast between the very short fourth line and the closing words, "and find another sweet man's gonna treat her with style," highlights the inconstancy of Betty, who not only does not mourn Dupree for very long, but also seems to be sleeping with the hanging judge ("Son, I know your baby well"). The final verse, which follows a repetition of the chorus, apparently returns us to the initial speaker and his reflections on Dupree's story.

Overall, the many shifts in narrative speaker and time frame in "Dupree's Diamond Blues" alternately distance the listener from, and draw the listener closer to, the events of the narrative, much in the fashion that the speaker of the song seems to be wavering between following in Dupree's footsteps and learning the lesson that the murderer's tale offers about the dangers of desire. So, while the Grateful Dead's contribution to the canon of songs about Frank DuPre follows the example of many predecessors in its inclusion of multiple voices, "Dupree's Diamond Blues" extends the possibilities of that trait to a radical degree, adding powerful ambiguities in narrative time and agency that universalize the DuPre story and subordinate it to another narrative—one that frames and, in some regards, mirrors that of the titular bad man. In this sense, it is not so much a song about DuPre as it is a parable illustrating the wisdom of the father's assertion that "you'll never get far." Hunter and Garcia would offer frame tales that function in similar ways in later years, as in the cases of "Wharf Rat" and "Terrapin Station."

Another way to contextualize what Hunter and Garcia have done in complexifying the tradition's relatively modest narrative structure is to approach the frame tale as a reflexive comment on the degree to which the Grateful Dead's present remains connected to the American musical past. New iterations of folk music, as Juniper Hill and Caroline Bithell argue, are typically understood to derive some of their power from the incorporation of sources deemed "authentic" within the context of a particular community.[49] The notion of authenticity can be so fraught, however, that it may be better to think of the musical past more in line with the terms proposed by Burt Feintuch, who conceives "*tradition* as a territory of the imagination rather than as a standard for some notion of authenticity."[50] From this perspective, Hunter and Garcia are not so much drawing on a pristine past that they have inherited, but instead exploring the territory of the imagination, opened when one ponders what the idea of a connection to the folk song tradition means for rock and roll bands in late 1960s California. Seen in this light, the song's initial speaker's reflections on the tale of Dupree—his effort to weigh his own desire's moral value against the lessons of the parable of Dupree—might be heard instead as the songwriters' meditation on the ways rock songwriters and musicians can learn from folk songs such as those about DuPre. We might therefore say that Hunter and Garcia do not so much give listeners a traditional song, but rather a version of tradition that recognizes that simply offering a narrative song about a familiar topic is not enough. "Dupree's Diamond Blues" is not only a song about DuPre, or about the initial speaker's thoughts about the moral value of Dupree's story, but also a critical commentary that calls listeners to reflect on how the musical past relates to the musical present.

To hear "Dupree's Diamond Blues" as a song about how new music is related to musical traditions brings reflection on the piece into territory amenable to Nancy's suggestion that the fragment's power is in part projective, anticipating and defining the terms of its own creation. For popular musics, the projective implications of a text are mediated by the folk tradition, which may lend a new performance the gravitas of authenticity, or, alternately, may bury the contemporary in the weight of the past. Hunter declared his

"Dupree" song one of his "studied efforts to continue the oral tradition"; but while Hunter emphasizes continuity with the past, Garcia's take on the piece is somewhat different, drawing attention to the contemporary context for the historical: "Hunter and I always had this thing where we liked to muddy the folk tradition by adding our own songs. . . . It's the thing of taking a well-founded tradition and putting in something that's totally looped."[51] So, while the Grateful Dead's "Dupree" is continuous with the past in some regards—including the attribution of the crime to the irresistible sweetness of "jelly roll," the formulaic direct introductions of a variety of speakers, and the generic expectations listeners bring to a bad man song—it is also a conscious effort to trouble the past, recognizing that the richest tales offer possibilities for their own realization that may stray from models that answer to the narrow standards of strict traditionalism.

If "Dupree's Diamond Blues" offers a model for engaging folk tradition while preserving and even foregrounding spaces for supplements to that tradition, other Grateful Dead lyrics explore the potential of other sorts of incompletion, ones no less entangled with traditions, but in this case, more conventionally literary. "Let It Grow," which is the second part of the longer composition "Weather Report Suite," enjoyed some longevity as an element of the Grateful Dead's performance repertoire. First aired in late summer 1973, it reappeared with regularity until the end of the band's career. The lyrics are a meditation on natural cycles and recount a revelatory encounter with divinity via the workings of the natural world. The degree to which "Let It Grow" focuses on the "work of men," such as hauling water, chopping wood, plowing fields, and planting and harvesting, as the "seasons round," allows one to recognize that the most direct literary predecessors to the song are the ancient and modern georgic poems. The term "georgic" derives from the influential example of Virgil's *Georgics*, which, like other poems of the type, describe human relations with the natural world, and especially such agricultural topics as caring for livestock, appreciating the plow and similar technologies, making wine, cultivating apiaries, and maintaining orchards. This genre is one of poetry's most persistent, informing countless works from the ancient world to those of such more recent poets as Robert Frost, Wendell Berry, and Gary Snyder.

Whatever the song's other inspirations, it is hard to deny the similarity between the lyrics of "Let It Grow" and some passages that appear early in the first of Virgil's *Georgics*. Here, for example, is Grateful Dead lyricist John Perry Barlow's fourth verse:

The plowman is broad as the back of the land he is sowing
As he dances the circular track of the plow ever knowing
That the work of his day measures more than the planting and
    growing
Let it grow, let it grow, greatly yield

And here are a few lines from Virgil:

The time has come for my groaning ox to drag
My heavy plow across the fields, so that
The plow blade shines as the furrow rubs against it.
Not till the earth has been twice plowed, so twice
Exposed to sun and twice to coolness will
It yield what the farmer prays for; then will the barn
Be full to bursting with the gathered grain.[52]

As one can see when excerpts like those above are set one after the other, Barlow's lyrics and Virgil's poetry share both topical and sonic similarities. In terms of the former, it is apparent that poem and song alike represent the farmer, the repetitive circularity of plowing, the sense that greater forces are invoked by honest labor, and the joy of a good harvest. Furthermore, Barlow also follows Virgil in his poetics. In the case of Virgil, as quoted above in David Ferry's translation, the repetition of words such as "twice" and "plow" across a handful of lines creates the sense of returning to the same place. In the original, the similar shaping and repetition of words and sibilants in two phrases that share the same line in this passage—"bis quae solem, bis frigora sensit"—establishes structural similarities between hot and cold, two states we generally think of as opposed rather than alike. That the sonic patterns are amenable to evocations of the psychological balance felt upon returning to the familiar, and to the parity between contraries, signals that the diverse topical elements are part of a unifying whole, one the plowman enacts as he comes around in his circle of labor. Barlow's lyric achieves something of the same effects with a variety of sonic strategies, including repetition ("growing / Let it grow, let it grow") and the reappearance of some key phonemes across the verse, as in the *gr-* of "growing" and "greatly," the *-owing* of the end rhymes ("sowing," "knowing," "growing") in the first three lines of the stanza, internal rhyme ("back" and "track"), and visual rhyme (the *-ow* of "plow" is sonically different from that of "sow," "know," and "grow," but it creates unity on the page). Like Virgil, then, Barlow finds in aural repetitions and variations a reflection of the meaning of the lyrics, enacting a wonderful instance of "the sound of sense," to borrow a phrase from Robert Frost.[53]

Because "Let It Grow" follows earlier examples of georgic poetry in its emphasis on the labor that defines our interactions with the earth, as well as the aptness of the cyclical to right living, it also participates in the genre's traditional recognition that even the humblest activities allow for the contemplation of moral considerations. Indeed, the genre typically presents agricultural work as a figurative lens for ethical comment, which is one of the reasons georgic poetry is usually considered more ambitious and rewarding than nature poems in the simpler, generally more static, and rougher traditions of the bucolic lyric or eclogue. The definitive georgic poem prior to Virgil is certainly Hesiod's *Works and Days*, which foregrounds the ethical via the speaker's declarations that the text intends to offer his less-than-scrupulous brother the knowledge necessary to earn an honest living. Because the speaker seeks to mount as many justifications for his advice as possible, the narrowly agricultural content of *Works and Days* is supplemented with mythic evidence in the form of stories about Prometheus and Pandora, rhetorically resonant animal fables, and a meditation on necessity driven by a vision of human history as slowly declining in grandeur across five eras. Additional support for the arguments of *Works and Days* derives from occasional nods to Hesiod's other (grander) poem, the *Theogony*, one of the greatest sources of ancient myth, which make it evident that the rightness of particular courses of action has been established by the gods, who alternately reward and punish mortals for their choices.[54] In short, the agricultural labor featured in the typical georgic poem is not only tied to the cycles of the natural world, but also informed by ethical concerns.

"Let It Grow" thus follows earlier examples of the genre not only in its focus on the degree to which agricultural labor is definitive of human existence, but also in its placement of that labor in relation to the divine. Unlike Hesiod, Barlow somewhat resists naming the divinity that governs the action described. When the song asks, "What shall we say, shall we call it by a name?" the response is a conventional figure of pointlessness: "As well to count the angels dancing on a pin." As speech fails, however, a space for the emergence of truth opens, and the speaker of the song recognizes that "the name is on the earth." Finally, the heavens roar an answer to the question to which human speech was unequal:

> We will not speak but stand inside the rain
> And listen to the thunder shout
> I am, I am, I am, I am.

These closing lines are deeply indebted to a variety of prior texts. Most directly, they unite the climactic final section of T. S. Eliot's great Modernist poem *The Waste Land* with a biblical episode. In the case of Eliot's work, the equation of the divine voice with thunder derives from the example of the *Brihadaranyaka Upanishad*, in which Prajapati, the Lord of Creation, speaks as thunder in order to recommend three virtues to mortals: self-control, charity, and compassion.[55] The other cultural element the song's thunderous voice brings into play is the "I am" observed in the Judeo-Christian tradition as the divine name. Fairly early in the biblical book of Exodus, the prophet Moses expresses concern that the message he brings from God will be disputed—on the basis that he is a false prophet or because he has been deceived by some power other than God—so he asks, "*When* I come unto the children of Israel, and shall say unto them, The God of your fathers hath sent me unto you; and they shall say to me, What *is* his name? what shall I say unto them?" God replies, "I AM THAT I AM: . . . This shalt thou say unto the children of Israel, I AM hath sent me unto you."[56] In other words, the final lines of "Let It Grow" draw allusions to moral virtues as described in one of Asia's great religious texts together with the spiritual authority of the Judeo-Christian tradition, and they do so in the context of the georgic, a poetic genre deeply informed by the historical and mythic aspects of ancient literary exercise. This daring mix of sources displays the sort of global reach the Grateful Dead's corpus exhibits, as when it moves from the Arabian Desert of "Blues for Allah" to the American Southwest of "El Paso," and from the "Copper-dome Bodhi" of "China Cat Sunflower" to the "El Salvador" of "Standing on the Moon." The wide cultural net Barlow employs celebrates the synthesis of various forces into a new form, unifying diverse elements in a fashion that reminds the audience that, as is often the case in the Grateful Dead experience, the harmony of the whole provides more than any one part could hope to offer.

"Let It Grow" concludes with the repetition of the chorus, with its divine voice, but before closing my remarks on this song, I want to backtrack slightly to the final verse. It begins, "So it goes," and concludes, "Seasons round, creatures great and small, up and down, as we rise and fall." The "round" of the "seasons," and, more powerfully, the "rise and fall" of the people who walk the path of life, would seem to offer the interplay between destruction and creation that signals, per Nancy's remarks on the fragment, the terms of creation more generally. The fall into chaos and the structured emergence of life are not only the passage from winter cold to spring planting, summer growth, and fall harvest, but also a figure of our lives. Here, then, is that image of the self Lacoue-Labarthe and Nancy assert will be offered by the fragment. The song's establishment of a congruity between agricultural labor and the shape of the individual life, both under the aegis of the divine voice, reveals the "the name . . . on the earth," the creative power that can be articulated as the act of self-recognition: "I am."

The power of "Let It Grow" is profound, but it is not exceptional in that sense among the Grateful Dead's songs, a fact that testifies to the remarkable abilities of the band's lyricists. As a third and, for this introductory chapter, final analysis of Grateful Dead lyrics in relation to tradition and to the fragment, I turn to the song "Saint of Circumstance." The band premiered this piece in concert on August 31, 1979, and included a studio version on the album *Go to Heaven* in 1980. Although it would persist in the repertoire for roughly a decade more than "Lost Sailor" (another song that debuted in the same era), "Saint of Circumstance" was almost always preceded by "Lost Sailor" prior to that piece's retirement in early 1986. The "Lost Sailor > Saint of Circumstance" medley is thus context for the song as many fans know it. In the following paragraphs, I want to approach "Saint of Circumstance" in relation to a few poetic predecessors and, via the insights they afford, to offer remarks on the relevance of Nancy's insights about the interplay of creation and destruction evoked by the fragment, his arguments asserting that the process of literary creation modeled by the fragment is aligned with the process that generates the philosophical subject, and his suggestion that the limit of thought is a space of freedom.

As many listeners doubtless recognize, there are significant lyrical connections between "Lost Sailor" and "Saint of Circumstance," especially in their nautical imagery and the repetition of variations on the theme of "dreaming." To the extent that one hears "Saint of Circumstance" as a sequel of sorts to its frequent partner, it would seem to relate a time when the titular "lost sailor" found, at least provisionally, a safe harbor. On the surface, the first verse offers something one might find in a typical love song. The speaker declares he has "crossed the line" to arrive in a place that "must be heaven," where he encounters someone who appears to "be [an] angel." The song is filled with images and figures of uncertainty that culminate in the speaker's departure from the apparent heaven, driven by a sense that the place has somehow fallen short of the mark. The nature of that insufficiency is, at least upon cursory consideration, fairly vague—a sense the speaker describes only as a "feelin.'"

The song's power deepens when one registers its several literary predecessors. There are, of course, many major literary nautical tales, from the stories of Sindbad in *The One Thousand and One Nights* and the whale of the Book of Jonah to Edgar Allan Poe's *The Narrative of Arthur Gordon Pym*, Herman Melville's *Moby Dick*, and Joseph Conrad's *Heart of Darkness*, among many others. Nonnautical narratives are also relevant to "Saint of Circumstance," especially those driven by the dramatic situation of the homeward journey undertaken by so many protagonists of narratives, both nautical and otherwise. Among the relevant pieces, two in particular stand out: Homer's *Odyssey* and Dante Alighieri's *Commedia*, especially for the latter's treatment of the intersection of erotic and religious discourse.

Erotic poetry has traditionally drawn on tropes of sainthood and divinity to describe the beloved. Examples can be found in Dante, Petrarch, John Donne, Sir Philip Sidney, William Shakespeare, and many others. For a single illustrative text, consider Romeo declaring Juliet at one point a "dear saint" who can support his "faith" and at another his "god."[57] There is also, however, a long history of erotic language serving as a means to explore sacred love, a phenomenon perhaps most familiar to Western readers in the form it takes in the Song of Solomon. As Aldo S. Bernardo explains, the convention extends across millennia, as when medieval mystics described the relation between God and the believer as a marriage—one involving, at its extreme, everything from wedding gowns and love games to marital beds and copulation.[58] The tradition thus treats the congruency between the erotic and the spiritual in a bivalent fashion, one consequence of which is that one may hear "Saint of Circumstance" as a song merely about a restless lover approaching a metaphorically heavenly beloved, or as a song about a spiritual searcher resorting to the language and imagery of everyday romance in order to explain his quest. Either way, the intersection of erotic and spiritual desires finds a powerful precursor in Dante's epic poem, the *Commedia*.

Whether one regards "Saint of Circumstance" as describing a search for earthly love or as a search for a spiritual home does not change a central point, namely that both sorts of seekers are assailed by difficulties. Such a challenge is described as wind in the first verse, which reveals the speaker as a Job-like (or, to keep L. Frank Baum in mind, Dorothy-like) victim of circumstance, "Driven by the wind / Like the dust that blows around." The idea of a sailor riding the wind is not much of a stretch, but to hear the song as one that uses nautical imagery in service of describing a love affair frames such a scene in a fashion that echoes a famous moment in Dante's *Commedia*. Dante's poem is about a spiritual seeker, a man who, midway through life, has fallen off the path of faith and must journey through the realms of the afterlife to return his soul to the right course. His journey begins with a descent into hell, which Dante envisions as an immense pit with different levels, or circles, to which various sorts of sinners are consigned by divine judgment. In the fifth canto of this first part of the poem, the *Inferno*, the pilgrim enters the second circle of hell, where the souls of the lustful are blown about eternally in a great whirlwind. Dante describes it as a place

> that
> groans like the sea in a storm, when it is lashed by
> conflicting winds.[59]

As with most of Dante's underworld, the punishment is suited to the sin. Just as lustful sinners were impelled by uncontrollable desire in life, so they are being pushed by irresistible forces in death. Here, Dante's character speaks with a pair of adulterous lovers from his own late-medieval Italy. The woman of the pair explains their condition and the sinful acts that earned them their spot in hell, a moment typical of the *Inferno* in the sense that it presents evil to teach good. Dante's pilgrim in this way learns by example, securing his own faith by confrontation with the horrors of sin. Dante's use of the image that Barlow employs to describe the speaker of "Saint of Circumstance," "Driven by the wind / Like the dust that blows around," is thus particularly illuminating. It allows listeners to recognize that the speaker, like Dante's pilgrim but unlike those unrepentant souls he meets in hell, has not yet gone so far astray as to be beyond redemption. Just as Dante's pilgrim knows he is back on the right track when he emerges from hell and can "look again at the stars," so the "Saint of Circumstance" will sight his journey by the "dog star."[60]

The "dog star," more conventionally known as Sirius, is among the brightest in the sky, and thus has served many cultures as a navigational aid. However, its literary valences are not insignificant; nor are they as promising as Dante's stars in terms of their value to spiritual navigation. Sirius is mentioned several times in ancient works, including Hesiod's *Works and Days*, Homer's *Iliad*, and Virgil's *Aeneid*. In all these poems, it is a harbinger of danger. The *Iliad* makes the point quite clearly: "Brightest of all is he, yet he is a sign of evil, and brings much fever on wretched mortals."[61] So, while Dante's poem would seem to be one ancestor of the star imagery in "Saint of Circumstance," the song is also indebted to ancient texts for images that regard such lights as having dubious or even harmful value to viewers.

The dangers the speaker of the second verse faces are also emphasized by Barlow's allusion to an episode from Homer's *Odyssey*. The reference is found in the following lines:

> When the night's about to fall
> I can hear the sirens call
> It's a certain sort of sound

Homer's work describes the homeward journey of the Greek hero Odysseus following the Trojan War. He is beset along the way by a variety of hardships. One of these is an encounter with the monstrous Sirens, about whom the enchantress Circe warns him, "Sirens . . . beguile all men who come to them. . . . with their clear-toned song, as they sit in a meadow, and about them is a great heap of bones of moldering men, and round the bones the skin is shriveling."[62] So, in "Saint of Circumstance," hearing "the sirens call" speaks either to a moral laxity on the part of the speaker, whose attention so easily slips that heaven itself cannot keep it; or serves as a means to register the fact that the heaven he has reached is a false one.

Intriguingly, Barlow's allusion to Homer very much resembles one employed by Dante in the second part of his *Commedia*, the *Purgatorio*. Whereas the lustful souls of the *Inferno* show Dante how debased love is a sin that leads to punishment, there are also purer forms of love—one of the most august of which is emblematized by the figure of Beatrice. When Dante's pilgrim finally encounters Beatrice face-to-face, in canto 30 of the *Purgatorio*, she takes him to task for his failures, particularly his susceptibility to distraction. In attending to so many other concerns, he has neglected to focus on her—whose way of loving is the expression not of lust's corrupting desire, but of the soul's wish to move toward God. Beatrice compares his temptations to the song of the Sirens, and instructs him in the art of resistance, telling him that she does so

> so that [he] may bear
> the shame of [his] mistakes, and when [he] hear[s]
> the Sirens another time [he] may be stronger.[63]

Beatrice's point is valuable in relation to "Saint of Circumstance" in a fashion that goes well beyond Barlow's use of an allusion earlier employed by Dante. She reminds her audience that seeming gratifications may be false ones—ones we need both intellect to identify and will to resist. In other words, a heaven "close enough to pretend" is no heaven at all. Ultimately, Dante's pilgrim will find satisfaction only when his soul is returned to the right path, just as Odysseus will reach home only after overcoming the call of the Sirens and others who hinder his efforts. Indeed, the similarity between the spiritual rectification of the sort Dante's pilgrim experiences and the homecoming voyage of Odysseus has encouraged readings of Homer's poem as an allegorical spiritual journey for centuries; an early example of such an argument can be found in Plotinus's *Enneads*.[64] As the speaker of "Saint of Circumstance" departs for a new adventure, he abandons the temporary shelter provided by the expired heaven and follows the examples of both Dante's pilgrim and Odysseus, moving closer to home because wiser with regard to temptation.

As the above points hopefully illustrate, the literary context of "Saint of Circumstance" brings the adventures it describes into sharper focus. The erotic dimension of the song does not disappear entirely in light of this context, but rather encourages listeners to hear such carnal distractions in the fashion of a reader of Homer or Dante. That is to say, the literary allusions in "Saint of Circumstance" make a reading of the song as primarily about romantic love more difficult to maintain, shifting one's understanding of it in the direction of a heroic or spiritual quest. In this sense, the speaker's reaching the end of the proverbial rainbow (another echo of Baum) mentioned in the second verse, in a place that "must be heaven," only to abandon it for an indeterminate future when his "sails are fillin'," dramatizes the sort of creative interplay between stability and disorder, or form and chaos, that Nancy and Lacoue-Labarthe found the German Romantics celebrated as the definitive component of creative power. From this perspective, "Saint of Circumstance" is not only about erotic, heroic, or spiritual adventure, but also about artistic development.

A reading of "Saint of Circumstance" as a reflexive comment on creative activity is further supported by the song's debt to Dante's presentation of Beatrice, who appears not only in the *Commedia*, but also in his earlier text, *Vita Nuova*. In both, she is cast as something of a muse, bearing the authority of one who can encourage and pass judgment on Dante's artistic development. As Maria Christina Fumagalli writes, "In the *Vita Nuova*, she is Dante's inspiring source for his artistic apprenticeship, and in the *Commedia* she reappears to sanction Dante's destiny as the founder of a new vernacular tradition."[65] Hearing "Saint of Circumstance" through the lens of Dante encourages a reading of the song's movements between tempestuous disarray on the one hand and calm on the other as a narrative about the singer's own development and creative power. In this sense, the song is its own origin myth, presenting the tale of the singer's self-creation. Returning to Nancy may remind us that such moments arise from the evocative power of the poetic fragment.

These final points deepen the conceptual implications that govern the end of the song. As Nancy and others in the philosophical tradition on which he draws argue, thought arises at the border between the comprehensible and the incomprehensible—a limit that opens into a space of freedom. "Saint of Circumstance" repeats numerous times the formulae of incomprehension that these philosophers view as characteristic of the liberating borderlands: "Well I never know, just don't know"; "Never could read no road map / And I don't know what the weather might do"; "Sure don't know"; "Holes in what's left of my reason"; and so forth. The song also indicates the speaker's compulsion to engage these gaps in understanding, as in

> Sure don't know
> What I'm goin' for
> But I'm gonna go for it
> For sure

The conclusion of the song,

> Maybe goin' on a feelin'
> Maybe goin' on a dream
> Maybe goin' on a feelin'

replicates both the failure of understanding—for feelings and dreams are very much outside the demesne of reason—and a willingness to enter the space of mystery, of not knowing, as a way of advancing the ongoing process that the German Romantic philosophers saw as the heart of creation and the foundation of freedom. In this sense, the song is a paean to risk-taking in the service of understanding, to the exercise of freedom to define oneself where conventional terms of subjective self-invention stumble. Like "Dupree's Diamond Blues" and "Let It Grow," "Saint of Circumstance" foregrounds for listeners these processes of creative exercise, resisting conclusion while offering for contemplation the definitive characteristics of creative work performed by Grateful Dead music.

Each of the following chapters extends the preceding introduction to the Grateful Dead's engagement with the literary tradition and philosophical aesthetics. In most cases, the arguments commingle the sort of close textual analysis exemplified by the readings above and remarks on cultural history and literary tradition. These extensions find additional focus via a roughly chronological examination of how the band's lyrical engagement with particular topics in these areas allowed the Grateful Dead to ponder publicly the course of its own career, even while teaching listeners what some of the central features of Grateful Dead music are—including its evocation of the productive exchange between creation and destruction that Nancy celebrates in his remarks on the Romantic fragment.

Chapter 1 launches this project with a consideration of the band's extensive interactions with and artistic debts to the Beat generation. Neal Cassady, in particular, offered the young musicians a sense that they were joining a contemporary movement that was very much invested in literary exercise. Although some aspects of these interactions are relatively well-documented, much remains to be thought and said about the degree to which Beat aesthetics helped transform a Bay Area dance band of moderate proficiency into the Grateful Dead proper. This book's reading of the early Grateful Dead will treat the band's connections to the literary Beats not only as a matter of historical record, but also as a way to apprehend the degree to which its engagement with Beat literature opened the door to the conditions of and possibilities for their art. The chapter's arguments gain focus via engagement with Sascha Pöhlmann's formulation of American literature as a "future-founding poetry." Pöhlmann argues that American poetry often conceives of itself as an exercise in national self-presentation, a vision of the cultural present that serves as a fragmentary foundation for the American future. Yet the poetry and fiction of the Beats, the first generation to write in the shadow of the Cold War's constant threat of nuclear annihilation, were crafted at a moment when there seemed to be a very real chance that there was no future at all. The tension between the impulse to undertake the work of the future, and the possible total futility of the effort, shaped the Beats' understanding of their relations to the American past and future, and, as chapter 1 will show, left its mark on the Grateful Dead on several fronts.

The following chapter begins with Garcia's fascination with Frankenstein's monster, a theme he raised in interviews repeatedly over the course of his career. Critical accounts tend to focus on the cinematic work that was his introduction to the creature, Charles Barton's 1948 feature film *Abbott and Costello Meet Frankenstein*. I elect a different starting point: the lyrical reference to Mary Shelley in "Ramble on Rose." That song is a sort of comic-book catalog of American popular culture, but beneath the fun hide some rather dark passages. Too, the piece numbers among those that may be regarded as material for an unrecorded third volume in the Americana trilogy that includes *Workingman's Dead* and *American Beauty*, a sequence of albums that features many thieves, brawlers, and other ne'er-do-wells in its songs.

Along the way, these records map part of the American gothic tradition, in which Frankenstein's creature would find a not inhospitable home. This chapter surveys that ground, defending the Grateful Dead's early 1970s songwriting as rooted in a tradition that is not only musical, but also literary, and that is very much amenable to my overall contention about the frequency with which the band confronted the central mysteries of its art and of our being. The songs "Dire Wolf" and "Friend of the Devil" are particularly illuminating on this front, and this book's readings situate them in relation to not only Shelley's *Frankenstein*, but also an array of other texts, including poems by Robert Burns, Arthur Conan Doyle's *The Hound of the Baskervilles*, and Goethe's *Faust*. This context helps one see the degree to which the Grateful Dead found in the exceptional fragmentation and distortions of gothic literature terms with which the band could articulate the challenges its community and its music faced in the early 1970s, as well as its possibilities for evolution as the cultural environment drifted away from the regnant conditions of the late 1960s.

The third chapter focuses primarily on "Althea," a song the band debuted live in 1979 and performed more in 1980 than in any other year. Although the title and some of Hunter's comments indicate classical sources for the lyrics—material to which chapter 3 devotes some attention—the primary interest here is the piece's several Shakespearean allusions. The chapter thus takes the form of three related inquiries: the nature of the song's Shakespearean material and its contribution to the work as a whole, the ways in which the uncertainties articulated by the song's primary speaker reflect the band's situation when this piece was most prominent in the repertoire, and the degree to which allusions to *Hamlet* allow a reading of "Althea" as a confrontation with the insoluble mystery that is the source of art. These inquiries are framed by commentary on Shakespeare's own debt to the ancient Roman poet Ovid and the Shakespearean influence on other Grateful Dead songs, from "Rosemary" to "Black Muddy River," but especially "Mountains of the Moon."

In the summer of 1987, Bob Dylan joined the Grateful Dead for a short tour as coheadliners, during which time the band found itself with a hit record and single, and a level of popularity and media attention greater than it had ever experienced. At the same time, Dylan's career was in something of the doldrums—after the "Christian phase" that divided his fanbase in the late 1970s, Dylan offered a relatively unremarkable sequence of albums in the 1980s. Much more than their shared dates with Tom Petty in 1986, the brief 1987 tour transformed both Dylan and the Grateful Dead. Dylan began singing and recording some of Hunter's songs—issuing in the early 1990s a couple of acoustic roots records that displayed a reconnection with some of his (and

American recorded music's) earliest inspirations—and, by the end of the decade, had entered a period of exceptional songwriting and performance. Too, selections from Dylan's catalog—rarely long absent from the Grateful Dead's set lists—became, at almost the same time, a regular part of nearly every concert that the Grateful Dead played.

While the *Dylan and the Dead* album that stands as the only officially sanctioned document of the collaboration usually receives low marks from fans of both artists, the transformation of Dylan's career in the following decade, and the shifts in the Grateful Dead's live repertoire during an era that was one of the high points in its performance career, point to a collaboration that was much more important than is usually recognized. My fourth chapter looks closely at the relationship between these artists on their own terms and in relation to the shared literary touchstone of Arthur Rimbaud. Rimbaud is important to both Dylan and Hunter, and his formulations of the poet and of poetry are rich in relation to the rethinking of the subject and the source of creative potential described in the German Romantics' discussion of the literary fragment.

The final years of the Grateful Dead saw fewer new original songs than some earlier eras, but several that emerged were quite remarkable. Too, Hunter began publishing more poetry than ever before, a phenomenon that points toward the cultivation of a more conventional literary identity by someone whose song lyrics were, after the success of *In the Dark*, reaching ever-wider audiences. The final chapter gives this phenomenon of Grateful Dead lyricists working as published poets its due, reading Hunter's books in particular as a contribution to the literary tradition on which the band had drawn for so many years. While there is some extant commentary on Hunter's work, most of it reads the poetry as the counterpart to the songwriting. This book looks instead at Hunter's poetry as a more purely literary exercise by acknowledging his debt to Modernist authors such as James Joyce, Eliot, and, especially, Rainer Maria Rilke. Hunter published translations of Rilke's two most important books of poetry; taken together with his other work as a wordsmith, these translations evince an ongoing debt to the Austrian poet's mystical efforts to reconcile art and the world.

As the preceding pages indicate, one implication of this book's argument as a whole is that the Grateful Dead was not merely influenced by the literary tradition, but in some real senses a participant in it. This book's conclusion assesses some of the most significant ways that the band's participation repaid the tradition on which it drew. Examples include a number of works by the late twentieth century's most notable journalists and essayists, such as

Tom Wolfe's *The Electric Kool-Aid Acid Test*, which engages the band's world throughout; Hunter S. Thompson's *Fear and Loathing on the Campaign Trail '72*, one of his books in which references to the band are sprinkled; and Joan Didion's *Slouching Towards Bethlehem*, which appraises the San Francisco Haight-Ashbury scene in part through interactions with the band.

Too, the conclusion looks at fictions and poems that mention the band and its music, either in passing or with sustained attention, such as James Merrill's "Self-Portrait in Tyvek™ Windbreaker," Richard Brautigan's "The Day They Busted the Grateful Dead," David Foster Wallace's *Infinite Jest*, Douglas Coupland's *Polaroids from the Dead*, and Philip K. Dick's *VALIS*. In all these works, one finds examples of the Grateful Dead's roles as an emblem of the conundrums of late twentieth-century popular culture and an inspirational embodiment of countercultural iconoclasm. Taken together, these literary texts show how the band members' activities contributed to the literary traditions that inspired them throughout their career.

That's When It All Began

BEAT LITERATURE, FUTURE-FOUNDING
POETRY, AND THE GRATEFUL DEAD

The Grateful Dead's literary identity takes many forms. As the following chapters will demonstrate, a tremendous number of literary figures, movements, works, genres, motifs, and modes left direct and indirect marks on the band's lyrics and approach to performance. Furthermore, many notable contemporary authors have biographical ties to band members, some of whose social connections were germinating even before the Grateful Dead formed. In addition, the musicians' comments in interviews not infrequently rely on literary texts, topics, and personalities as touchpoints for articulating thoughts about their individual and collective ambitions, artistic achievements, and cultural position. The Beat writers of the 1950s and early 1960s are, in many ways, foundational on all these fronts, and the Beats' place in the imagination of the band, its inner circle of friends and family, and its wider scene is difficult to overstate. As Regina Weinreich explains, Beat texts "favor aspects of instinct over intellect, fresh experience over canned. All... working to express human experience that may be beyond the radar of most people, whom" the Beats view "as hypnotized by the language of advertising and commodification."[1] These qualities, conjoined with the celebration in Beat fiction and poetry of improvisation, mysticism, spontaneity, intoxication, antimaterialism, mobility, and general nonconformity, were central to the Grateful Dead's music and its surrounding social world. However, the value of the Beats to the Grateful Dead went beyond these tendencies, for the Beat writers not only practiced, described, and embodied such artistic and cultural values, but also served as an initial gateway for many in the Grateful Dead's generation to thinking and speaking about traditions of American art and literature. Jerry Garcia expressed the point quite clearly: "I owe a lot of who I am and what I've been and what I've done to the beatniks from the Fifties and to the poetry and art and music I've come in contact with." He then took that assertion as a launching pad for reflection, both expanding and historicizing the initial frame of reference: "I feel like I'm part of a continuous line in American culture.... My life would be miserable if I didn't have those little chunks of Dylan Thomas and T. S. Eliot. I can't even imagine life without that."[2] Garcia's remarks on the Beats as a movement tied to a particular decade, the 1950s, provide terms on which a proximate history of the literary inspiration for the Grateful Dead's project can be conceived, but his additional recognition that Beat literature offers readers a door that opens onto a profoundly enriching past of music, art, and poetry is perhaps even more illuminating, for it signals that the Grateful Dead was conscious of its place in relation not only to the pasts of American music, but also to those of the visual arts and literature.

This chapter's exploration of relations between the Grateful Dead and the Beats follows the lead of Garcia's comment. On the one hand, it accounts for many of the literary texts and personal connections that inspired and fostered bonds between the Grateful Dead and Beat generation writers, in terms of both intertextual relations and biographical fact. On the other, it treats the Beats as ciphers or conduits, reading their fictions and poems as a means by which the Grateful Dead indirectly engaged aspects of literary tradition. The materials, questions, and artistic legacies that Beat writing opened to the Grateful Dead could easily justify a book-length study; this chapter finds focus by attending to three foundational and mutually supportive points of particularly sympathetic intersection between the Beats and the Grateful

Dead. First is that they share a concern with the invention of works marked as genuinely American in their preoccupations. Second, they develop or discover similar formal innovations that are useful for lending their works a sense of contemporaneity. Finally, both preceding contentions unfold in conversation with a view of America's cultural potential as one of productive incompletion characterized on terms congruent with those Nancy and Lacoue-Labarthe find definitive of the Romantic fragment.

"I'm Uncle Sam": The Grateful Dead and the Beats' America

Beat writers were motivated by a variety of factors to articulate what was meant by the term with which they were labeled. While Jack Kerouac claimed to have been the first to use the word *beat* to describe certain aspiring writers of his generation in the 1940s, he gave credit to Herbert Huncke—whose rent for room 828 in the Chelsea Hotel was for some time covered by the Grateful Dead—for being the person who initially brought it to their awareness and used it in a fashion that resonated with their experiences.[3] In these earliest instances, the phrase signaled someone who is broke, physically tired, and down and out in spirit.[4] Despite the pessimistic register that characterizes Huncke's use of the label, the Beats' writings were not exclusively, or perhaps even primarily, a matter of documenting exhaustion and exclusion—but also an effort to find in such a state inspiration for new means of literary expression, one that could reinitiate literature on terms that would hopefully overcome or avoid the stultifying and totalizing restrictions that they felt characterized mid-twentieth-century America.

The Beats' efforts to recover or invent language and modes that could speak convincingly for possibilities inherent in American culture and speech that they perceived their historical moment as lacking or frustrating have been read by Sascha Pöhlmann as those of a "future-founding poetry." As Pöhlmann asserts, the notion of a new beginning is ideologically central to Americans at both individual and collective levels, and the particularly American version of this beginning presumes that the future is not simply coming, but rather is something created in the work of the present. This work of creating a future, when valid, entails a careful interrogation of current possibilities, and it is consequently likely to reject or to critique national values, even as it sometimes celebrates them.[5] Among the goals of strong American writers, then, is the creation of a voice that both offers grounds to examine the culture of their nation's historical moment with a critical eye and verifies the paths to possible futures that such a critique unveils. This sort of project, Pöhlmann contends, necessarily entails some negation of or blindness to earlier formulations of American poetic beginnings, and inventing America anew is therefore not only an essential, but also a complex part of any serious American artist's agenda. Pöhlmann's view of American poetry as an openness to the productive possibilities of the present is remarkably amenable in the political register to the conception of the fragment discussed in this book's introduction. America and truly American poetry are, at the intersection of Pöhlmann's reading of American culture and Nancy and Lacoue-Labarthe's reading of the Romantic fragment, consistently enacting a struggle between form and chaos, out of which emerge possibilities for their own joint future, not as determinate goals, but as an ongoing process or operation that adapts to changing conditions. Such self-production is not only the means of presenting specific literary texts or realizing particular political possibilities, although it is at least some of the time both of these, but also, and more importantly, an ongoing openness to potentiality—a pointing to that endless reserve of possibility, out of which literary texts, philosophical thought, and, following Pöhlmann, political possibilities emerge. The first section of this chapter considers the ways that the Beats' notion of American identity is shared by the Grateful Dead, considering especially the degree to which the band's lyrics brought Beat sensibilities, as first described by Kerouac and Huncke and then developed by their friends and successors, together with both the critical and productive aspects of the American poetic impetus to newness delineated by Pöhlmann.

There can be little doubt that the Grateful Dead saw its project as an especially American enterprise. Even the iconography that surrounds the band joins the lyrics in repeatedly driving home the point, as we turn from its red, white, and blue, skull-with-lightning-bolt emblem to Jerry Garcia and the others singing "I'm Uncle Sam" in the song "U.S. Blues," or from the 1966 photographs by Herb Greene that present Jerry Garcia in front of a massive American flag to the motorcycle-riding Uncle Sam who appears roaring through the opening of *The Grateful Dead Movie*. In *Searching for the Sound*, Phil Lesh relates an anecdote that prompts him to make this aspect of the band's sensibilities explicit. In 1980, the management of Radio City Music Hall attacked the band for exceeding the limits of propriety in the decorations it prepared for a run of shows at that venue, going so far as to suggest that its intentions were un-American. Lesh's take on the accusation neatly encapsulates a central attitude of the band: "Un-American? Why, there's *nothing* more American than the Grateful Dead."[6] The Grateful Dead may have ignored or sought to transcend various conventions, but an abiding devotion to certain national ideals, particularly those of liberty and self-reliance, remained central to its work. This is not to say that the band members were mindless flag-wavers or saw themselves as engaged in some sort of political project, but comments like Lesh's do indicate they were aware of and sensitive to their place in the nation's culture.

The sociocultural conditions of the United States in the mid-twentieth century were a particularly challenging context for writers seeking to develop new terms for the sort of poetry Pöhlmann describes. Beat writers, working in the shadow of the atom bomb and mounting evidence of the industrial age's terrible impact on the natural environment, faced a historically unprecedented hurdle in the genesis of a poetry oriented toward the future. The dawn of the Cold War meant that the Beats were the first generation to create art during an era when not only a given community or nation, but our entire species, faced the possibility of having no future at all. The paranoia the global situation inspired was reflected in domestic politics. As Dennis McNally writes, "By March of 1950, . . . the American future had arrived, and it seemed like [Orwell's] 1984. Suspicion, paranoia, and dull fear settled . . . over the official land": Alger Hiss had been convicted; McCarthyism was on the rise; and espionage charges were being issued.[7] Many Beat writers responded to the possible closure of the future by making poetry of the regnant cultural despair. Such were the conditions that fomented the frustration that remains on the surface throughout texts such as Allen Ginsberg's "Howl," filling the poem with characters running the gamut from those "who poverty and tatters and hollow-eyed and high sat up smoking" to the ones "with the absolute heart of the poem of life butchered out of their own bodies."[8] The sense of exclusion, dehumanizing persecution, and confusion upon confrontation with mid-century American life that characterize so much of Ginsberg's early poetry was shared by other Beat writers, and the recording of its insults to the more noble aspects of the human spirit and the search for alternative social and spiritual frameworks of understanding allow a poet to write of the future even while recognizing that the future is very possibly a dead end.[9]

The cultural trauma and disorientation that Ginsberg and the other Beats delineated in their poetry and fiction also emerge repeatedly in the Grateful Dead's lyrics. They are there in the earliest compositions, such as the "uniforms on nighttime beats" who "ask . . . where I'm going and what I eat" in "Can't Come Down," the anonymous subject lamenting, "They took away my name and gave me a number instead" in "Standing on the Corner," and the reflective plea, "If I could only be less blind / If only I knew what to find," of

"Mindbender." Too, some of the earliest songs committed to vinyl, such as "Cream Puff War," likewise incorporate the situation of the displaced via lines like "You're both out in the streets and you got no place to go" (although this latter instance has a sharply personal edge that owes much to the attitude expressed in songs like Bob Dylan's "Positively 4th Street"). These sorts of lyrics not only capture the spirit of "Beat" as originally conceived, but also anticipate the impoverishment represented in pieces across the Grateful Dead's career, from the indigent despair of "Wharf Rat" and the Depression-era hardship of "Brown-Eyed Woman," to the fugitives' urgency of "Jack Straw" and "Friend of the Devil," and the directionless confusion of "Althea" and "Lost Sailor."

One who is relatively unfamiliar with the Grateful Dead's lyrics and Beat poetry may see the distress of the characters encountered therein as a call for some sort of political reform, in the mode of a manifesto or protest song. This interpretive inclination resonates with some aspects of Beat poetry. Ginsberg, for example, examines both the damage the social climate of the moment effected on the figures in his poetry and the forces—militarism, mechanization, and consumer capitalism—that contribute to the problems he describes. This tendency is especially evident in the anaphoric second section of "Howl," which is characterized in large part by lines like "Moloch the vast stone of war! Moloch the stunned governments! / Moloch whose mind is pure machinery! Moloch whose blood is running money!"[10] Yet, while lines like this may lend themselves to being read as presenting a voice amenable to progressive political agendas, Ginsberg's intent was not, especially in his early poetry, about sociopolitical reform in any narrow sense. Reflecting on "Howl," he writes, "A word on the Politicians: my poetry is angelic ravings, and has nothing to do with dull materialistic vagaries about who should shoot" whom.[11] In the place of such intentions, Ginsberg aligns himself with a sphere of experience both more abstract and more noble, declaring his poetry of "no use to this world, except perhaps to make it shut its trap and listen to the music of the spheres."[12] A decade and a half later, the Grateful Dead found itself following Ginsberg's lead in response to a perhaps even more charged cultural moment.

While the early Grateful Dead was hardly supportive of late 1960s points of contention such as the American military action in Vietnam, and despite the band's proximity to centers of youth protest like Berkeley, it shared with Ginsberg a resistance to politicking, strongly and consistently objecting to the use of the stage as a platform. In a 1982 interview, for example, Garcia reflected on the band's position regarding the protests of the 1960s, "I remember once being at a be-in or one of those things, and the Berkeley contingent—Jerry Rubin and those guys—got up on stage and started haranguing the crowd. . . . All of a sudden it was like . . . every asshole who told people what to do. The words didn't matter. . . . It made me sick to my stomach."[13] Other members of the band and their circle also expressed this sentiment, as when Bob Weir dismissed rumors that they would turn their July 8, 1970, concert into a fundraising event, stating, "We're not political at all. . . . It's . . . music for music's sake."[14] Even songs so oblique in their arguments as "Mason's Children" and "New Speedway Boogie," which were penned in reaction to the murder and general disarray at the Altamont Speedway Free Festival but are marked in no way as particular to that event, were too topical to get much space in the performance repertoire. Like Ginsberg, then, the band regarded its work as operating in an entirely different sphere. By not turning its performances into advocacy for political positions or socioeconomic agendas, the band avoided what it joined the Beats in regarding as the condescending and spiritually vacuous terms of power.[15] Instead, the band followed the Beats in dealing with the preoccupations of its day in part by electing life on the cultural margins. It is important to recognize that this is not essentially a turn of detachment or indifference; instead, the counterculture exists via the discovery or generation of space for a relationship of critical separation from the status quo, a sociopolitical opening that is necessary to cultivation of the sort of future-oriented art Pöhlmann describes. Yet, the production of this space does not mean its immediate population. Having rejected the norm, the Grateful Dead and the Beats both faced the challenge of how to define an art that could grow on the ground they were clearing. The problem is essentially that of an incomplete exchange between assemblage and dispersal, an exchange from which, Nancy and Lacoue-Labarthe argue, possibilities of poetic production may emerge. A cultural dropping out may register the necessity of disorder in creation, but to fulfill the promise of the fragment by taking the resultant freedom for generative creation in hand requires that the wheel be advanced by another turn.

Writers as central to the Beat movement as Kerouac and Ginsberg explicitly address the difficulties of devising a style and finding a voice that were equal to their generation's American experience, and they do so in passages regarded as offering essential insights into their careers. Kerouac, for example, when asked about his remarks on the "spontaneous prose," which he understood to be the best bearer of the frantic energy he sought to deliver in his writing, addressed the point with reference to a text by Neal Cassady known as the *Joan Anderson Letter*:

> I got the idea for the spontaneous style of *On the Road* from seeing how good old Neal Cassady wrote his letters to me, all first person, fast, mad, confessional, completely serious, all detailed, with real names in his case however (being letters). I remembered also Goethe's admonition, well Goethe's prophecy that the future literature of the West would be confessional in nature; also Dostoevsky prophesied as much and might have started in on that if he'd lived long enough to do his projected masterwork, *The Great Sinner*. Cassady also began his early youthful writing with attempts at slow, painstaking, and-all-that-crap craft business, but got sick of it like I did, seeing it wasn't getting out his guts and heart the way it *felt* coming out.... The letter, the main letter I mean, was 40,000 words long, mind you, a whole short novel. It was the greatest piece of writing I ever saw, better'n anybody in America, or at least enough to make Melville, Twain, Dreiser, Wolfe, I dunno who, spin in their graves. Allen Ginsberg asked me to lend him this vast letter so he could read it. He read it, then loaned it to a guy called Gerd Stern who lived on a houseboat in Sausalito, California, in 1955, and this fellow lost the letter: overboard I presume.[16]

Here, Kerouac's remarks vacillate rapidly between the poles of innovation and inheritance, and they do so in a manner that grounds Cassady's style in the literary canon even as they simultaneously undermine the authority of the canon in the present. He first declares Cassady's style to be the source of his own, describing it as the fulfillment of ideas that tie the validity of literary voice to a level of energetic, confessional authenticity that was called for but ultimately unrealized by canonical authors of the Old World, such as Johann Wolfgang von Goethe and Fyodor Dostoevsky. This assertion suggests that the Cassady-Kerouac style both overcomes the past and is rooted in a specifically American (rather than European) context. Furthermore, Kerouac suggests that the letter's prose was of a quality that at least approached and perhaps even surpassed that of canonical American forebears, including Herman Melville and Mark Twain. The rejection of both European and American nineteenth-century models is an argument for unequaled contemporaneity. The letter, he effectively argues, realizes the voice toward which others have striven, but that they could not attain. Kerouac's rhetorical maneuvering is extended by the alleged loss of the letter (it was, in fact, merely misplaced, and was brought to light in 2012), which enacts further violence on the possible origins of the style, even as it advances Kerouac himself to the pole position. In the absence of the letter, the implicit argument contends, Kerouac's prose is the definitive example of Beat writing and the grounds on which any potential post-Beat possibilities for American fiction must be established.

For the Grateful Dead, the possibilities of Beat literature that Kerouac advances in his remarks on the *Joan Anderson Letter* were mediated by a handful of figures who embodied direct social connections between band members and Beat writers and artists. One such person is artist Wally Hedrick, who began working as an artist in San Francisco in the late 1940s and was part of the city's burgeoning Beat scene throughout the 1950s. He was one of the six artists and writers who established the Six Gallery at 3119 Fillmore Street and subsequently helped conceive the poetry reading held there on October 13, 1955, which is when Ginsberg first read "Howl" to an audience.[17] The event was monumental in terms of bringing attention to this literary generation. Although John Clellon Holmes' *Go* and William S. Burroughs's *Junkie* had been published, the three books that best define the Beats in the minds of many readers—Ginsberg's *Howl and Other Poems*, Kerouac's *On the Road*, and Burroughs's *Naked Lunch*—were still in the future. Furthermore, Ginsberg was not alone on the stage, but shared it with a handful of emerging authors who would come to occupy a place among the leading lights of the "San Francisco Renaissance": Philip Lamantia (who read not his own works, but rather selections by the late John Hoffman), Michael McClure (who helped organize the evening), Gary Snyder, and Philip Whalen. Kenneth Rexroth, at the time essentially the leading figure on the San Francisco poetry scene, served as master of ceremonies. Like the performers, the audience included both East Coast Beats and West Coast poets. Kerouac was there, and later recounted a slightly fictionalized version of the event in his novel *The Dharma Bums*.[18] Lawrence Ferlinghetti was in attendance, and his recognition of the importance of Ginsberg's work would lead to the publication of *Howl and Other Poems* as part of City Lights Books' Pocket Poets series.[19] To claim, as some suggest, that the event signaled that Beat poets and those of the San Francisco Renaissance were a unified group may be to overreach—some works by figures like Jack Spicer do not sit easily in the Beat mold, and, on the other side of the coin, Burroughs was more often traveling south to Texas and Mexico, and then overseas, rather than looking much to the West Coast—but shared dissatisfactions and certain innovations in form and subject matter affirm significant common ground. Whatever its other implications, the reading put both groups on the map to a degree previously unrealized, and Hedrick's involvement was essential.

While Hedrick's position at the Six Gallery placed him at ground zero in terms of the emergence of Beat literature, he also served a foundational role in awakening the early Grateful Dead to the movement. His effecting the connection was largely possible because he taught at the California School of Fine Arts, where Garcia took classes in a precollege extension program in the late 1950s.[20] Hedrick recognized something of promise in Garcia and took an interest in turning him on to the local bohemian scene, which, at the time, was centered in the coffeehouses, bars, and bookstores of San Francisco's North Beach neighborhood. Thus, Garcia was sent to City Lights Bookstore to check out Kerouac's writing, and to coffeehouses to listen to Ferlinghetti and others read.[21] The experiences were eye-opening. McNally explains that the encounter with Kerouac's works "changed" Garcia's "life forever," continuing, "Kerouac's hymn to the world as an explorational odyssey, an adventure outside conventional boundaries, would serve as a blueprint for the rest of Garcia's life."[22] Furthermore, Hedrick lived the life of the Beat artist. While he would go on to become friendly with the Grateful Dead as a collective, Garcia tends to discuss Hedrick as someone who embodied ideas that otherwise would have remained, to at least some degree, abstractions.[23] He was, in Garcia's words, someone who showed that "art is not something you do, but something you are as well."[24] In these ways, Hedrick served as a point of intersection between the relatively older bohemian San Francisco represented by Rexroth, the Beats, and the San Francisco Renaissance poets of the 1950s, the ongoing early 1960s arts activity of the Bay Area, and the many young people who would become part of the Grateful Dead and its circle as the 1960s unfolded.

Certainly, Hedrick served a key role in bringing the young Grateful Dead to awareness of the Beats, but another, and even more direct, link between the band's world and that of Beat writing was also developing in the early 1960s—the group members' friendship with Neal Cassady. On December 4, 1965, the Grateful Dead performed at an Acid Test in San Jose, California, and it would appear at several more during the following year. These events grew out of parties that author Ken Kesey hosted at his home in La Honda, where an increasing number of the area's cognoscenti gathered to take psychedelics, socialize, and see what the night's mixture of people and chemicals made possible. By mid-1965, the evenings involved not only Kesey's coterie of comrades, known as the Merry Pranksters, but also literary stars like Ginsberg, aspiring writers such as Hunter S. Thompson, members of the Hells Angels Motorcycle Club, and the Grateful Dead. When these parties outgrew the available physical and psychological space, Kesey and the Pranksters took them to the streets, renting venues and opening the doors to those among the public who were interested and clever enough to decipher the advertisements. Like the initial parties at Kesey's, these Acid Tests were multimedia happenings incorporating fluorescent paint, film projectors, theatrical attire, homemade sound experiments, and any other elements participants wished to include. The formlessness of the experience, which had among its aspects the option for the Grateful Dead not to play and the expectation that everyone in attendance was in some way a creative participant, created conditions that greatly diminished traditional understandings of the distinction between performers and audience and unseated just about every other conventional expectation of how a musical performance might unfold, ultimately leading Jerry Garcia to go so far as to identify "the Acid Test . . . [as] the prototype for" the Grateful Dead's "whole basic trip."[25] This declaration of the band's genealogy foregrounds exactly the features Lacoue-Labarthe and Nancy highlight as essential to the creative urge signaled by the Romantic fragment: an interplay between order and disorder that provides the opening for freely realized creative production.

When the young Grateful Dead began developing its friendship with Cassady in 1965, the band was interacting with someone who possessed an unassailable countercultural reputation. Central to this was Cassady's appearance as a semi-fictionalized character in several Beat works, most famously Kerouac's *On the Road*. In that novel, he is cast as Dean Moriarty, the companion of narrator and authorial stand-in Sal Paradise on high-speed, cross-country trips undertaken in pursuit of pleasure, self-knowledge, and opportunities for liberating adventure in America. Cassady's centrality to Kerouac's essentially confessional text blurred the line between fiction and art, and, as with Hedrick, Garcia saw Cassady as someone whose very identity rejected the distinction between the work of the artist and the art of living. In one interview, for example, Garcia described Cassady as someone whose movement through the world spoke even to "musical things . . . rhythm, you know, motion, timing." He continues, "He was like a 12th-dimensional Lenny Bruce in a way, some kind of cross between a great stand-up comedian like Lenny Bruce and somebody like Buster Keaton. He had this great combination of physical poetry and an incredible mind. He was a model for the idea that a person can become art by himself, that you don't necessarily even need a forum."[26] In the cases of both Cassady and Hedrick, then, Garcia saw art modeled as embodied performance. Theirs was not the static experience of paint on canvas or words on the page, and it became a component of the Grateful Dead's identity as a group that prioritized spontaneity and improvisation as central to its praxis.

Cassady had entered the world of Kesey and the Merry Pranksters in the early 1960s, and his time with them only enlarged his already legendary countercultural status. He now not only emerged from the pages of Beat literature as a living embodiment of the central events, values, and attitudes of that movement, but also accrued experiences that ensured his place as a prominent personality in the post-Beat Bay Area bohemian world in which the Grateful Dead germinated. Most central among the contributions of recent events to Cassady's reputation in the period during which the Grateful Dead came to know him was his celebrated adventure with the Pranksters on a cross-country journey that unfolded in 1964. In that year, Kesey and a band of coconspirators set out for New York in a 1939 International Harvester bus christened *Furthur*. They took with them not only a significant amount of audio and video equipment, as one intention was to produce a film about the journey, but also a variety of mind-altering substances, including especially a substantial supply of LSD, to which Kesey (like Hunter) had been introduced via the CIA-funded and Stanford University–organized MK-Ultra research experiments a few years earlier.[27] Cassady's famous skills as an automobile-age wizard behind the wheel landed him in *Furthur*'s driver's seat, where he admirably distinguished between real and hallucinated obstacles for thousands of miles. While the ostensible goals of the journey were an appearance at a book release event for Kesey's second novel, *Sometimes a Great Notion*, and a visit to the World's Fair in Queens, its documentation in Tom Wolfe's *The Electric Kool-Aid Acid Test* made of it the definitive post-Beat, proto-hippie experiment in seeing what would happen when the budding psychedelic freak culture of the West Coast moved through the spaces and places of straight Middle America.

The Grateful Dead's friendship with Cassady and its prominent role at the Acid Tests signaled, among many other things, a rearrangement of the hip constellations, one that was, at some level, a barometer of the transition from a post-Beat to a hippie counterculture. Just a few years earlier, the future band members had been looked on as something of annoying kid brothers to Kesey's crowd. Garcia, Lesh, and Hunter lived at points in the early 1960s in a house known as the Chateau, alongside Prankster Page Browning. Before moving to La Honda, Kesey's circle gathered socially around Perry Lane, an area close to but socially distinct from the more roughshod inhabitants of the Chateau. Consequently, relations between the groups were at that point something less than comradely. From the viewpoint of Kesey's crowd, Garcia, Hunter, and Lesh represented "no-counts, lumpenbeatniks" whom "you had to throw ... out when they came over and tried to crash the parties." Garcia, Hunter, and the others, for their part, saw Kesey's social scene as that of *"the wine drinkers"*: bohemian, yes, but only so far as possible while within sight of the perimeters of middle-class America.[28] Such discriminations faded as the Tests became a shared project. To use the insider slang of the Pranksters, one was either "on the bus" or not. The members of the Grateful Dead may not have been part of the earliest Prankster gatherings, but they very much were "on the bus" by the end of 1965. At that point, several manifestations of Bay Area countercultural bohemia, which had been running for some time on similar but somewhat distinct paths, finally converged.

The early connections between the Grateful Dead and Cassady and other Beat figures were strengthened by the rise of the former's cultural capital on the San Francisco scene. Consequently, intersections of the two worlds became increasingly apparent, and were especially strong during the first years of the Grateful Dead's career. Too, it should be noted that while the *Furthur* adventure and the Acid Tests played an important role in bridging the gap between Cassady-as-Beat-icon and the Grateful Dead, they were not the sole means through which the future band members came into direct or indirect contact with him. For example, a very early Warlocks gig—back when the band was still performing under its original name—ended with Garcia, Weir, and Lesh getting stoned with one of Weir's friends, who had scored some marijuana from Cassady.[29] Too, Robert Hunter spent time with Cassady even before he became part of Kesey's circle, as Brian Hassett explains. Hunter remarked of that period that "[Cassady] used to visit me a lot. He paid me the compliment of saying that when he goes to New York, he visits Bill Burroughs, and when he comes here, he hangs at my house."[30] Furthermore, Beat writers and artists found space to coexist within or alongside the countercultures of later eras. On January 22, 1966, for example, McClure read to the audience at the Trips Festival, a three-day Acid Test held at the Longshoreman's Hall in San Francisco, at which the Grateful Dead also performed, and he was a frequent visitor at the Grateful Dead's home when the band resided at 710 Ashbury Street (McClure lived nearby on Downey Street).[31] McClure would again share the bill with the Grateful Dead at a benefit for the Straight Theatre held at the Avalon Ballroom on May 19, 1966, and at the Trips Festival at the PNE Garden Auditorium in Vancouver on July 31 of the same year. The following year, on January 14, McClure, Ginsberg, Snyder, and Lenore Kandel were featured along with the Grateful Dead at the Human Be-In, with the Doors in attendance due to McClure's influence.[32] The Human Be-In stands as an especially rich point of intersection between Beat literature and the burgeoning San Francisco rock music scene. The poets who participated not only represented the ongoing compatibility between those worlds, but also, as Erik Mortenson explains, contributed to a movement aimed at presenting contemporary poetry to a broader audience through live performance, as Ginsberg, Spicer, Whalen, Lew Welch, Robert Creeley, Robert Duncan, Denise Levertov, Joanne Kyger, Charles Olson, John Wieners, and Amiri Baraka had done at the Vancouver Poetry Conference of 1963 and the Berkeley Poetry Conference of 1965.[33] This catalog of intersections between Beat writers and the Grateful Dead could be greatly extended in length and time, particularly when the writers' presence as audience members at concerts is considered, as Welch's attendance at the February 4, 1970, show at the Family Dog or Allen Ginsberg's visit backstage at Madison Square Garden on September 20, 1987, attest.[34] In the end, one might wonder, given everyone involved in the *Furthur* bus journey, the Acid Tests, the explosion of cultural change represented in the popular imagination by the Summer of Love, and the ongoing development of Bay Area bohemianism in general, to what extent the Grateful Dead in particular were perceived as the inheritors of the legacy of the Beats and the Pranksters. For his part, Jon McIntire declares little doubt that the band members were anointed as keepers of the flame—of the period during which Cassady was most often in the Haight and not infrequently staying at 710 Ashbury Street, McIntire says, "This was the moment of the shift from the beatniks to the hippie movement. The baton was passed on by Neal Cassady directly to the Grateful Dead."[35]

Part of the band's assumption of this cultural significance was its allegiance to the ongoing American adventure Cassady represented, and this devotion remained a defining element of the Grateful Dead's scene not only in the 1960s, but throughout its career. Decades after Cassady's death, Garcia and Weir discussed his role as being that of a father figure, a perspective perhaps especially notable since Garcia's father died when the future guitarist was only five years old, and Weir would not meet his biological father until long after the 1960s had ended. Weir asserts, regarding relations among the group, "We're all siblings, we're all underlings to this guy, Neal Cassady."[36] Garcia agrees with the notion, adding, "He was the guy speaking to us from the pages of Kerouac. . . . He was a breeze, some kind of incredible super-American, mythos personality blasting through the highways of 1947 America."[37] Too, it is worth noting that, for Cassady, the habit of holding forth with a stream of freely associated topics was to some extent an intentionally literary exercise. For example, Garcia and Weir discuss an effort to annotate one of Cassady's monologues (probably that of July 23, 1967, during which the band very patiently comps its musical way to a performance of "Turn on Your Love Light" while Cassady talks), recalling that it includes references to works by authors ranging from Kerouac to Rainer Maria Rilke.

Cassady was in some ways closer to Weir than to the other band members, and John Perry Barlow describes some striking examples of the ways they complemented each other. One such narrative is tied to the kitchen of the group's home at 710 Ashbury Street. At the time, Weir followed a macrobiotic diet, which requires extended low-heat cooking and slow eating. As a result, he spent a lot of time in the kitchen, painstakingly preparing and silently eating his meals. For whatever reason, Cassady often chose the same space to exercise his amphetamine-fueled logorrhea, with the result that "there would be Neal, a fountain of language, issuing forth clouds of agitated, migratory words. And across the table, Bobby, his jaw working no less vigorously, producing instead a profound, unalterable silence. Neal talked. Bobby chewed. And listened." Thus passed the days. At night, the two could be found in the front room on the second floor, where Weir bedded down on a couch in what served during waking hours as a communal music room. Around him circled Cassady, dancing, talking, and generally performing: "While the God's Amphetamine Cowboy spun, juggled and yelped joyous *doo-WOP's," Barlow writes, "Weir lay on his couch in the foreground, perfectly still, open eyes staring at the ceiling. There was something about the fixity of Bobby's gaze which seemed to indicate a fury of cognitive processing to match Neal's performance. It was as though Bobby were imagining him and going rigid with the effort involved in projecting such a tangible and kinetic image."[38] The seemingly symbiotic connection between the two was central to one of the group's strongest early compositions, the monumental "That's It for the Other One." This piece is not only an example of relatively mature songwriting from the early part of the band's career, but also a sign of the degree to which their biographical connections to Cassady and the search for American adventure, central to Beat writings, were woven into lyrics that resonate with the future-founding poetics that Pöhlmann identifies as eminently American and the sort of fragmentary aesthetic Nancy and Lacoue-Labarthe discuss.

"That's It for the Other One" is a multipart suite that entered the Grateful Dead's performance repertoire in late 1967 and saw its first official release as an innovative mix of live recordings and studio work in 1968, on *Anthem of the Sun*. The various sections of the track range from threnodic ballad to experiments with tape and prepared piano, by way of raging acid rock improvisation. The piece opens with a section titled "Cryptical Envelopment," the lyrics of which describe a judgment and execution that unfold around repeated variations of the phrase "Solemnly they stated, 'He has to die, you know he has to die.'" In the reprise of the song later in the piece, tense shifts signal that those calling for the execution have apparently seen it carried out and persist unchanged regarding their verdict: "Their minds remained unbended, / He had to die, oh, you know he had to die." A comment by Garcia suggests that one hear the song as the record not only of persecution, but of martyrdom: "I think that's an extension of my own personal symbology for 'The Man of Constant Sorrow,'" he says, "which I always thought of as being a sort of Christ parable."[39] Garcia's point makes the central event one of holy sacrifice. The attitude echoes the spiritualism of the Beats. As David Stephen Calonne has explored, Kerouac saw the virtues of the beatitudes as central to Beat identity, and Andrew Vogel emphasizes Sal's anxious need in *On the Road* to make it clear that Dean is no simple fool, but instead a saintly clown.[40] For these reasons, "Cryptical Envelopment" can be heard as of a piece with the other Beat-inflected works of the early Grateful Dead— abuse of hegemonic power causes the suffering of the disenfranchised in the present, the closure of their futurity becomes a mark of sacrifice, and poetry and lyrics respond to that closure by documenting the horrors it engenders.

While the titles assigned to the movements of "That's It for the Other One" have not been consistently applied, the section between the initial "Cryptical Envelopment" and its reprise was initially known as "The Faster We Go, the Rounder We Get" and, after 1971, most often referred to as "The Other One." Whatever it is called, this piece is the most direct declaration of the band's connection to Cassady. The two verses in this section of the suite are worth replicating in full:

> Spanish lady come to me, she lays on me this rose.
> It rainbow spirals round and round,
> It trembles and explodes.
> It left a smoking crater of my mind,
> I like to blow away.
> But the heat came round and busted me
> For smilin' on a cloudy day.
>
> Escapin' through the lily fields
> I came across an empty space
> It trembled and exploded
> Left a bus stop in its place
> The bus came by and I got on
> That's when it all began
> There was Cowboy Neal
> At the wheel
> Of a bus to never-ever land

Anecdotes about the composition of these lyrics reveal that they are entangled with those stories illustrating the power of magical thinking that have accrued to the Grateful Dead over the years. Fans talk about changes in weather occurring as songs like the "Weather Report Suite," "Cold Rain and Snow," "Rain," "Here Comes Sunshine," and "Looks like Rain" unfolded on stage. Mount Saint Helens seems to have erupted as the band launched into "Fire on the Mountain" at the Portland Memorial Coliseum, just over an hour's drive south of the volcano, on June 12, 1989. In the case of "The Other One," as recordings suggest, such magic shaped Weir's struggle with the lyrics. Those of the piece's premiere on October 22, 1967, are somewhat different from what fans hear on *Anthem of the Sun*, and recordings of several intermediate performances make it clear that the song did not emerge in something like its final form until February 3, 1968. That date fell late in a short tour that the Grateful Dead undertook of the Pacific Northwest, during which it performed eight shows over the course of a demanding fortnight. February 3 was also the evening on which Cassady, "[a] couple of thousand miles south," fell into a coma "on railroad tracks near San Miguel de Allende, Mexico." Found the next morning and carried to a hospital, Cassady died of exposure on February 4, 1968, the final day of the band's West Coast jaunt.[41] The band members would not learn about his death until their return to San Francisco, but many regard the strong bond between Weir and Cassady as having played a part in bringing the Grateful Dead's best song about him to fruition just as he passed out of the world. In the end, the point of these stories is not that they are true tales or products of misremembered timelines; whether factual or not, they speak to the perceived power of the band and the way that power unfolds in songs under the right conditions. Weir would evoke Cassady in later songs, most explicitly in "Cassidy." However, "The Other One," with its mystical origin story and premiere position as a comment on his importance to the Grateful Dead, remained a durable part of the repertoire, culminating in a final performance on July 8, 1995. Its longevity attests to the song's power and expresses the degree to which Cassady and the Beat legacy he represented for the Grateful Dead persisted as a guiding light throughout the band's career.

No small part of the song's signification of its participation in an especially American discourse derives from its treatment of space. As the quoted verses above make evident, the final lines of "The Other One" speak volumes in terms of the future of the band and the traditions with which it aligned itself by declaring and commingling an intriguing set of spatial markers. The emergence of the bus stop from the explosion of "an empty space" signals a need for reinvention, and Weir's lyrics bring together a reference to Cassady ("Cowboy Neal") and his display of frenetic power at the wheel of *Furthur* ("the bus") with an oblique allusion to Peter Pan—oblique because "never-ever land" is not quite "Neverland"—a distinction that not only nods to pre-Beat literature but ties the Pranksters' cross-country journey to a space of magical possibility outside history. This treatment of space brings the Grateful Dead at its most Beat-inflected very close indeed to the sort of interchange between chaos and systematization, between destruction and creation, that Nancy regards as essential to the productive power of literature. The experience of the sublime in the "smoking crater of" the "mind," conjoined with the openness of the explosive "empty space," strongly turns attention from past to future, materializing itself as the bus stop from which additional adventure may proceed and generative energy may flow.

To the catalog of spatial openings Weir adds the "Cowboy," that fundamental metonym for certain regions of the American imagination that Garcia once described as the place "where the laws are falling apart and every person is the sheriff and the outlaw."[42] The Beat writers followed the example of idealized cowboy tales in presenting the West as a land open to redefinition of the self and reconceptualization of American community. As Roy Kozlovsky argues, the Beats' cross-country journeys saw them speeding at one point or another to every point on the compass, but they followed predecessors in regarding the West as the promised land of opportunity and freedom.[43] Kerouac recognizes as much early in *On the Road*, at a moment when Sal Paradise, on an afternoon in Des Moines, thinks, "I was halfway across America, at the dividing line between the East of my youth and the West of my future."[44] And Kerouac, especially among the Beats, valorized the automobile as a tool for achieving a more egalitarian access to that frontier space of the West, allowing for the sort of mobility between the predetermined experience of the American East and the liminal fringe of the West. Kozlovsky explains that the social experience of the automobile in the mid-century served as more than a tool for movement into unregulated space. As the motorized transcontinental journey shortened from sixty-six days in 1903 to four days by 1945, the car became a portable embodiment of the possibilities that open space signified.[45] On these grounds, Kerouac's Sal Paradise regards the geographic site not as the goal so much as the tool that makes it available—he describes Dean and himself realizing that they "were leaving confusion and nonsense behind and performing [their] one and noble function of the time, *move*."[46] In these ways, the horses and wide-open ranges of cowboy mythology are revitalized in the mid-twentieth century as cars and highways, and especially as cars on highways leading westward.

Beat texts and the Grateful Dead's "The Other One" go further, recognizing that movement, and especially movement toward the American West or south to Mexico, is not only a search for the liminal zones that allow for social reconfiguration, but also a means to subjective redefinition. In Des Moines, Sal Paradise finds himself in a place that is geographically forward-looking and simultaneously recognizes that it is a place for the redefinition of the subject, in keeping with Arthur Rimbaud's "Je est un autre" (I is an other).[47] Kerouac writes, "I didn't know who I was. . . . I wasn't scared; I was just somebody else, some stranger . . . a ghost."[48] Likewise, we find that the speaker's experience with *Furthur* in "The Other One" follows the spatialization of the song's action with a focus on personal involvement with the scene—the ground clearing that leaves the "smoking crater" of the speaker's "mind" dispenses with the old self, and sets the stage for the moment at which the speaker can recognize that it is only when "I got on" the bus that "it all began." Taken together, the innovative, prophetic, and predominately American components that "The Other One" combines not only presage much of the Grateful Dead's later work, but also effectively serve as a catalog of the possibilities they encountered in the works of the Beat writers. Again, as Pöhlmann argues, Beat poetry confronted the closure of the American future that Ginsberg and others regarded as defining the 1950s by making that closure the subject of Beat poetry, even as they persisted in finding alternatives to it. Whereas "Cryptical Envelopment" embeds its martyrdom within the spiritual offenses of mid-twentieth century culture, "The Faster We Go, the Rounder We Get" points to a space that sidesteps that cultural dead end of Cold War anxiety. Cassady, at the wheel of *Furthur*, explodes conventional emplacement, not in the manner of a nuclear holocaust, but by remaining mobile, shaking up the old even as *Furthur* forges into spaces that promise new beginnings.

To think about "That's It for the Other One" and other early Grateful Dead compositions in relation to Beat literature is to demonstrate how compatible the band's vision of America is with that of Kerouac, Ginsberg, and other Beat writers. In its expression of dissatisfactions with mid-twentieth-century culture, and its simultaneous declaration of renewed attachments to the promise of the possibilities afforded by the future, the band performed an eminently familiar trope of renewal that Pöhlmann finds to be characteristic of strong and definitive expressions of the American literary tradition. Too, the presentation of those expressions and renewals within a process that unfolds through the exchange between creation and destruction proffers to readers a version of the Romantic fragment's model of play between those opposing forces, which serves as the shifting ground of productive energy. Yet, these conceptual continuities between the band and the Beats are by no means the entire story. As the following section of this chapter explores, the degree to which the innovations in poetry's management of the materials discussed so far are supported by innovations in literary form is another important consideration in adjudging the degree to which Beat poetry and Grateful Dead song lyrics render the sound of expression as forward-looking as the ideas expressed.

Contemporary Voices: (Re)Inventions from Whitman to Weir

It barely stands repeating that the Grateful Dead redefined several aspects of how rock and roll is understood. Some of the band's innovations were matters of music-business practice, but others were more fundamental, pertaining to how the structure and performance of music could unfold. One aspect of its achievement concerns development of a viable lyrical voice. This voice depended, in part, on a verbal idiom that, again following Pöhlmann, conveys a sense of American contemporaneity. It also entailed the recovery or invention of forms for a singable line that can support that idiom. On both fronts, the Beats' poetry is instructive, demonstrating some of these characteristics on its own terms while also serving as an example of Garcia's point, introduced earlier in this chapter, about its function as a doorway into the literary tradition.

Looking at the Beats on both their own terms and as participants in a tradition finds them engaged with a wide array of predecessors. Prominent among them are the literary Modernists, including William Carlos Williams. Williams was seen by Ginsberg and other Beat writers as a particularly strong example of an author of the literary generation immediately prior to their own, one who established a specifically American poetic diction and a self-consciously contemporary poetic form. One can see, even at the level of superficial content, certain points that would have drawn the Beats to Williams. His "For Elsie," for instance, anticipates some of the definitive passages in Beat literature. The poem's

> devil-may-care men who have taken
> to railroading
> out of sheer lust of adventure,

appear, when seen through the Beat lens, almost like a comment about Cassady, who worked the Southern Pacific railyards in San Francisco.[49] The same poem's claim that "the pure products of America / go crazy" returns in Ginsberg's description of the "best minds of my generation destroyed by madness" and in Kerouac's assertion, "The only people for me are the mad ones, the ones who are mad to live, mad to talk, mad to be saved."[50]

In Beat writing, diction marked as contemporary and American reinforces in a more substantial fashion the sort of content described in the immediately preceding paragraph. Some part of this sense is advanced via what one might call the lexical furniture of Beat texts, namely, the sorts of modern consumer and technological items that populate them. This kind of feature is evident in the "American jet fighter plane" of Gregory Corso, the "hydrogen jukebox" of Ginsberg's "Howl," and Welch's admixture in one line of "Bulldozers" and "Baseball Players."[51] Another source for contemporary diction is slang adopted from jazz and street culture. For instance, Kerouac asserts that the author recording an uninterrupted and authentic burst of literary inspiration is one who can "blow" like a jazz horn player, and Cody Pomeray (another literary incarnation of Cassady) can draw attention in *Visions of Cody* to "a cool bop hepcat."[52] Even the term labeling the generation as a "beat" one comes from street slang. As mentioned at the start of this chapter, Kerouac and Holmes picked up the word from writer and street hustler Herbert Huncke. As John Tytell explains, speech heavy in slang terms and phrasing offers alternatives to standard English. More musical in nature, it advances its content in a private code and, through constant mutation, serves the vehicle of "fugitive intentions."[53] As a result, Albert Gelpi asserts, Beat writing is "quick and syncopated, brassy and spontaneous" in its efforts "to wail the woes and sound the highs of human existence."[54]

"The Other One" participates in the Beats' lexical tendency to the current and the popular, rather than the traditional. Its "bus stop" and use of "heat" as slang for the police mark it as especially contemporary at the level of diction, and other early Grateful Dead songs fill in the picture. Examples include the "Asbestos boots" of "Can't Come Down," the "neon-light diamond" of "The Golden Road," and the name-dropping of such Haight hot spots as the Fillmore and the Avalon in "Alligator." By the time of songs like "Truckin'" or late-career numbers like "Standing on the Moon" and "West L.A. Fadeaway," the employment of recent additions to the lexicon as markers of contemporaneity became even more evident.

More important to the Beats than any anticipations of Beat content and diction is Williams's development of a poetic form that is at once contemporary and clearly American, a form produced by a variety of technical innovations, some of which are more salient than others in evaluating the work of the Beats. One such innovation is Williams's admonition to write about "no ideas but in things," a dictum that owes much to ideas that were in the air during the period of his involvement with Imagist poets in the 1910s.[55] A second, closely linked with the first, is a compression of poetic speech achieved via the exclusion of abstractions and any other words that do not contribute to the effect of the whole. These two factors resulted in a spare but powerful poetry: direct, concrete, and highly charged. A third factor in Williams's aesthetic is his short line lengths, which grew out of his effort to liberate poetry from traditional meters and move toward the patterns of natural speech, particularly language tied to the experiences of people in American places.[56] In this context, the compression of the poem was among the factors dictating the placement of the line break, with the result that Williams's line lengths fall far short of conventional examples of English meter, such as John Milton's blank verse. Indeed, in Williams's much-anthologized poem "The Red Wheelbarrow," one sees lines that range from two to four syllables, with one or two stressed syllables, which are sometimes given over to single words:

> so much depends
> upon
>
> a red wheel
> barrow
>
> glazed with rain
> water
>
> beside the white
> chickens[57]

By the 1950s, when he was in communication with Ginsberg, Williams was experimenting with other innovative strategies. He was much at work on his epic, *Paterson*, in the second part of which (along with several other books produced in the 1940s), he began using a triadic stanzaic structure. This approach sees three lines increasingly indented, as in the following:

> I have learned much in my life
>   from books
>   and out of them.[58]

As this example demonstrates, Williams does not adhere to conventional metrical patterns. Instead, the length of the line is defined by what he calls a "variable foot," which takes advantage of free verse's liberties while nodding in the direction of consistent form. For better or worse, later critics and poets have not found themselves entirely on the same page regarding Williams's definition of the variable foot or his intentions for it, but one can see that he employs typographical arrangements that give line breaks a strong rhythmic function. This is not a strategy that depends on the conventional meters of English prosody. Williams has found a form that breaks not only with the rhythms of England's use of the language, but also with the pre-twentieth-century poetic tradition, in favor of a structure more amenable to the physical and social rhythms of American speech in the present. His aesthetic responsiveness to variations in spoken expression, and his willingness to experiment with variations on conventional prosody, speak to Williams's recognition that the poetic oeuvre is a work in progress, a fragment that points to the larger whole of American verse and to creative energy in general.

Early in his career, Ginsberg also struggled with the problem of line length, a matter that he recognized was relevant to the seeming contemporaneity of the poem. When Ginsberg undertook his own experiments with the rhythms of American speech, he initially followed the example of Williams, a tendency that Ginsberg saw acknowledged in the few appreciative remarks Williams offered in letters, and, more publicly, in his composition of an introduction to *Howl and Other Poems*.[59] Ginsberg's attachment to the short lines and triadic arrangements that Williams developed remains in evidence in the extant typescript version of "Howl," as the opening lines demonstrate:

> I saw the best minds of my generation
>   generation destroyed by madness
>   starving, ~~mystical~~, naked.[60]

Other poets associated with Ginsberg were also tending toward the shorter line, at least in some poems: McClure is a strong example; Snyder and Welch are others. As the final version of Ginsberg's "Howl" shows, however, these short lines, arranged in triads, were traded during revision for much longer ones that do not necessarily rely on the three-part arrangement that Williams developed. The opening line thus becomes "I saw the best minds of my generation destroyed by madness, starving hysterical naked."[61] The justification for Ginsberg's choice to move away from the shorter lines is twofold. One aspect is that his ideas manifest themselves in lines amenable to longer breaths. He was not, in other words, rejecting the example of Williams in turning to long lines, but adjusting Williams's precepts for his own natural physical and mental rhythms. Ginsberg stated, "Ideally each line of *Howl* is a single breath unit. My breath is long—that's the measure, one physical-mental inspiration of thought contained in the elastic of a breath. It probably bugs Williams."[62] As Ronna C. Johnson explains, the argument of Olson's essay "Projective Verse" concerning the accurate regulation of the poet's "heart" via the "breath" and the "line" reinforces Ginsberg's ongoing work on this front, and it would inspire Joanne Kyger, Kerouac, McClure, and Diane di Prima as well.[63] Stefanie Heine has made the point that this movement on the part of Beat poets connects the poetic to the corporeal; it is an embodied literature that finds authenticity in performance.[64] One can see how such a poetry would appeal to the Grateful Dead, whose prioritization of performance is a definitive feature of its musical identity. Another explanation for Ginsberg's movement from short lines to longer ones concerns his attachment to the example of an earlier American free verse poet, one often regarded as the father of American poetry: Walt Whitman.

Whitman was, like Williams after him, devoted to free verse as evidence of an American break from older, and specifically Old World, poetic forms, but whereas Williams moved toward greater compression and condensation, Whitman's approach was a project of expansion. This aspect of Whitman's work was true not only in terms of the typographic line, but also in terms of the management of content. In Whitman's poetry, the people, places, and experiences of America are lifted in a swell of exuberance that is at once specific and universal. As Bonnie Costello writes, "Any reader of 'Song of Myself' is immediately impressed by the sweep of American life that it takes in, especially through the poet's famous catalogs, his 'enumerations.' He makes long, even canto-long, lists, in sentences paced by syntactic repetition. These create a better sense of America's unity in diversity than any generalization."[65] The result is a sequence such as the following:

> The bride unrumples her white dress, the minute-hand of the clock moves slowly,
> The opium-eater reclines with rigid head and just-open'd lips,
> The prostitute draggles her shawl, her bonnet bobs on her tipsy and pimpled neck
> . . . .
> The President holding a cabinet council is surrounded by the great Secretaries

> On the piazza walk three matrons stately and friendly with twined arms,
> The crew of the fish-smack pack repeated layers of halibut in the hold[66]

Whitman here moves between social realms with ease, from a bride to a prostitute, from the president to a group of fishermen. Elsewhere in the poem, he does the same with race and place, bringing everything together in a great mélange of American life, which he generally presents as worthy for its egalitarian impulses. He also anticipates Williams in avoiding, at least in this passage, abstract speculation in favor of a concrete image. This ancestor, then, modeled for Ginsberg the way in which the long line and repetition can serve as a means of celebratory inclusion, one that resonates with both the individual mind and the national consciousness. Whitman's poetry is, in short, an eminently American one, crafted by what Linda Freedman fairly calls a "democratic personality."[67] Ginsberg's use of concrete images, catalogs, and long lines resound with echoes of Whitman's poetry, as in the following lines from "Howl":

> who went out whoring through Colorado in myriad stolen night-cars, N.C., secret hero of these poems, cocksman and Adonis of Denver—joy to the memory of his innumerable lays of girls in empty lots & diner backyards, moviehouses' rickety rows, on mountaintops in caves or with gaunt waitresses in familiar roadside lonely petticoat upliftings & especially secret gas-station solipsisms of johns, & hometown alleys too,
> who faded out in vast sordid movies, were shifted in dreams, woke on a sudden Manhattan, and picked themselves up out of basements hung-over with heartless Tokay and horrors of Third Avenue iron dreams & stumbled to unemployment offices,
> who walked all night with their shoes full of blood on the snowbank docks waiting for a door in the East River to open to a room full of steam-heat and opium[68]

As these three lines demonstrate, the catalogs of Ginsberg's poetry, even though they have traded Whitman's excited incorporation of all that his mind meets for a tonal shift appropriate to their focus on the dispirited and distressed, on the "beat," are well-served by the extended line.

"Howl" was by no means the end of the question. Even a decade after the Six Gallery reading, when he was working alongside and socializing with the Grateful Dead more often, Ginsberg was still exploring the spaces Williams and Whitman opened with their formal innovations. His "Wichita Vortex Sutra," for example, which was written in 1966 and thus more or less contemporary with his earliest interactions with the Grateful Dead, employs in part the tripartite line of Williams that Ginsberg reformulated under the influence of Whitman's example:

> Blue eyed children dance and hold thy Hand O aged Walt
>   who came from Lawrence to Topeka to envision
>   Iron interlaced upon the city plain[69]

As this excerpt demonstrates, there is an ongoing negotiation between Whitman and Williams in poems across Ginsberg's career. No little part of his works' dynamism derives from the tension he creates by bringing together the compressed and "modern" triadic stanzas of short lines Williams developed and the expansive and "American" long lines of Whitman. Ginsberg's proposed compromise delivers both contemporaneity and a strong native spirit. The challenges and possibilities of rhythm, timing, and phrasing, which are part of what Ginsberg, Williams, and Whitman explore as an aspect of their development of an American voice, are, of course, also key aspects of music. For any singer, the suitability of the line in terms of voicing, breath, and musical accompaniment is an essential consideration. Garcia noted that a lot of the songs that fell out of the Grateful Dead's repertoire over the years did so because they failed on this front, with something like "Cosmic Charlie" being "cumbersome" because it demanded "really complex chord voicings" that were hard to play while also focusing on the "vocals." That and other songs from the early part of the band's career are, he states, "overwritten," so "packed with lyrics" that they fail in performance.[70] In other words, the maturity of the band's songwriting depended on the accommodation of their concerns about the line, essentially the same problem that drove some of Ginsberg's most important engagements with the innovations of Whitman, Williams, and Olson.

Intriguingly, the lyrics of Weir's "The Other One" functionally resemble Ginsberg's middle ground between the rhythms of Whitman and those of Williams, and they are of a piece with the Grateful Dead's effort to play music that departs from the tired clichés of pop standards and expands the music's possibilities. Just as Ginsberg developed his prosodic experimentations with line length in relation to rhythm as part of an effort to find a form that delivered a sense of modernity equal to the experiences of the Beat generation, so the Grateful Dead explored time signatures, rhythms, and phrasings that differed from those of traditional popular music, which tends to rely on standard time or waltz time. The band practiced extensively, especially in its first few years, with less familiar options, including the 11/8 of "The Eleven," the 10/4 of "Playing in the Band," and the 7/4 section of "Uncle John's Band," among others. Even when the time signature the band used was not too exotic, the phrasing could make it sound so. The percussion line of "The Other One" is a strong example of this latter strategy. It has been described by band members as generating a "tiger paws" rhythm, something that is especially evident in performances that include two drummers.[71] "Tiger paws" is an evocative description that captures the power and idiosyncratic rhythm of the line, even if it is more than a bit imprecise in terms of musicological specificity. This rhythm and the song that unfolds in relation to it depend on a tension between the vocal line and the time signature of the song, a time signature that, although not in itself particularly unusual, evokes figures of different lengths for the musicians. The result, as David Dodd explains, is a "roiling music, with" a "tumbling 12/8 beat" that "can sound like it's in a fast three or a slower four or even a moderate six."[72] This variability, via which the 12/8 is heard in three or four different ways simultaneously, shapes the delivery of the vocal lines, which are sometimes paired with instrumental lines that unfold in different phrasings. As a result, there is some ambiguity in the listeners' experience, an ambiguity reflected in the typographic inconsistencies evident in Trist and Dodd's book of lyrics. Here, again, is the first verse as they present it:

> Spanish lady come to me, she lays on me this rose.
> It rainbow spirals round and round,
> It trembles and explodes.
> It left a smoking crater of my mind,
> I like to blow away.
> But the heat came round and busted me
> For smilin' on a cloudy day.

The general alteration between longer and shorter lines suggests a loose ballad stanza, but, even in light of that observation, the first line, at thirteen syllables, is obviously extended in comparison to the others. To insert a line break at the comma, however, brings it into the range of its fellows. Listening to the song reveals that Weir's delivery typically offers a short rest at the commas and a longer one at the periods, although the exact length of each varies a bit by line and depends on the intonations of a given performance, especially in those late-career shows during which Dan Healy added effects to Weir's singing. In print, however, it is immediately apparent that Weir's song offers vocal lines that are stimulating by virtue of their ambiguity in relation to the lengths of phrases allowed by competing understandings of the piece's time signature.

Ultimately, the idiosyncratic phrasing of vocal lines in "The Other One" results in verses that can be heard and read as a series of either eight short lines or four longer ones, each of which marked by a strong caesura. There is an intriguing echo of a typical Old English verse form here, but even more immediately relevant is the similarity of Weir's lines to those Ginsberg developed, which balance Whitman-like expansiveness against the compression of Williams's variable foot as a means to stage the terms of twentieth-century American speech.[73] Like Ginsberg, Weir has composed lines of variable length and meter that allow for the sort of contemporary syntax and diction required for writing or singing about Neal Cassady and the America through which he moved. At the same time, Weir has honored the limits that the breath imposes on the length and rhythm of the sung line. Just as the other instrumental lines present figures of varying lengths and thus challenge easy apprehension of the song's time signature, so the vocal line works in tension with itself, creating a sort of aural equivalent to the exploding, swirling, and trembling described in the lyrics and manifest in the music.

Such qualities as those enumerated above show that Weir employs songwriting strategies in "The Other One" akin to those Beat writers developed in pursuit of their own artistic ends. Furthermore, Cassady's presence in the song reinforces a listener's sense of these similarities. In particular, the Beat poets' discovery of markers that signaled their poetic voices as contemporary and distinctively American was understood by Whitman and Williams, and then, as well, by Ginsberg and other Beat writers, in a fashion that found them pursuing innovations in rhythm, line length, and phrasing—some of the same features that make "The Other One" so powerful.

This chapter has largely focused on "That's It for the Other One" for two reasons. First, the direct allusion to Cassady offers an irresistible entrance into consideration of the shaping role that Beat texts and personalities played in delineating the Grateful Dead's sense of American identity. Most centrally, the piece demonstrates exactly the sort of future-founding qualities that Pöhlmann sees as fundamental to American poetry, including the Beat poetry of the mid-twentieth century. That the piece, and particularly the movement titled "The Faster We Go, the Rounder We Get," remained for so long—indeed longer than any other original composition—and so consistently central to the band's repertoire indicates not only the band's persistence in its devotion to the allegiances declared therein, but also its recognition that the piece offered the sort of openness to possibility that a truly successful future-oriented poetry makes manifest. The opportunities it afforded are in these senses central to an America that explores, critiques, and generally articulates possibilities for liberty, dignity, adventure, and beauty. Furthermore, the presentation in "That's It for the Other One" of the sorts of poetics that engage past models as launchpads for the development of new terms amenable to future efforts very much supports a view of the Grateful Dead's aesthetic as one that answers to the conditions of the fragment as understood by Nancy. The interplay between destruction and creation in the lyrics, as in the improvisatory passages allowed during performances of the piece, honors creativity as an adaptive process rather than a movement toward an exhaustive product, as an ongoing openness to generative possibility.

"That's It for the Other One" is, in the ways described above, not only a direct engagement with Beat literature but also a powerful statement about the band's aesthetics during the late 1960s. The following chapter will look more closely at the Grateful Dead's work from the very late 1960s into the early 1970s. This was a period in which new material, best read in relation to literary models other than that of the Beats, extended the band's consideration of America's past, present, and possible futures. It is worth keeping in mind, however, that these later avenues were opened to exploration in part due to the foundation of Beat literature, and, in this sense, the arguments of this chapter must remain a factor in the next, as well as in those that follow.

Just Like Mary Shelley

THE GOTHIC TRADITION,
THE AMERICAN PAST,
AND THE GRATEFUL DEAD

Audience recordings of the Grateful Dead's July 22, 1972, show at the Paramount Northwest Theatre in Seattle include a bit of stage chatter as the band tunes up for the second set. Phil Lesh remarks, "That thing is pretty weird looking, believe me. I can't even describe it. It defies description. Suffice to say, it's got a skull and a bunch of bones on it, and it just kinda . . . haaaaangs there." Bob Weir chimes in with a comment or two, then Lesh adds, "I don't know. It reminds me of Gormenghast, reeking and dripping." Lesh's mention of Mervyn Peake's *Gormenghast* series of novels is consistent with the appreciation for speculative fiction—including fantasy, horror, and science fiction—that members of the Grateful Dead expressed over the years. Kurt

Vonnegut and Theodore Sturgeon are perhaps the most frequently mentioned figures in this regard, but their novels shared space with a lot of fellow travelers on the band's bookshelves. In the case of Jerry Garcia, we can get a sense of the extent of his devotion to this sort of fiction from Ozzie Ahlers, who explains that, on a Jerry Garcia Band tour, Garcia "had almost no clothing. He'd just brought two suitcases, almost entirely filled with science fiction books. He loved science fiction. . . . He was an avid fan and anything that I had read he had read twice and all the books surrounding it."[1] Rock Scully also notes Garcia's fascination with science fiction, writing of a flight to the East Coast, "Jerry's immersed in a science fiction novel. You always know when Jerry has a good book because he'll share it, quote from it, give you a synopsis. By the time he snaps it shut, everybody wants to read it next."[2] Too, one could recall Garcia's unrealized interest in adapting Vonnegut's novel *Sirens of Titan* for film, having gone so far as acquiring the necessary legal rights for the effort, working on a script, and meeting with film-industry figures.[3] Robert Hunter also tipped his hat in the direction of speculative fiction, as when he joined a band called the Nazgûl, which was to record music for and perhaps appear in an unrealized cinematic version of George R. R. Martin's novel *The Armageddon Rag*.[4] Unlike most of the writings of Sturgeon, Martin, and Vonnegut, Peake's *Gormenghast* books—the novels *Titus Groan*, *Gormenghast*, and *Titus Alone*, as well as the novella *Boy in Darkness* and the fragments of the unfinished *Titus Awakes*—emphasize the eerie. The first two volumes in the series, in particular, are dominated by the "reeking and dripping" castle that is their central setting. While Peake's works are not often discussed in relation to the band, Lesh's reference to a work of weird fiction is hardly an isolated incident in the context of the Grateful Dead as a whole.

The aspects of supernatural horror that inform *Gormenghast* are also evident in many of the band's other enthusiasms. The EC horror comics for which Garcia expressed so much love are one example.[5] Another is Garcia's spoken-word recording of the short story "My Pretty Pony" for the audiobook release of Stephen King's *Nightmares and Dreamscapes* collection.[6] Several of these strands came together when the Grateful Dead became involved with the 1980s revival of *The Twilight Zone* television show. Not only did the band join Merl Saunders in contributing recordings of the show's theme and incidental music, but Mickey Hart signed on as sound designer for the series, and Hunter wrote the screenplay for one episode, "Devil's Alphabet."[7] Hunter's episode is an adaptation of Arthur Gray's 1910 short story "The Everlasting Club," which features a promise by seven nineteenth-century Cantabrigians to meet annually, a pact that binds them to return even after death. Gray's piece may be a minor example of the Edwardian ghost story, but the notion that a shared agreement draws seven men inexorably back to the same ritual, creating a bond that transcends even death itself, may well have resonated with Hunter and the rest of the band. Indeed, Hunter's choice to work with the tale seems to have been almost supernaturally prescient when one notes that the episode first aired just a few months before Garcia's near-death experience, followed by his subsequent return to the stage after a diabetic coma in 1986. Furthermore, this revival of *The Twilight Zone* in the late 1980s would see Hunter earning writing credits alongside a who's who of speculative fiction writers, including King, Sturgeon, and Martin. Given the broad importance of supernatural horror to the band's imagination, this chapter undertakes an investigation into connections between the Grateful Dead and the tradition in which most contemporary horror narratives are rooted, that of the gothic novel. More particularly, this chapter argues that traditional gothic characteristics, and especially American variations on those traditional qualities, allowed the early 1970s iteration of the band to question American history and redefine the project that was the "Grateful Dead" in a changing national culture.

The Gothic Tradition

The gothic narrative made its debut with Horace Walpole's 1764 novel *The Castle of Otranto*, although it was not until the very late 1780s that the genre began to gain its widest appreciation. Essential to that early popularity were Ann Radcliffe's novels, particularly her 1794 *The Mysteries of Udolpho*. These works are the ancestors of the modern horror novel and film and are recognizable by conventions of setting, incident, and character. Familiar features include decaying castles and abbeys filled with secret passages and cobwebs, supernatural events, corruption, cannibalism, incest, necrophilia, live burial, addiction, violence, mystery, the grotesque, nightmares, and a gloomy antihero. More significant than these relatively superficial trappings are the gothic's conceptual preoccupations. As Leslie Fiedler writes, the "gothic ... is committed to portraying the power of darkness."[8] It is motivated by "guilt ... and the fear that ... the West has opened a way for the inruption [sic] of darkness: for insanity and the disintegration of the self."[9] Its aesthetic is one "that replaces the classic concept of nothing-in-excess with the doctrine ... that nothing succeeds like excess."[10] Here, too much of everything is just enough. Fiedler's remarks are certainly foreboding, but some perspective might allow one to see them as the negative image of the exchange between creation and destruction that Nancy declares true of the subject as understood in light of the fragment. The Fichtean self that posits itself may not be entirely compatible with the fragmentary subject to which Nancy points, but both Fichte and Nancy recognize in the dissolution of the subject no dead end of total dispersal, but instead an opportunity for production. This is the self as disunified, uncertain, and even divided against itself, but its energy is a force that can serve assemblage; as in literature, dissolution marks the beginning of self-production.

As the dates and titles of the literary texts mentioned in the preceding paragraph suggest, the birth of gothic literature is entangled with the maturation of the Romantic movement, even if it is not entirely one with it. While Romantic literature in general is by no means obsessed with the darker side of human experience and is more inclined to assume a coherent self than the distorted and fragmented one often encountered in gothic texts, it does represent a cultural critique of both the rationality and order that governed neoclassical aesthetics and broader cultural sensibilities of the Enlightenment and thus celebrates not only the fanciful poetic romances of the Middle Ages, but also the role of intuition and imagination in the apprehension of truth. This celebration of the irrational capacities sets the ground for Romanticism as a movement that was enchanted by the awesome power of the sublime, as expounded by Edmund Burke on the basis of the Pseudo-Longinus, and that preoccupation sits comfortably alongside the excess that is so common a feature of the gothic scenario.

Regardless of its gothic dimensions, the Romantic movement's role in shaping the sensibilities of the Grateful Dead is difficult to overstate. In the first place, as Colin Campbell and others argue, the similarities between the values of the 1960s counterculture and those of the late eighteenth- and early nineteenth-century Romantics are hard to ignore, even if, as Maarten Doorman points out, they are also difficult to articulate with rigor.[11] There is, however, a much more proximate connection between the Grateful Dead and Romantic poetry: Robert Hunter (né Robert Burns) is a great-great-grandson of Scotland's most notable Romantic poet, Robert Burns.[12] Burns is famous for having championed the cause of poems in Scottish dialect within the canon of English poetry, and some part of his success stems in part from his introduction of engaging idioms and phrasings from Scottish popular song. In this regard, his poetic achievement is something like that of the Grateful Dead in its music. Just as the band infused its rock and roll with components of American and European folk music traditions, so Burns incorporated traditional Scottish folk sources in his poetry, and thereby not only found source materials for his own songs and poems, but contributed to the construction of Scottish national identity.[13] "Auld Lang Syne," which Burns built on a folk lyric that may otherwise have been lost to us, is perhaps the most famous result of this process. Burns's impulse toward the definition of a national identity in song, his enshrining of the Scottish popular arts in the high literary canon, even as the kingdom of Scotland opened to greater communication with London, is, in its way, commensurate to the Grateful Dead's embrace of its American folk-musical roots as the 1960s came to an end.[14] There are more incidental correspondences, as well. Aside from "Auld Lang Syne," the best-known of Burns's works is likely his poem "A Red, Red Rose," which—while inspiring Bob Dylan and contributing to the Grateful Dead's imagery—offers its "And fare thee weel, my only luve! / And fare thee weel a-while!" as a bridge between Shakespeare's use of such phrases and the "Fare you well" and "Fare thee well" that appear in "Smokestack Lightning," "Brokedown Palace," and "Cassidy."[15]

Furthermore, Burns, too, had his gothic bent. We are indebted to him for his poem "Halloween," which played a notable role in popularizing that Scottish name for the holiday, but the greater achievement in this vein is "Tam O'Shanter." The latter is a narrative poem that tells the tale of Mr. O'Shanter, who has a habit of getting drunk at the local pub before heading home to his unhappy wife. After leaving the tavern late on one especially dark and stormy night, Tam and his trusty horse, Meg, glimpse something dreadful:

> Warlocks and witches in a dance:
> Nae cotillion brent new frae France,
> But hornpipes, jigs, strathspeys, and reels,
> Put life and mettle in their heels:
> A winnock-bunker in the east,
> There sat auld Nick, in shape o' beast;
> A towzie tyke, black, grim, and large,
> To gie them music was his charge[16]

Surrounding the frightful dance are corpses in open coffins, candles, and the weapons of murderers. While unsettled by the gruesome scene, Tam, bolstered by his Dutch courage, lingers to watch. One of the witches is both attractive and scantily clad, facts from which he derives further spectatorial motivation. Eventually he is overcome with spirit for her, at which point, "Tam tint his reason a' thegither, / And roars out, 'Weel done, Cutty-sark!'"[17] At the appreciative shout, the witches notice and chase after him. Knowing such magical persons cannot follow him more than halfway across a river, he flees across a homeward bridge, reaching it just in time to save his neck. His horse is less fortunate—poor Meg's tail is lost to the pursuers. Burns's excursions into the gothic were clearly offered with a sense of humor, but their subject matter nevertheless demonstrates a preoccupation with the eerie. That Burns gives us gothic elements is, in itself, of interest, but that they are commingled in his poetry with a project of Scottish national definition is worthy of note, for a similar mélange of gothic horror and history can be found across the Atlantic.

The Grateful Dead and Frankenstein

In the lyrics of the Grateful Dead, the most explicit nod to the gothic literary tradition appears in "Ramble on Rose." The song's catalog of characters turns, in its penultimate verse, to a major author of the literary gothic and her most famous character:

> Just like Mary Shelley
> Just like Frankenstein
> Clank your chains and count your change
> Try to walk the line

While the jaunty rhythm may suggest to a casual listener that "Ramble on Rose" playfully enumerates American pop-cultural figures and scenes (Billy Sunday, a ragtime band, New York City, Wolfman Jack) and appropriates lines from the superficially innocent "Jack and Jill" nursery rhyme, the piece very much has its darker side. It begins, after all, by name-checking Jack the Ripper and closes the first verse with a reference to the destruction of Jericho. The introduction of destructive powers calls the listener to rethink the tone of the song while also revealing how the piece tests the terms of productive tension that Nancy finds staged by the Romantic fragment.

Furthermore, while the song's later mention of Frankenstein extends the reach of British monstrosity introduced at the very start, it also offers an intriguing ambiguity in terms of the formulation of the subject at the border of death and life. In Shelley's novel *Frankenstein*, the main character is a scientist who bears the family name Frankenstein, and he brings to life a body assembled from the parts of several corpses. On the other hand, in many later representations, Frankenstein's creature bears the name of its creator, with the consequence that there is a slippage in the popular imagination between creator and creature. To take the measure of the Frankenstein story—at once in reference to Shelley's original version and its reformulations in American culture over the past two centuries—thus requires that one consider the scientist at its heart and the being he creates. Intriguingly, the ambiguities of naming are maintained even as one hears Garcia sing of Frankenstein clanking his chains. Among the more striking scenes in the cinematic representations of the creature is one showing his escape from chains in a jail cell in James Whale's 1935 *The Bride of Frankenstein*, and Whale's 1931 *Frankenstein* also shows the creature in chains. In Shelley's novel, however, Dr. Frankenstein is the only one of the two to be imprisoned, first as the suspected murderer of his friend Clerval, and later as a man driven to madness by the death of his wife. Of the latter period, Shelley's Frankenstein relates, "Chains and darkness were the only objects that pressed upon me. Sometimes, indeed, I dreamt that I wandered in flowery meadows and pleasant vales with the friends of my youth, but I awoke and found myself in a dungeon."[18] In both the cinematic and the literary tradition, then, chains are part of the Frankenstein story, albeit in different regards. The dead being brought to life, and the man who made that possible, thus "walk the line" not only to avoid the grasp of the authorities, but also to tread the border between such binaries as living and dead, as well as self and other. The improvisatory interplay that their initial space allows is one, Nancy argues, that is liberating—it is a state of true freedom, and one that resonated with members of the Grateful Dead.

While Hunter's lyrics point to Shelley's novel, Garcia's interpretation was likely shaped by Hollywood's depictions of Frankenstein's creature. In one interview, Garcia declares a family excursion to see the 1948 film *Abbott and Costello Meet Frankenstein* a foundational encounter with the unsettling, explaining that he spent much of the film hiding behind the theater's seats. Frankenstein's creature, "a dead thing brought to life," he continues, was especially resonant, given that his father had died the year before. Furthermore, he attributes his ongoing personal fascinations to the depiction of the three monsters that feature in the film—Dracula and the Wolfman among them—not only as a source of imagery that contributed to the expansion of his artistic sensibilities, but also as a path that led to German Expressionism and an interest in cinema in general. More broadly, he adds, the film fostered a sense that "there are things in this world that are really weird. I don't think I knew that before I saw that movie. There are things in the world that are really weird, and there are people who are concerned with them. . . . I thought to myself on some level, I think I want to be concerned with things that are weird. . . . That seems like fun."[19] "Fun" would remain a key term in Garcia's evaluative lexicon, and the form that his most famous brand of fun weirdness took, the

Grateful Dead, shares more than a few similarities with both Frankenstein's creature and its creator—not least of these is the centrality of electricity.

Frankenstein's creature is brought to life—quite dramatically in the films, somewhat more subtly in the novel—via galvanism, the use of electricity to cause movement in otherwise dead organic tissue. That the Grateful Dead followed Dr. Frankenstein in using electricity to bring new life to the old is a theme that stands in the background of countless aspects of the band's projects. The Grateful Dead even had its own mad scientist, in the figure of Augustus Owsley "Bear" Stanley III. Bear's contributions to the scene are to some degree stylistic. He helped develop, for instance, the design of the band's red, white, and blue skull-with-lightning-bolt logo. More important was his support as the early patron and live sound engineer of the band. The latter role was motivated, in part, by the dismal conditions governing electric amplification of live music in the early to mid-1960s. In his efforts to address these sonic shortcomings, Bear cobbled together pieces of movie-theater PA systems, home stereo components, and custom-made gear. The diversity and inherent fickleness of the equipment involved, his idiosyncratic perfectionism, and the improvisational wiring demanded by the many venues that hosted performances but were unequipped to power or stage sound gear properly led to a system that was hard to transport, took a long time to set up, and was subject to endless breakdowns.[20] The Grateful Dead, and its offshoot, Alembic, would eventually become leaders in the field of live concert sound—a legacy made possible by Bear's commitment to the alchemical generation of a new whole from various bits and pieces of otherwise separate systems and bringing that misshapen thing to life with electric power. The attendant complexities, however, meant that the first systems had a short stage life, and it is not too surprising that Weir recalls that the band referred to the earliest incarnations of Bear's system, which they regarded with no little trepidation, as "Owsleystein."[21]

Bear was a shaping factor in the band's sound in other ways too. In the late 1960s, he—along with Melissa Cargill and various comrades such as Rhoney Gissen-Stanley and Tim Scully—helped manufacture a tremendous amount of LSD, estimated at 1.25 million hits by Jesse Jarnow, introducing a new consciousness later termed "electric." For some time, only sources like Albert Hofmann, who not only first synthesized the drug but did so within the infrastructure and budget of the Sandoz corporation, would likely be able to promise purer materials in larger quantities. But unlike a big corporation, Bear would give away a lot of his product and much of his profit to feed the brains and ears of the West Coast counterculture.[22] He was, to put it otherwise, a head and a part of the scene, dramatically unlike both the early military-industrial pioneers of psychedelic experimentation and the more elitist Millbrook / Harvard University crowd centered around Timothy Leary and Ram Dass, which included in its legacy the Miracle at Marsh Chapel, held at Boston University. LSD was legal in the early days of the Grateful Dead, of course, and it had its cultural proselytizers in figures like Ken Kesey.[23] With these points in mind, one can see that Bear's identity as a Frankenstein-like electrical reanimator must be understood as having at least two facets: the first sparkled on the high-powered sound stage, while the other, even-higher-powered, performed its work in the psychochemical register.

Yet, Bear's electrification of the Grateful Dead, which brought the band to life in a new way, was as much psychedelic-mental as acoustic-physical, meaning that the chemical systems could go haywire just as the sound systems did. Among the more famous low points is Hunter's experience on June 8, 1969, an evening that once again foregrounds Bear's identity as an echo of the problematic Victor Frankenstein. As could happen at Grateful Dead shows, the backstage beverages were dosed, although miscommunications and mischief meant that this night saw an earth-shattering amount of acid—Dennis McNally proposes a full gram of crystal LSD—dropped into the apple juice.[24] The evening went downhill fast for several musicians and people in the entourage, including Hunter. Things worsened when his girlfriend Christie Bourne was temporarily kidnapped, leaving him on a very bad trip indeed, one during which he saw blood gushing from Janis Joplin's mouth and felt as if he "experienced every assassination he knew of, dying with JFK and with Lincoln, among many other deaths."[25] While the various extant narratives of the evening vary somewhat, several feature Hunter taking a swing at Bear, screaming, "Owsleystein!" and "The monster you created destroyeth you."[26] Hunter was no novice with psychedelics. Aside from being part of the Grateful Dead's inmost circle, he had been a subject in the same MK-Ultra experiments as had Kesey, but this night was exceptional.[27] He later estimated his consumption at 250,000 micrograms (which is about one thousand times greater than strong recreational doses), adding, "My time is still scrambled from that era. It took me a full two years after that to get back to where I felt creative or could feel any joy in life, or much of anything else."[28] Nevertheless, he turned the straw of the experience into gold. His psychedelic brush with death became the basis for the powerful "Black Peter," which can thus be heard as joining "Casey Jones" and the "Sweet Jane" passage in "Truckin'" in warning listeners about the dangers of reckless use of illicit substances.[29]

We might argue for at least one other sense in which the Grateful Dead resembled Frankenstein's creature. In a passage given over to its construction, Shelley writes, "I collected bones from charnel-houses and disturbed, with profane fingers, the tremendous secrets of the human frame.... The dissecting room and the slaughter-house furnished many of my materials."[30] The hodgepodge nature of the creature's form resembles the diversity of talents and traditions that were united under the aegis of the Grateful Dead. From the model of "bleshing," as derived from Sturgeon's fiction, to Bill Walker's description of the band as a multiheaded entity—captured in his cover artwork for *Anthem of the Sun*—the notion of the Grateful Dead as a whole comprising many parts, including the musicians, the audience members, the performance space, and all the crew and family involved in a given night's experience, persists. While that new whole, synthesized and brought to life in performance, may not be as obviously monstrous as Hollywood's image of Frankenstein's creature tends to be, neither is it always naively innocent and pure. The ways the impurities found a space are many, but their eruptions led the band to a critical examination of itself as the 1960s turned into the 1970s—an examination that follows the gothic tradition, drawing attention to the darker corners of both the past and the present.

The Grateful Dead's American Songbook

No listener could fail to register the strong shift in the sound of the Grateful Dead's music as one proceeds from the heady psychedelia of 1968 and 1969, as represented on *Anthem of the Sun*, *Aoxomoxoa*, and *Live/Dead*, to the roots-rock, songwriting-focused sensibilities of *Workingman's Dead* and *American Beauty*, both from 1970. While the tracks on the former records, with the exception of "Dupree's Diamond Blues," had been intentionally and aggressively unconventional, the latter two albums, as Buzz Poole argues, incorporated pieces that clearly draw on the long history of American popular music, both in terms of form, with vocal harmonizing and songs with "hooks and bridges," and in terms of subject matter, with settings and character types drawn from American history—and, particularly, the mythic agrarian American past that stretches from the hard times of Appalachian mines and the rough backcountry of the Louisiana Delta to the dusty roads of the Wild West.[31] The three records released after *American Beauty* are, aside from some studio overdubs, live: the self-titled album (generally known by fans as *Skullfuck* or *Skull and Roses*) from 1971, *Europe '72*, and *The History of the Grateful Dead, Vol. 1 (Bear's Choice)*, recorded in February 1970 and released in July 1973. Hunter explained that he thought the original compositions first released on those live records, if given the studio treatment, could have made a worthy follow-up to *American Beauty*, thus forming a trilogy of Americana-inflected albums.[32] Garcia adds that some of the tunes from the era even trickled through to the band's next studio album, *Wake of the Flood*, released on October 15, 1973.[33] For fans making it to the concerts, the Grateful Dead's turn to a more folk-inflected mode began well before the release of *Workingman's Dead* in June 1970, in part because acoustic or partially acoustic versions of *Aoxomoxoa* songs had been performed on stage at that point for some time. Garcia played acoustic guitar on "Rosemary" during the performance on December 7, 1968; "Mountains of the Moon" usually featured Garcia on acoustic guitar starting December 20, 1968, with Weir and Tom Constanten joining on acoustic guitar and harpsichord, respectively, on some performances; and beginning in February 1969, "Dupree's Diamond Blues" would usually be performed on acoustic guitars. Too, the airing of what would become *Workingman's Dead* tracks started with the debut of "Dire Wolf" on June 7, 1969. The following months and years saw the unveiling of a tremendous number of new compositions that pursued this new-old direction, with eight more tracks in 1969, twelve or thirteen (depending on whether you count "Sunshine Daydream" as part of "Sugar Magnolia") in 1970, eighteen in 1971, and four in 1972, prior to the debut in April of "Stella Blue," which marks the arrival in concert of songs that would be recorded for *Wake of the Flood*.

In other words, even if one sets aside the eighteen (or nineteen) pieces that appeared on *Workingman's Dead* and *American Beauty*, "The Wheel" (which was composed during this period but did not see its live Grateful Dead debut until 1976), the four songs that were recorded for Garcia's first solo record but were part of the Grateful Dead's repertoire, "Cassidy" (which was composed during this period but did not debut as part of the Grateful Dead live repertoire until 1974), and the other six songs that were recorded for Weir's solo album *Ace* but were part of the Grateful Dead's repertoire, there are still thirteen original compositions that would have been contenders for a never-realized third volume of Grateful Dead Americana: "Mason's Children," "Bertha," "Wharf Rat," "Mister Charlie," "Brown-Eyed Women," "Empty Pages," "Tennessee Jed," "Jack Straw," "Comes a Time," "Ramble on Rose," "Chinatown Shuffle," "The Stranger (Two Souls in Communion)," and "He's Gone." The band ended up keeping "Mason's Children" in the mix for only a couple of years, and the four songs that were sung by Ron "Pigpen" McKernan would disappear from the repertoire after he stopped performing in 1972. But the other eight were strong enough to work on their own and together, appearing in performances for decades, with one, "Comes a Time," later earning a spot on Garcia's second solo studio record. The preceding skeletal performance and recording history suggests that the band could indeed have followed Hunter's vision and offered the record company and fans another strong volume in sequence with *Workingman's Dead* and *American Beauty*. But it also helps one to see to what extent the era was more than the *Wunderjahr* of 1970, and rather a highly productive period that began germinating in late 1968 and ran through 1972 or 1973. Too, it is an era in which songs appeared that would shape the band's repertoire for the rest of its career.

The reasons for the notable change in the band's sound and approach to songwriting are several, and while the causes are ultimately of much less concern than the results in this instance, some of the more notable among them might be enumerated as follows: Prior to the formation of the Warlocks in 1965, most of the Grateful Dead's members had already engaged with folk, blues, country and western, and bluegrass, making their 1968–69 turn toward these genres more of a revival than a departure. In early 1969, Garcia became interested in playing the pedal steel guitar, which was historically affiliated with country music, and he sought an outlet for that exploration. Hunter and others were attracted to country-inflected rock music, like that of Bob Dylan's *John Wesley Harding* and the Band's *Music from Big Pink*, which was beginning to appear in the late 1960s. Garcia was taken with the acoustic British folk rock of the Pentangle, which opened for the Grateful Dead several times in February and March 1969. More prosaically, music that demanded less studio wizardry could be recorded more quickly, and thus less expensively—a fact that could not be ignored in light of the massive debt the group accumulated while working on some of its 1960s albums.[34] Whatever combination of causes is responsible, these songs have proven perennial favorites with performers and fans alike. The following pages turn to examinations of a handful of songs from this key period in the band's history, drawing inspiration equally from the mention of the canonical gothic author Mary Shelley in "Ramble on Rose" and the band's turn toward American country-folk—a change in style that is part of the basis for Garcia's assertion, "There's nothing more American than the Grateful Dead."[35] As readers will see, considering these songs in relation to such interpretive guideposts reveals that the compositions pull simultaneously in two directions. Evaluations of the darkness that characterized many aspects of the band and its world as the 1960s counterculture took stock of itself on the cusp of the 1970s are weighed against and situated within the lyrics' implicit evaluations of America, whose mythic past offered the band the full spectrum of shadow and light.

"Dire Wolf": Performing the Divided Self in Fennario

The first song that the Grateful Dead premiered as the band more intentionally turned away from the baroque psychedelia of its late 1960s incarnation was "Dire Wolf." The dramatic situation of the song is simple and grim, as Hunter explains: "It's the middle of winter, and there's nothing to eat for anybody, and this guy's got a little place. Suddenly there's this monster, the dire wolf, and the guy is saying, 'Well, obviously you're going to come in, and why don't you pull up a chair and play some cards?' But the cards are cut to the queen of spades, which is the card of death, and all the cards are death at this point."[36] Like many of the songs that emerged over the next few years, the action of this one unfolds within a space that is paradoxically both specific and amorphous—a duality that allows for a strong sense of emplacement while simultaneously fostering disorientation. Another way to voice the point is that these songs give listeners home ground but take away their compasses at the same time. Listening, we know at some level where we are, but we have little sense of how that place is connected to anything more familiar. This simultaneous evocation of contrary states sits well with the feeling of the uncanny that drives just about every ghost story, gothic or otherwise, including "Dire Wolf."

In this case, the place within which the action unfolds is given the name "Fennario." Fans will know that the Grateful Dead also sing about "Fennario" in its version of the traditional song performed under the title "Peggy-O," and although that piece would not join the repertoire until 1973, one or another version of it—many readers are likely most familiar with Bob Dylan's 1962 "Pretty Peggy-O," and a 1979 studio recording of the piece, under the title "Fennario," included as a bonus track on the expanded edition of Garcia's *Run for the Roses* solo album, collected in the *All Good Things* boxed set— served as inspiration for Hunter's use of the term in "Dire Wolf." The history of "Peggy-O" is not irrelevant, insofar as it is likewise a history of this nonplace. The song seems to be an American adaptation of the old Scottish tune "The Bonnie Lass o' Fyvie," with the real-world location of Fyvie transformed by the Appalachian folk tradition into the invented New World space of "Fennario." According to the *Good Ol' Grateful Deadcast* episode devoted to "Dire Wolf," the earliest version of a ballad with a "Fennario" lyric was transcribed in 1908 by Katherine Jackson French.[37] That is also how it appears in Olive Dame Campbell and Cecil J. Sharp's classic 1917 collection, *English Folk Songs from the Southern Appalachians*, on its way to "Dire Wolf."[38] So, "Dire Wolf" marks the band's shift toward a certain tradition, a shift rooted in a touchstone song and setting that derive from a transatlantic displacement that gives it a distinctly American twist. The Fennario of "Dire Wolf" is a space with a past, but it is also a nonplace, geographically speaking, a place of imaginative exercise. Because it is nowhere specific, it is potentially on the border of any map, and thus a consideration for everyone, everywhere. It is a space of creation and destruction, like the bus stop of "That's It for the Other One," or the line between life and death in "Ramble on Rose." Such a place offers the sort of looming sense of inescapable and strange possibility that is the perfect context for the murder at the song's heart.

There are some other ingredients in the witches' brew of "Dire Wolf" beyond "Peggy-O." Among them is the real-world unease and violence perpetrated by a murderer known as the Zodiac killer. In discussing "Dire Wolf," Garcia stated in a 1985 conversation, "I wrote that song when the Zodiac killer was out murdering in San Francisco. Every night, I was coming home from the studio, and I'd stop at an intersection and look around, and if a car pulled up, it was like, 'This is it. I'm gonna die now.' It became a game. Every night I was conscious of that thing, and the refrain got to be so real to me: 'Please don't murder me.'"[39] The Zodiac killer was in the public eye starting only in August 1969, which means Garcia implicitly postdated the composition of the song's lyrics in his comment, but it is certainly the case that the killings could have shaped the mood of the song during its formative early live performances. (The band tried it many ways between its May 1969 composition and its release on *Workingman's Dead*: Garcia vocals, Weir vocals, backup vocals, no backup vocals, acoustic guitars, electric guitars, with pedal steel, without pedal steel, lyrics sung once, lyrics sung twice in their entirety.) Garcia not infrequently introduced it with statements like that of October 26, 1969: "This song is dedicated to the Zodiac, and also to paranoid fantasies everywhere." With the Tate-LaBianca murders in the recent Californian past, and the Zodiac killer at large, the paranoid fantasy of "Dire Wolf" very much had its real-world counterparts. Decades later, Garcia would return to the song with a similar carefree grimness. Death threats prior to the September 6, 1979, and July 2, 1995, Grateful Dead shows had security on high alert.[40] Garcia's typically sly reaction was to sing the song that fans initially called "Please Don't Murder Me." Although no shots were fired either night, the queen of spades was nonetheless drawn. This 1995 date marked the final public performance of "Dire Wolf" by the Grateful Dead.

While the reference to Fennario grounds the composition of "Dire Wolf" in a tradition of folk music, and the Zodiac killer and Manson Family provide some contemporary context for the song's refinement, there is also a literary-historical component for which to account. Intriguingly, like *Frankenstein*, this component is for the Grateful Dead partly cinematic. McNally relates, "One night Hunter and M.G. had sat up and watched *The Hound of the Baskervilles*, and she'd remarked that the hound was 'a dire wolf.'"[41] Hunter's memory diverged from McNally's report on a minor point. In a July 29, 1996, journal entry, he wrote about composing the lyrics one morning after "watching the Hound of the Baskervilles on TV with Garcia" the previous night.[42] In any case, Hunter and either Garcia, Carolyn "M.G." Adams, or both are likely to have seen Terence Fisher's 1959 adaptation of the novel featuring the renowned detective Sherlock Holmes, which, as the "Dire Wolf" episode of the *Good Ol' Grateful Deadcast* explains, aired in the San Francisco area on May 25, 1969.[43] Like the book on which it is based, the film includes a murderer hiding in the gloomy wilderness of a moor; a peatland known as the "Grimpen Mire," in which animals and people sometimes sink to their death; and, of course, a killer dog.[44] Too, attention is paid to the west-facing windows of Baskerville Hall, for it is through them that signals pass between certain members of the household and the murderer hiding on the moor. All this has been drawn into the song, with its repeated plea not to be murdered, a "black and bloody mire," dangerous canines in the form of "wolves . . . running 'round," and a killer "grinning at my window." Furthermore, just as the locale of Fennario links Hunter's lyrics to a folk tradition, so the Fisher film and Arthur Conan Doyle's novel, on which it is based, draw on the many English folktales about demonic black dogs, which have been prevalent, as Theo Brown explains, since the medieval period.[45]

The moor, as presented in the novel and film, is complex in its functioning, an aspect of the works that deepens the resonance of place in "Dire Wolf," as introduced with the invocation of Fennario. The novel profits particularly in this regard from a juxtaposition of the primitive and the modern, delivering a sense that to travel to Baskerville Hall is to leave the latter behind. The text mentions a handful of times the remains of prehistoric dwellings, with Holmes's confidant and chronicler Dr. Watson writing, "When you are once out upon its bosom you have left all traces of modern England behind you, but, on the other hand, you are conscious everywhere of the homes and the work of the prehistoric people. On all sides of you as you walk are the houses of these forgotten folk, with their graves and the huge monoliths which are supposed to have marked their temples."[46] The film does include several ruins, although most of them look Roman rather than properly prehistoric.

Whether prehistoric or merely ancient, these ruins are fragments in the literary-philosophical sense. From their dramatic staging emerges not nostalgia for the lost past, but rather a revelation of the strange possibilities in the present. On their own, especially in the novel, the structures evoke the sort of chthonic weirdness we might associate with H. P. Lovecraft or Arthur Machen more than Doyle. Taken together with Holmes, the ruins and the moor also introduce a counterpoint that drives the narrative: Holmes is Apollonian, the embodiment, as Nils Clausson argues, of ratiocinative clarity and faith in science. Yet, like most Holmes stories, the novel is narrated primarily by Watson, who is absorbed by the gloom of the setting. And, as Clausson further notes, this is a tale in which Holmes finds the solution to the mystery not by careful scientific inquiry, as is usually the case, but by hiding out in those ruins and following a hunch about human nature and the power of greed.[47] In this fashion, the novel and film both stage a competition between reason, the present, and light, on the one hand, and unreason, the past, and darkness, on the other, and while Holmes seems triumphant, it is a qualified victory, one that the hero of reason effects by an uncharacteristic reliance on the irrational. In all these ways, the novel and film take their audiences out of the everyday, turn away from rationality, and return to deep mysteries, violence, and the unnatural (there are hints of incest, as well). These components, along with a fairly complex narrative framing, are much more evocative of the gothic tradition than they are of the conventional detective tale. What comes to the surface, then, is a tension between a late gothic novel and the Victorian novel of civilized progress, a tension that Clausson describes aptly: "What is really at stake in the novel is something much deeper . . . than the solution to a puzzling murder: namely, the unfathomable mystery of criminality, and, ultimately, of evil itself."[48] In the end, that mystery is not definitely eradicated. The villain of the story is not caught, but disappears into the moor, where his death is presumed on the basis of several clues, though never confirmed. With these considerations in mind, one can see to what degree this place of primitive evil drives the narrative, whether one focuses on the novel or the film. The Hall, the moor, and the Mire are together, and at once, a clearly characterized place, but also a nonplace. With their relics from the ancient past, they exist outside the normal workings of time, disconnected both temporally and geographically from the world in which Holmes and Watson—and, indeed, the rest of us—normally move. It is here that the setting of the Holmes tale overlaps with the legacy of folk music. This place is the generally mysterious Fennario gone profoundly dark, a lawless place of atavistic truths. This place is the Fennario of "Dire Wolf."

Hunter once said that the situation of "Dire Wolf" is "a barren setting, stripped; there's no setting really, just blank white, and these characters in the middle of it."[49] In placing so much emphasis as this chapter so far has on the important setting of "Dire Wolf," the other part of Hunter's remark has been neglected—some scrutiny of the characters, including the narrator and the wolf, would not be misplaced. Perhaps with the "blank white" aspect of Hunter's remark in mind, McNally compares the wolf of the song to "Melville's white whale."[50] Hunter himself painted in strokes at once broader and more explicit, asserting that the wolf "is Behemoth; that monster, the Id; the subconscious."[51] Behemoth has been linked to Melville's Moby Dick by, among others, Perry Miller, so McNally's point is apt.[52] Less attention has been given to Hunter's assertion that the wolf is the incarnation of an internal, rather than an external, threat. This goes a fair way to explaining the setting. Regardless of whether the Fennario of the song evokes the black hound of folklore, it is a nonplace because it is the manifestation of an interior rather than an exterior geography. This territory of the mind is the sea under Melville's *Pequod*. It is perhaps a distant corner of the world in which we might strive for the Grateful Dead's Terrapin. It is cold and lonely, and death is the only card that is ever drawn there. It is, perhaps most especially, a suitable home for the flourishing of the gothic.

The proposal that we are in a gothic realm, rather than that of a folk tale or a detective novel, is reinforced by Hunter's remark, "The dire wolf is the shadow of the man in the song who is dead at this point. It's a song by a ghost."[53] The narrator of the song does say that, after he went to bed, "that's the last they saw of me," so it is somewhat easy to understand that our character speaks from beyond the grave. It is more challenging to grasp fully what that means, and even harder to approach Hunter's claim that the "wolf is the shadow of the man." In what sense can a man and his monster be united in such a fashion? Here, too, the gothic tradition is illuminating, and perhaps especially so insofar as it includes Shelley's *Frankenstein*.

The introduction of a protagonist's double—as an unknown twin, a supernatural shadow self, a psychopathological mirror self, or in some other conception—is not unique to gothic literature, but certain manifestations of the motif find their natural home in that realm. The foundational critical text on the topic is Otto Rank's *Double*, but the definitive work on the motif in relation to *Frankenstein* can be found in Irving Massey's *The Gaping Pig*. As

Massey explains, one may read Victor Frankenstein's tale as the dramatization of a split consciousness, one in which the enlightened, rational mind of Frankenstein endeavors to impose itself on brute matter, and in doing so, isolates itself from communion with others. Victor does isolate himself from family and friends as he creates and struggles with his creature, and he extends his isolation by rejecting the creature immediately after he brings it to life, as well as by resisting its entreaties so strongly that it attacks those he allegedly loves.[54] His mind, having twice made itself an exile, cannot bridge the gap between himself and the creature, which leads him to seek to destroy it, even as it becomes an emblem of all that he has chosen to lose: sociality, friendship, pleasure, and everything else that depends at least in part on the physical and the workings of the irrational in us.[55] The creature, on the other hand, wants nothing so much as admission to human society and love from its creator, but finds that the only way to earn attention is through the perpetration of increasingly gruesome violence.[56] As a consequence, one struggle that drives the novel is the conflict between Victor's identity as a coolly rational man of science and everything in us that such an identity rejects, including our emotions, our bodies, and our affective connections to community. The similarity to the dynamic of the Doyle novel is not inconsequential. In both cases, one can discern a divided self, as Holmes-psychopath (or, more generously, Holmes-Watson) and Victor-creature are both portions of a whole subject, one divided against itself in the agonistic relations that drive the narratives. The victory of certain sympathetic characters in the plot suggests a resolution, but the ambiguities of the texts preserve the possibilities of less strictly determinate positions: Frankenstein's creature disappears, but its death is not witnessed; the murderer in Doyle's novel is presumed dead, but no corpse is recovered.

    Shelley's text develops a rough symbology for that struggle between different manifestations of the self, and it is a symbolic economy partially echoed in "Dire Wolf." In the latter case, the narrator is alone in an icy place, as "The winter was so hard and cold / froze ten feet 'neath the ground." That cold isolation with which the ghost's tale begins is juxtaposed in the final line with an image of a warm, if somewhat desperate, community, one of "the boys" who "sing round the fire." Fire (which—as lightning—was key to the creature's creation) also stands in *Frankenstein* as the emblem of that which can both cause pain and promise comfort. It is too neat an encapsulation to say that the fire represents all that Victor rejects, thus ensuring that he will lose the warmth of family and friends, even as he trades the pain that relations with others can bring for a struggle with the self, but the sense of the point is not inaccurate. While fire may thus be read as the emblem of the creature, it is juxtaposed, although not always in a symmetrical fashion, with ice. The glaciers, snows, and Arctic wastes of the novel are the only territories left for the creature, who finds space to live only in the chilly, crystalline, unfeeling north, which can be read as an exteriorization of Victor's cold mind and rejection of his creation. The book's final image of the creature, setting off to pursue self-immolation on the polar ices, suggests that he finds in a fiery death in that setting the only possible union with the frozen heart of his creator. In thinking about the symbology of fire and ice, it is useful to keep in mind that the track order on *Workingman's Dead* was not accidental.[57] By the time listeners get to "Dire Wolf," they have the context of "Uncle John's Band" in hand, which tells them, "You know all the rules by now / and the fire from the ice." In any case, the audience of *Workingman's Dead* should be attuned to the hot and cold imagery. If we are wise to the metaphors, as "Uncle John's Band" tells us we should be, we can find respite from the chaos of the world, sing with the boys around the fire, and hear the band play to the tide.

There is, however, more to the "Dire Wolf" narrative, and one aspect so far unexamined concerns the relation between the song, its characters, and its creator-performers. As Gero Guttzeit argues, the creator-monster duality of many gothic narratives is not only a means to dramatize the fragmentation of a coherent self, but also a mirror of the relations between the author and her text, as well as between the author as implied by the nature of the text she composes and the dominant conception of authorship at the time of the text's composition. From this perspective, one can view Victor as creating his creature in a sense similar to that in which Shelley creates her novel; without Shelley, there is no text, but it is equally true that, without the text, Shelley is no author.[58] The fraught interdependency of gothic monstrosity and its creator, then, serves as a commentary on the relations between artist and work, with the former being subject to the fragmentation and violent incompletion that the latter dramatizes, and the images, incidents, characters, and structure of the latter infected by disruptive forces that the author at once acknowledges and represses. Similarly, Massey writes of Frankenstein's creature, "He is imagination ... in ... symbiotic relationship with the artist, in the love-hate struggle that goes on between itself and its creator, within his mind."[59] He adds, "The monster is a real thing doomed because he stems from an unreal cause. His 'author' is also the author of the book, who reflects the hollowness of all writers."[60] More powerfully, perhaps, as Guttzeit explains, the gothic author challenges the dominant idea of the Anglophone author during the Romantic era, which was that of a strongly individual and highly original white male who produced works of organic coherence. Figures like Shelley and her characters instead foreground fragmentation, incompletion, and transgression.[61] In the case of "Dire Wolf," the song is the child of Garcia and Hunter, and also of the Grateful Dead as a whole. However, the deadly wolf of the title is also an aspect of the band that performs the song, whose members are in some senses responsible for it. And while performing, it embodies an aspect of them, with its idiosyncratic conglomeration of past sources, with its commentary on contemporary murderers, with its literary background. To present the creature that is the dire wolf is to accept the responsibility for bringing a dangerous power to life from the reassembled fragments of folk music (Fennario), 1960s culture (Zodiac), and the literary tradition (Doyle, Shelley). To assert that the wolf is at the heart of the song is not to contend that the song is somehow out to get the listener, or that the band saw itself as performing a dangerous feat by singing the piece. Instead, it demonstrates that "Dire Wolf" is more than just another song in the folk tradition or simply a change in sound for the band; it is a song that uses gothic monstrosity to dramatize the band's intuitive grasp of its responsibility to its art and its audience, providing an opportunity to meditate on the dangers of innovative composition, and a means to challenge the dominant notion of popular music as the 1960s ticked to a close. A song like "Dire Wolf" stands outside several measures of coherence, two of which are particularly relevant here. It is not like the other songs the Grateful Dead had been performing in the late 1960s, and thus challenges listeners' ideas of the band's identity. At the same time, the Grateful Dead was still more or less an underground band, one that operated on terms that challenged the status quo of the music industry. Thus, "Dire Wolf" is a nod to the band's outsider status, while also serving as a means to resist pigeonholing by its fans' expectations.

The contention that the text can be seen as both the monstrous double of its author and a dramatization of the struggle between that which is evident and that which is repressed, or of the author's desire for the suppressed, sits well with Hunter's argument that the wolf is the Freudian id. Furthermore, the preceding paragraph's proposal that one can hear the song as a comment on the Grateful Dead's relationship to the music industry encourages one to think about additional ways in which "Dire Wolf" works as a meditation on the band's relationship with Warner Bros. and the broader landscape of corporatized music as a whole. Hunter implied as much when he remarked that "the situation" of the victim in relation to the wolf "is the same as when a street dude, an up-against-the-Establishment guy, approaches the Establishment and says, 'We can coexist.'"[62] You can play cards with the Man, but the deck will be stacked, and you will always be outdrawn at the end. From this perspective, we can hear the Grateful Dead using "Dire Wolf" to dramatize its predicament. The band had not yet been eaten by the wolf, but it had played a few hands with it since signing with a major label. Its unconventional business enterprises of the 1970s and 1980s, especially those designed to circumvent the worst aspects of the conventional music industry—the establishment of its own record label, the development of in-house mail-order ticketing, and the granting of permission for recording to audience members—might be seen through the lens of "Dire Wolf" as a race against death, one that succeeded better than could have been imagined, in part because the band had an ace up its sleeve: its fans.

There is something in "Dire Wolf" that promises a reprieve from the danger, a sort of escape hatch that many gothic narratives lack. This is not to say that the gothic elements of the song are resolved away, as the conclusion is not enough to save the speaker of the song from the wolves, but it is perhaps a guard against the loss of the band to the queen of spades. Massey writes of Frankenstein's creature, "Most of the time, the monster is experienced as a disembodied voice coming from within. Perhaps he is hideous because he is an unseen inner image, a truth that we cannot admit, cannot face, and his ugliness is, like Mr. Hyde's, psychological in origin, felt rather than seen."[63] Many of Garcia's early introductions to "Dire Wolf" externalize this inner voice by including a relatively rare request for audience participation. His remarks before playing the song on January 2, 1970, are an example: "This is a song with an easy chorus, and you can even sing with it. It's fun!" In this fashion, Garcia makes the audience members part of the equation. They share the burden of the piece and take on some of the risk that comes with confronting its monstrosity. In doing so, they become one with the group, becoming "the boys" who "sing round the fire." The fragmentation of the author thus becomes, in performance, a means to foreground the danger of the wolf. Too, in encouraging the audience to sense this shared threat and the responsibility to which it calls us, Garcia saves the band; its members, no longer the sole author-figures, now share the dangers of artistic parturition. The move unites band and audience, trades the "I" of authorship for the "we" of performance, and expands the figure of the author via a shared dramatization of the danger of death. The nod to the audience members implicitly acknowledges their importance to the Grateful Dead's broader enterprises, to the sense of community they cultivated in so many ways, including, most notably, the *Dead Heads* mailing list launched in 1971, just a year after *Workingman's Dead* was released. Singing along with Garcia at a concert might not stop the Zodiac killer, exactly, but it does give everyone a common tune to whistle in the dark as they travel home from the show and try to walk the line.

The Grateful Dead and Faust: "Friend of the Devil"

Siehst du den schwarzen Hund durch Saat und Stoppel streifen?
—Johann Wolfgang von Goethe, *Faust*, 1808

The Grateful Dead was beset by various significant challenges and losses during the era this chapter discusses. Some of these were broadly cultural, while others were eminently personal. Taken together, they signaled a contextual shift that the music marks and weighs. One such change had to do with the close—or at least the fragmentation—of the countercultural moment in which the band was born. Hunter S. Thompson captured something of the feeling of the early Haight when he wrote that "San Francisco in the middle sixties was a very special time and place.... There was a fantastic universal sense that whatever we were doing was right, that we were winning.... We had all the momentum; we were riding the crest of a high and beautiful wave."[64] But his text continues, in a passage that does for the 1960s what the final paragraph of *The Great Gatsby* does for the roaring twenties: "Now, less than five years later, you can go up on a steep hill in Las Vegas and look West, and with the right kind of eyes you can almost see the high-water mark—that place where the wave finally broke and rolled back."[65] *Workingman's Dead*, *American Beauty*, and the related songs of the very late 1960s and early 1970s mark this change in a variety of ways.

"High Time" is emblematic, and prescient, regarding the complications of this change, as when Garcia sings, "Tomorrow come trouble / Tomorrow come pain" and "Nothing's for certain / It could always go wrong" at the dawn of the 1970s. Other songs are foreboding in their own ways. As previously mentioned, "Black Peter" and "Casey Jones" are informed by experience with the dangers of overconsumption. "New Speedway Boogie" and "Mason's Children" are Hunter's comments on the violence and total disorganization at the Altamont Speedway Free Festival of December 1969, which left one fan dead and many more injured. McNally suggests that Altamont was on the verge of disaster even before it started, as Emmett Grogan observed when he wrote on a blackboard in the band's offices, with reference to the event's plans, "Charlie Manson Memorial Hippie Love Death Cult Festival."

The Grateful Dead bore some of the brunt of and much of the guilt for that debacle, having been embroiled with the decision to use the Hells Angels as security.[66] Altamont was violent, but violence was generally in the air—with the Manson Family murders and trials, as Grogan's comment indicates, at the forefront of the collective consciousness; the Zodiac killer active and eluding apprehension; US military involvement in Vietnam dragging on, spreading its tendrils into Laos and Cambodia; and the Ohio National Guard killing four unarmed student protesters at Kent State. Furthermore, as the band entered 1970, its year of heaviest touring, the travails of life on the road were more acutely felt, as "Truckin'" acknowledges. Especially notable is the song's nod—"Busted—down on Bourbon Street"—to the night most of the band was arrested by the New Orleans Police Department Narcotics Squad, an event that resulted in, among other things, the loss of Bear from further touring, due to problems with travel across state lines and parole violations.[67] There were financial troubles, too, as when Mickey Hart's father, Lenny, who had been working as the band's manager, absconded with around $150,000 of the band's money, a treachery commemorated in "He's Gone."[68] To all the above, one must add the deaths during that period: of fellow traveler Jimi Hendrix; of Garcia's mother, for whom "Brokedown Palace" would serve as a threnody; of Lesh's father, whom "Box of Rain" commemorated; and of the band's friend and sometimes co-performer Janis Joplin, eulogized in "Bird Song."[69] Perhaps most importantly, Joplin's erstwhile lover, the band's own Ron "Pigpen" McKernan, missed months of performances after being hospitalized in 1971, retired from touring entirely in 1972, and died in 1973. For some fans and band members, the musicians who remained were no longer the Grateful Dead.

The troubles ahead and behind made recording sessions and concert performances welcome reprieves from a world going wrong, but they also served as a space in which the dangers and complications of that world could be tested. As is noted above with reference to "Dire Wolf," the band performed songs that turned the stage into a space in which challenges and ambiguities could be dramatized, explored, and contemplated, with the result that many of the songs from this troubled era are preoccupied with crime, victimization, guilt, loss, and violence. Some of these topics were expressed in "bad man" songs, like "Candyman"—a meditation on dangerous drifters and grifters who know how to tempt. Others presented and turned about for consideration the plights of what McNally calls "the fundamental Grateful Dead character, a workingman, an underdog without pretense or slickness, part of the old gritty America."[70] These are the laborers of "Easy Wind" and "Cumberland Blues"; the men driven by guilt, fear, or vengeance in "Mexicali

Blues," "Jack Straw," and "Sugaree"; the lonely lovers of "Empty Pages," "Looks like Rain," and "Operator"; the unwelcome and beleaguered soul of "Tennessee Jed"; the Depression-era strugglers of "Brown-Eyed Women"; the unlucky gamblers of "Loser" and "Deal"; and the desperate, indigent August West of "Wharf Rat." In the case of several of these songs, violence, heartache, uncertainty, and the general burden of the past are not only local problems, but also aspects of the broader condition that Weir and John Perry Barlow would bring to audiences in the vision of the "Mother American Night" in "Black-Throated Wind"—a dark expression of uncertainty, insufficiency, and longing at the heart of the national experience.

The consubstantiality of American reality and the alienated cry expressed in songs like "Black-Throated Wind" is eminently well-suited to exploration in terms of the gothic, for, in the American tradition, the gothic not only emerges in those novels filed under the generic label of "horror" at a bookstore or in the films of the Halloween season, but is also woven into the national sensibility. There is a deep historical context here. Even if some ideals of some aspects of European colonialism are noble in themselves, no datum can outweigh the double burden that the displacement and genocide of American Indian populations and the legacy of chattel slavery impose on the collective conscience of the United States. Consequently, the dream of escape from the constraints of the Old World is intertwined with the sins of the New World. Fiedler finds that this historical picture, which entangles the search for liberty with violation and guilt, makes the American imaginary particularly susceptible to the gothic, a point best expressed when Mark Twain's Huck Finn asserts, "All right, then, I'll *go* to Hell."[71] This is the strand of the American literary tradition that runs from Charles Brockden Brown to Edgar Allan Poe, and from Nathaniel Hawthorne and Herman Melville to Ambrose Bierce and William Faulkner. Coincidentally, Bierce was also a former owner of the house in which Buena Vista Studio was located. That is to say, the Grateful Dead made its second slate of demo recordings, in 1966, in a space that had been inhabited by the author of "An Occurrence at Owl Creek Bridge."[72]

In developing the gothic-inflected songs of the era this chapter considers, Hunter and the band's other lyricists turn repeatedly to the rich regional storytelling traditions of the American South and West. This turn not only opens a door to the sounds of southern Appalachian folk tunes like "Peggy-O" and country-and-western classics like "You Win Again," but also to the distinctive settings and character types of American folk legend—from pre-emancipation tricksters who get the best of work bosses to rootless adventurers who live on the edges of luck and law in the desert Southwest. Hunter once asserted that one of these compositions was "the closest we've come to what may be a classic song"—he was speaking of "Friend of the Devil."[73] Even setting aside the two songs' shared participation in the Grateful Dead's late 1960s–early 1970s turn to a country-folk sound, "Friend of the Devil" shares much with "Dire Wolf," not least because the former offers an idiosyncratic extension of some of the key ambiguities that made the latter song so powerful.

Among the more substantial of the correspondences between "Dire Wolf" and "Friend of the Devil" are several that come into focus when the songs are considered in light of a folk motif that Fiedler declares "identical with the American myth itself," that "of Faust and of the diabolic bargain."[74] The story of Faust has its origins, as does so much of the American imaginary, in Old World legends. It begins with a series of tales concerning the rumored supernatural powers of the historical figure of Johann Georg Faust, a scholar of the late fifteenth and early sixteenth centuries. While versions of the Faustian tales vary somewhat in details, their central episode is a bargain struck between Faust and the Devil, in which Faust offers up his soul in exchange for the gratification of his insatiable desire for worldly experience and preternatural knowledge. These legends entered print late in the sixteenth century, most notably in the 1587 chapbook *Historia von D. Johann Faustus*, also known as the *Faustbuch*, published by Johann Spies. This and similar collections inspired, among other later texts, the English Renaissance playwright Christopher Marlowe's sixteenth-century *The Tragical History of Dr. Faustus*, as well as several pieces featuring Faust by Johann Wolfgang von Goethe in the late eighteenth and early nineteenth centuries. Goethe's most ambitious work concerning Faust—the two-part play *Faust*—is arguably the greatest literary text in the German language, and a definitive entry in the tradition of Faust literature. That Faust was on the minds of those in the world of the Grateful Dead is no mere speculation. Hunter once remarked, regarding his works in progress, "I've got my Faust tucked away, that I've been working on for years and years."[75]

There has been some debate about the degree to which Faust's tale, in any of its versions, answers to the standards of the gothic, which finds its purest form in novels rather than dramatic poetry. Several scholars have, however, accumulated evidence that frustrates efforts to dismiss Faust as irrelevant to discussions of the mode, and some of their points bear directly on "Dire Wolf" and "Friend of the Devil." Jane K. Brown and Marshall Brown have been especially diligent on this front, gathering, among other evidence of intersections between the gothic tradition and Goethe's *Faust*, examples of shared foregrounding of supernatural figures and dark magic, character types like the tormented scholar, plot motifs such as illicit sexuality, torturous settings like prisons, disturbed psychodynamic states, and formal characteristics such as the inclusions in the text of ballads and multitudinous fictional frames.[76] Brown and Brown further emphasize that the Faust legends and the gothic tradition also share, as a key element, "a certain ambivalence of tone and a self-conscious playfulness . . . often reinforced with themes of playing or gambling."[77] A text's presentation of a dangerous contractual arrangement—whether in the form of a game of cards with a wolf or a wager with the Devil—is clearly pertinent not only to tales about Faust, but also to both "Dire Wolf" and "Friend of the Devil." This chapter's contention regarding "Friend of the Devil," as explored in the following pages, is that it centralizes ambiguity by selectively extending tensions introduced in "Dire Wolf." Essential to this reformulation of the earlier song's gothic dynamics is the presentation of a more subtle construction of the tension between threat and speaker. In the former case, the speaker of the song was left to the mercy of the wolf and his deadly cards; in the latter, the situation is more complex, with a less sharply delineated boundary between salvation and loss, as it pertains to the individual outside certain definitions of American community.

Some of the similarities that encourage consecutive readings of the two songs are superficial, but not for that reason any less intriguing. The "wolves . . . running round" the woods of Fennario in "Dire Wolf," for example, work in conceptual tandem with the "twenty hounds" on the trail of the central figure in "Friend of the Devil." The change in canine species pushes readings of the beasts of the later song more in the direction of the traditional folk motif of the infernal black dog, mentioned above in reference to *The Hound of the Baskervilles*. Yet, while the transformation occurs, it by no means elides the connection between the two songs and the situations they describe. Furthermore, given that we are in the territory of tales about Devil's bargains and popular song, one thinks immediately of Robert Johnson, and Trist and Dodd remind us of the echo in this part of "Friend of the Devil" of Johnson's "Hellhound on My Trail."[78] In the background of all these songs' canines stand the Faust texts, and Goethe's masterwork in particular. Among its other incidental features is the appearance of the demon Mephistopheles as a black poodle that follows Faust home, before revealing its true form and proposing the wager essential to the story.[79]

One might turn to more substantive points of intersection between the Faustian tradition and "Friend of the Devil" by noting that the complex presentation of the possibilities inherent in the Devil's bargain in this song relies partly on its spatial markers and temporal modes. Movement through both time and space is keyed to visions of different sorts of regression, arrival, termination, and salvation. Consider, for example, the temporal qualities of the song's opening. The first verse describes the speaker fleeing from Reno so frantically that he "didn't get to sleep that night / Till the morning came around." The moment is paradoxical. With dawn, the lyric asserts, comes the chance to sleep at "night." Of course, sleeping at night during the early day is no nighttime sleep at all. The confused conflation of temporal periods delivers the sense of urgency for the fleeing man, using language that resonates with a song found on the flip side of *American Beauty*, "Till the Morning Comes." More important, the urgency of the speaker's flight from his pursuers resembles a particular experience of time offered, as Brown and Brown argue, by Goethe's *Faust*—namely, time as *Schwindel*, a kind of vertiginous, mad rush that disorients and is especially germane to Faust's wilder supernatural experiences.[80] The chorus of "Friend of the Devil," however, resists that unnatural and frantic impulse, even as it is introduced, pairing "I set out running" with "but I take my time." In this way, the speaker presses the accelerator and applies the brakes at the same moment, and, given that resisting time-as-*Schwindel* is, within the Faust tradition, a means to resist the supernatural, this dual action contributes to our sense that the speaker either retains some measure of resistance to the diabolical powers or that those powers are not as hostile as they initially seem.

To the ambiguities of time in "Friend of the Devil," we may, following the lead of Fennario in "Dire Wolf," add those of space. Our speaker leaves "from Reno" at the song's start, with the possibility that his wandering will take him "home before daylight." He ends up spending "that night in Utah / In a cave up in the hills," so he did not end up making it home initially, although the repetitions of the chorus—with its refrain, "If I get home before daylight"—remind listeners that the speaker is convinced of the possibility of a homecoming, even as his days of wandering unfold. Travel on foot from Reno to the hills of Utah is an unlikely journey for a day, and the locations mentioned later in the song, Chino and Cherokee, are likewise problematic in terms of travel time. The difficulty is partially mitigated if we follow Trist and Dodd's observation that the song's action may be transpiring between 1850 and 1861, during which period Reno was part of the Utah Territory.[81] To resolve some of the song's spatial ambiguities in this fashion is by no means to eliminate them entirely, but it does situate the action in an era during which the formation of the national territory, and the territory of the imagined nation, were still far from fully defined.

Taken together, the song's ambiguous temporal and spatial markers create a sort of liminal and porous American geography, one in which day and night, physical distances, determinate locations, and speed of motion are repeatedly blurred. There are nevertheless several coordinates, however ambiguous, in relation to which the speaker's wandering unfolds. One of these is "prison," for "the sheriff's on my trail." Others are the hometowns of two wives, Chino and Cherokee. The one in Chino "says she's got" the speaker's "child / But," he asserts, "it don't look like me." Faust, too, avoids the declaration of paternity for an infant—one whom his abandoned lover, Gretchen, drowns.[82] In the end, the song's speaker seems no more drawn to a domestic future than to the prospect of prison. Both possibilities would be the circumscription of motility, a characteristic that, as this chapter is in the midst of arguing, may well be ideal for the song's speaker. The resistance to the immobilities of prison and domestic life are likewise definitive of Goethe's Faust, who pushes back against any slide in the direction of the sort of temporal experience Brown and Brown characterize as *Langerweile*—time as a sort of aimless boredom that contrasts with time-as-*Schwindel*.[83]

While one may be inclined to add "sweet Anne Marie," the "heart's delight" of the speaker of "Friend of the Devil," to the list of spatially determined spiritual mires that the protagonist must dodge, her name demands more careful consideration. Anne Marie bears a name that doubly honors the maternal line of Jesus—his mother, Mary, and her mother, Anne. The name therefore opens the devotion to Anne Marie in the Grateful Dead song to consideration in light of holy redemptive mothers, ones who offer succor from both infernal (the Devil) and earthly (the sheriff) authorities. The possibility of rest—the possibility that the song's speaker will "get home before daylight"—is a key distinction between this song and "Dire Wolf." In that song's Fennario, the threat was endemic and unavoidable. In "Friend of the Devil," the chance for salvation, as embodied in Anne Marie, balances the dangers of both the sheriff and the Devil. Furthermore, the song treats the spatial identity of Anne Marie in a manner different from that of the sheriff or the wives. They are tied to particular locales (jail, Chino, Cherokee), while Anne Marie exists unattached to any particular place. In this way, she serves as a more general emblem of salvation pursued as a possibility than as a symbol of salvation attained. Her lack of certain positioning not only prevents her from being associated with stagnation but also adds motivation to the speaker's wandering. In this fashion, too, she is the counterpart of the Devil, who is tied to no place and can appear and disappear at will. He first appears in an unspecified locale in the second verse, then at "the levee" in the third, before "he vanished in the air." The various coordinates for the speaker's wandering flight in "Friend of the Devil" thus offer two intersecting and, to some degree, overlapping spectra. One of these runs from motility to stagnation, while the other operates between redemption and damnation.

The more-than-natural maternal identity of Anne Marie also opens another door for hearing "Friend of the Devil" in relation to *Faust*, especially as regards the complex presentation of the maternal in Goethe's plays. Robert Anchor finds in the plays a competition of sorts between two maternal principles. One is the Magna Mater, the positive principle of motherhood "as the abundantly fruitful, eternally replenished matrix of the fullness and recurrence of life, out of which the purposeful and constructive, conscious and active personality could arise and, after a lifetime of striving, return again to be reborn on a higher level."[84] The other is that of Mother Night, the "mother archetype in its negative aspects," including all the despair, disorientation, and violence with which nighttime is affiliated. This is the vision of dark maternity that we find in Hesiod, when Night gives birth to death, sleep, grief, deceit, and vengeance, among other ills. Furthermore, although it may offer a reprieve from the ills of night, Day itself is presented as a child of Night in its most ancient manifestations.[85] This darker and more profound aspect of the maternal manifests in the second part of *Faust* as the primeval conceptual realm of the "Mothers," with which Faust comes into contact—a realm of "shaping, reshaping, / the eternal minds in eternal recreation."[86] Faust, in other words, moves between the worlds of the positive and negative maternal principles, and their play between darkness and light. These imposing yet playful exchanges are the terms for creation based on the model of the Romantic fragment. The playfulness is that of freedom manifested in the ongoing exchange between birth and death that marks the ephemeral, even as the exchange points to the eternal "work in progress," which is the truth of, and the condition for, literary production. These are the ramifications of the passage the speaker of "Friend of the Devil" must navigate while on the run, both drawn to and resisting the manifestations of this process that rolls between light and dark, among "tonight," "morning," "daylight," and "night."

The song's positioning of its protagonist within this complex array of contrary states and impulses—including light and dark, determinate place and indeterminate space, creation and destruction, liberty and imprisonment, stagnation and motion, ephemerality and eternity, and the Devil and salvation—results in a profound ambiguity, one that leaves the listener uncertain about the song's locus of narrative authority. For Nancy and the German

Romantics, such a space—one that exists between and beyond terms that would otherwise circumscribe and define it—is the space of the literary absolute, and it is a space of freedom. That freedom is not only the condition from which thought and art are generated, but also is itself a persistent potentiality. As Teresa A. Goddu has argued, such resistance to closure and stability is also fundamental to the gothic's implications for historical understanding. Because the genre opens the door to what is outside the norm, to what is excluded from the official and the commonly accepted, it admits what is otherwise given no voice and can challenge narratives that underpin the dominant terms of subjective identity, communal existence, and national mythography.[87] Consequently, the gothic helps foreground, as Carlos Gallego argues, "the marginalization and disenfranchisement of whatever and/or whoever is considered too different to be integrated into the majority: the unassimilable and thus expendable others who are classified as subhuman, if not monstrous, and treated accordingly, as exemplified in the strategic genocidal violence against Native Americans, the institutionalization of African American slavery and its Jim Crow legacies, and the ongoing domestication of women in general."[88] Arthur Redding adds to this point, emphasizing that the hauntings of the gothic are not always the spectral return of past sins, but also sometimes the manifestations of frustrated potential—hauntings carried out by what did not happen. Historical ghosts can therefore emblematize the scars on the national tapestry of past lives unlived or future opportunities foreclosed.[89] In this sense, the monstrous violence of the gothic is not just a potential marker of past traumas, but also a means to acknowledge lost pasts, unrealized presents, and impossible futures.

This chapter's several avenues of inquiry regarding "Friend of the Devil" converge at this point. Brown and Brown point out that a wager or game in a gothic text serves to mark, or even emblematize, deeper and potentially productive ambiguities. The song offers a Faustian Devil's bargain and foregrounds a rich array of general ambiguities that honor the overarching freedom that is the context within which those productive ambiguities develop. Goddu, Gallego, and Redding note that such ambiguities, when historicized, can bring repressed voices and populations into focus. Moreover, the song presents the typical Grateful Dead character of the American underdog-everyman, as described by McNally, fleeing an array of forces that want to pin him down in particular categories. That all these factors come together in what seems to be the mid-nineteenth century space of the Utah Territory (again, the song's action seems to occur between 1850 and 1861) encourages reflection on the composition as a comment on the dangers of, and opportunities for, sociopolitical inclusion that America faced as the Jacksonian period drew to a close and the tensions that would lead to the Civil War became more acute. The 1850s saw the late stages of America's westward expansion unfold, and those steps forced more urgent conflicts between American Indian populations and American military forces, even as the nation had to determine whether its new territories and states would extend the practice of chattel slavery. Hunter and Garcia, in discussing their own music of the early 1970s, praised the historical awareness of songs like the Band's "The Night They Drove Old Dixie Down," so the context of the American nineteenth century does seem to have been on their minds during the period in which "Friend of the Devil" was composed.[90]

Read in relation to the gothic's tendency to undermine the authority of generally accepted historical narratives, the song's positioning of the speaker in the relatively amorphous and porous American West of the 1850s, together with the incorporation of Faustian motifs, encourages a view of the song as a comment on the curtailment of liberty that occurs as sociopolitical life becomes more about the rule of law and less about the preservation of possibility. For this reason, the sheriff and his hounds must be avoided. Operating at another level than restrictions on individual liberty are those that occur across several registers concurrently with, and because of, the expansion of social conventions emblematic of enlightened, Euro-American conceptions of progress and civilization. For this reason, traditional domestic life—whether with the wife in Chino or the one in Cherokee—must likewise be avoided, as it serves merely as an emblem of mere convention. On the other hand, as Gallego argues, the gothic's interrogation of firm hierarchies is brought to life through the presence of the monstrous other—such as Frankenstein's creature—which can proffer examples of unconventional modes of living that are morally sounder than those of the cultural dominant.[91] The preservation of such possibilities is among those values that the Grateful Dead consistently and unabashedly tried to instantiate in its music: the openness of songs to improvisation, the assurance that no concert would too closely resemble one from the night before, and the presentation of space for creative freedom.

If, as the gothic tradition suggests, the seemingly monstrous other is not an absolute threat so much as an emblem of deficiencies in the dominant narrative, then a friend of the Devil, or even the Devil himself, may indeed be a source of positive help. Maybe deals with the Devil are not so much routes to eternal damnation as playful expressions of intentions much less grave than the Devil's participation in the bargain makes them seem. Such an understanding is very much of a piece with Fiedler's analysis of the American gothic tradition, which he argues implicitly adheres to a "secret belief that damnation is not all it is cracked up to be." He adds, "In a strange way, the naturalized Faust legend becomes in the United States a way of denying hell in the act of seeming to accept it, or suggesting that it is merely a scary word, a bugaboo, a forbidding description of freedom itself!"[92] Maybe, then, there is a reason the song's speaker takes his time. In this world, liberty is preserved by maintaining the perspective needed to look critically at both heaven and hell, and by choosing to live by one's own lights rather than those of earthly or supernatural authorities. According to this attitude, the song follows Goethe's *Faust* in showing the possibility of salvation even for those who seem to have abjured it—as when Faust himself is saved at the conclusion of the play despite having agreed to trade his soul for a life of extraordinary encounters granted by the power of Mephistopheles.

Thus, "Friend of the Devil" shares with Goethe's *Faust* a sense of what it is to be at liberty in the world. Such freedom, truly realized, opens doors to exceptional experiences, but it also requires a willingness either to weather or to dodge the slings and arrows of authorities who would foreclose the productive ambiguities of the frontier, seeking to bring the spaces of freedom within the pale of secular power. As Astrida Orle Tantillo explains, the reason God finally saves Faust's soul in Goethe's plays is a point of some debate among scholars. It could be that Faust tricks the infernal tricksters, finding a loophole of some sort in the bargain he made. Alternatively, maybe he feels some little-expressed remorse for his deeds, a remorse that justifies his salvation. Or, perhaps, he is saved because he conforms to God's vision of human nature as expressed in the work's "Prologue in Heaven," which sees in Faust's striving the spirit of our species—a sort of built-in guarantee that we will not allow ourselves to be frustrated in pursuit of the good.[93] Whatever the reason, Faust is saved, and the similarities between Faust and the speaker of "Friend of the Devil" therefore suggest that the latter may also be on the right track.

It is asserted above that "Friend of the Devil" is not only a song written after "Dire Wolf" but also, at least in some regards, a development or extension of it. While both songs deal, to some degree, with death, damnation, and salvation, their sense of what happens on the way to those final things differs considerably. The distinction is clearer if we compare Victor Frankenstein to Faust. Frankenstein is Faustian in several ways. Both are embodiments of the flawed, antiheroic protagonist typical of the gothic, and, in the case of both characters, that flaw is the desire to know more than is typically allowed to humans—the secret of life and the secrets of the universe. Yet Shelley's character, as Manuel Aguirre argues, does not only deal with the infernal, but becomes like "a satanic entity" himself, roaming a world that has become a hell because he remains excluded forever from the one thing he comes to truly desire: human society.[94] In this, he is much like Cain, to whom the Grateful Dead would turn in 1972's "Mississippi Half-Step Uptown Toodleloo." Too, insofar as this is the case, the ghostly speaker of "Dire Wolf" remains forever outside the proscribed bounds of community envisioned as the "boys" who "sing round the fire." The Faustian antihero, on the other hand, differs on this last point. He elects his own exile, finding the paths of his wandering not emblems of a confining labyrinth, but rather opportunities that are in themselves redemptive. From this perspective, the speaker of "Friend of the Devil" has no need to chase Anne Marie. She, as his salvation, is with him, as long as he keeps moving, and as long as he "takes his time."

Perchance to Dream

OVID, WILLIAM SHAKESPEARE, AND THE GRATEFUL DEAD

To use the English language is to evince the influence of William Shakespeare, and it is therefore no surprise that there are extensive connections between Shakespeare's writings and the Grateful Dead's lyrics. This chapter is devoted to several of the songs in which the Grateful Dead makes use of Shakespeare's language and imagery, and includes considerations of "Rosemary" in terms of *Hamlet*'s Ophelia, the various aspects of *King Lear* in "Mountains of the Moon," and—most extensively—the several Shakespearean texts that inform the lyrics of "Althea." In these and other songs, Shakespearean language allows for more extensive and subtle considerations of the pieces' poetics and thematic content, especially when the songwriters turn to the topics of love, fate, and betrayal. Furthermore, the images and language in "Althea" that derive most directly from Shakespeare allow listeners to hear the band performing the piece as an act of self-reflection, commenting on the somewhat complicated situations characterizing the career of the Grateful Dead during the transitional period in which the song debuted.

In addition, Shakespeare's exceptional prominence in the canon means that the band's engagements with the texts discussed in this chapter illuminate with particular intensity the degree to which the Grateful Dead manifests its creative activities in terms of an aesthetic of the fragment. That the band's intertextual engagements with the Shakespearean texts discussed below are much more likely to result in evocative suggestion than in rigidly defined, determinate, or totalizing musical or lyrical expression illustrates the band's lack of interest in mere replication or reiteration of musical ideas, its resistance to lyrical closure, and its sympathy for and practice of openness to incompletion as a means of signaling devotion to the productive power of the literary absolute. Several of the fragmentary qualities discussed in the preceding chapters, including especially the playful dance between destruction and creation, as well as the generative possibilities of inconclusion, are strongly evident in the Grateful Dead's exploration of Shakespearean territory.

Consideration of two explicit references to Shakespeare in the Grateful Dead's performance repertoire, both of which appear in songs penned by Bob Dylan, is a useful illustration of the way the band employs allusions to Shakespeare's works in its own songwriting. The Grateful Dead performed one of these Dylan songs, "Stuck Inside of Mobile with the Memphis Blues Again," seventy-six times, beginning on Independence Day, 1987. After six performances of the piece as a backing band for Dylan, the Grateful Dead made the song its own during a concert on St. Patrick's Day, 1988. Dylan would join them for the song on stage at least once more, on February 12, 1989, although the Grateful Dead also played it without him many times. The second Dylan song with an overt mention of Shakespeare to be played by the Grateful Dead is "Desolation Row," which the band performed a total of fifty-six times, starting on March 25, 1986. In this case, too, Dylan joined the band for a handful of performances, beginning on July 7, 1986. Both songs remained in the Grateful Dead's repertoire, with at least one performance per year, until the band's retirement in 1995. As these dates and figures indicate, they were fairly strong presences during the final third of the band's career.

The Shakespearean content of these Dylan songs differs in degree of complexity. In the case of "Stuck Inside of Mobile with the Memphis Blues Again," the lyric's reference to Shakespeare is a rather superficial blend of irony and metonymy:

> Well, Shakespeare, he's in the alley
> With his pointed shoes and his bells
> Speaking to some French girl
> Who says she knows me well
> And I would send a message
> To find out if she's talked
> But the post office has been stolen
> And the mailbox is locked.

Here, Shakespeare's name stands in for a class of people who are, or who at least consider themselves, poets. The "pointed shoes" and "bells" with which Shakespeare is here associated may well remind listeners of the many fools in his plays. As this chapter will explain, the Shakespearean fool is a character type of no little significance to later songs by the Grateful Dead.

The references to Shakespeare in "Desolation Row" are richer. In the second verse, Dylan combines an allusion to *Romeo and Juliet* with a glance at his own earlier song, "She Belongs to Me":

> And in comes Romeo, he's moaning
> "You Belong to Me I Believe"
> And someone says, "You're in the wrong place my friend
> You better leave"

Two verses later, the song's cast of characters expands to include Ophelia, a character from Shakespeare's *Hamlet*:

> Now Ophelia, she's 'neath the window
> For her I feel so afraid
> On her twenty-second birthday
> She already is an old maid
> To her, death is quite romantic
> She wears an iron vest
> Her profession's her religion
> Her sin is her lifelessness
> And though her eyes are fixed upon
> Noah's great rainbow
> She spends her time peeking
> Into Desolation Row

Dylan's Ophelia at once is and is not Shakespeare's. While the character's name directly recalls the Ophelia of *Hamlet*, who sings of being "a maid at your window," her position in Dylan's song also gestures to the balcony scenes of *Romeo and Juliet* and *Much Ado About Nothing*.[1] In this way, the lyric combines a dramatic situation experienced by a female character in one play with that of male and female characters from others, uniting and reconfiguring materials from multiple works. As is the case with Shakespeare's Ophelia and Romeo, the fate of Dylan's Ophelia is hardly glorious. Yet, the differences between Shakespeare's Ophelia and Dylan's are not negligible. While Shakespeare's Ophelia goes mad and dies heartbroken and grieving, Dylan's is a young woman who has doomed herself to lonely discontent because of her unwillingness to engage with life—yet her prurient curiosity results in her hypocritically "peeking into" the abject scenes the song describes. In sum, Dylan's refashioning of Shakespeare's Ophelia preserves the original's tragic isolation and distress, even as it departs somewhat from her example.

To consider the method of Dylan's adaptation of material from Shakespeare is instructive. While his adaptations honor the literary sources that are their intertextual forebears, the adaptations proceed in a highly selective manner. The verse of "Desolation Row" in which Dylan offers his vignette of Ophelia, for example, approaches the language, images, and performative dynamics of Shakespeare's works as portions of a common fund on which he may draw in service of his own compositions. These several fragments of image, dialogue, and dramatic attitude claimed from Shakespeare's oeuvre here serve the individual work that is "Desolation Row," but they are by no means merely backward-facing allusions. They are, instead, reaching in all directions at once, taking shape not only in relation to the predecessor texts that undergird them, but also interacting even more immediately with the maelstrom of other fragments of narratives and lyrics that "Desolation Row" presents. In employing such an approach, Dylan's intertextual uses of Shakespeare's language and dramatic action—both in their simple factuality and in their exploration of terms for engagement with the earlier poet's corpus—take shape in relation to the other fragments among which they are presented, highlighting the process of fragmentation itself and paying tribute to the fundamental productive energy described by the aesthetics of the Romantic fragment. Dylan's treatment of the Shakespearean source as an emblem of the fragment is an instructive case as regards the compositional strategies he was employing in the late

1960s, but also very much prefigures the Grateful Dead's use of Shakespearean materials in its own songs.

While Dylan's lyrics may have provided the Grateful Dead with the only songs of its standard performance repertoire in which Shakespeare is explicitly named, several of its own compositions have lines that evoke the playwright's works.² Among these are pieces the band began to play live in 1968 and 1969. A number of lyrics from these years contain lines that nod to the Bard of Avon's writing, as in the way "Sink beneath the waters / to the coral sand below" of "The Eleven" echoes a passage from *The Tempest*, "Full fadom five thy father lies, / Of his bones are coral made." "You needn't gild the lily, offer jewels to the sunset / No one is watching or standing in your shoes" from "Doin' That Rag" reminds one of *King John*'s

> To gild refined gold, to paint the lily,
>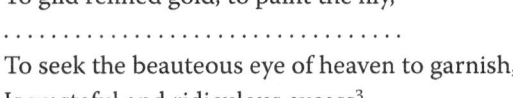
> To seek the beauteous eye of heaven to garnish,
> Is wasteful and ridiculous excess³

Too, the last words of the chorus of "Mason's Children," "When I'm dead and gone / don't you weep for me," owe something not only to several folk songs, but also to the opening of Sonnet 71, "No longer mourn for me when I am dead." However, some other Grateful Dead songs offer more complex engagements with Shakespeare's poetry, among them "Rosemary" and "Mountains of the Moon."

"Rosemary" is a rarity among Grateful Dead songs in that extant live recordings include only one performance, from Kentucky's Bellarmine College in late 1968. As Vivian Thomas and Nicki Faircloth explain, the song's titular plant has a long and varied history in herbal lore and is widely acknowledged as an emblem of remembrance.⁴ Shakespeare draws on that traditional knowledge in several works. The herb is mentioned in *Winter's Tale*, *King Lear*, *Pericles*, and multiple times in *Romeo and Juliet*. Perhaps its most relevant and familiar appearance, however, is in *Hamlet*. By the fifth scene of the fourth act, Ophelia has gone mad. Her father has been murdered; her boyfriend, Prince Hamlet, seems to have rejected her; and Elsinore and Denmark in general are in disarray. She enters singing fragments of songs, ones scholars believe would have been largely familiar to Shakespeare's original audiences.⁵ Among her verses are some that speak, as do many lines in the Grateful Dead's "Rosemary," to the theme of departure and return. Consider, for instance, the following, from Ophelia:

> To-morrow is Saint Valentine's day,
> All in the morning betime,
> And I a maid at your window,
> To be your Valentine.
>
> Then up he rose and donn'd his clo'es,
> And dupp'd the chamber door,
> Let in the maid, that out a maid
> Never departed more[6]

in relation to the Grateful Dead song's many references to isolation, entrance, departure, return, and loss, such as "Her mirror was a window / She sat quite alone"; "She came and she went / and at last went away"; and "No one may come here / since no one may stay." While Hunter's lyrics share with the Shakespearean song a general sense of absence and time, they do not focus, as Ophelia's do, on the loss of sexual innocence in particular. As a result, the song sung by Garcia challenges listeners to contemplate the more general question of what is lost, and what may persist, at various types of leave-takings. The song demonstrates Hunter's early use of Shakespearean content to direct, supplement, and enrich listeners' contemplations.

A view of "Rosemary" as engaging the characters, ideas, and action of *Hamlet* is supported by several additional indications. After her first appearance in the fourth act's fifth scene, as discussed above, Ophelia wanders offstage, only to return about eighty lines later, raving even more incoherently than before. She carries and wears as decoration several herbs and flowers, in keeping with the Grateful Dead song, in which Hunter writes:

> All around her
> the garden grew
> scarlet and purple
> and crimson and blue

Among her remarks is one seemingly directed to her brother, Laertes, to whom she hands certain stems and sprigs, along with a message: "There's rosemary, that's for remembrance; pray you, love, remember. And there is pansies, that's for thoughts."[7] The court is thrown into confusion by her appearance and behavior, and she again exits. This is the character's final appearance in the play before the news of her death is revealed later in the act. The entrances and exits of Ophelia during this scene align her closely with the female character at the center of "Rosemary," who likewise comes and goes among flowers, before leaving forever:

> She came and she went
> and at last went away
> The garden was sealed
> when the flowers decayed

The final line of this verse again reminds one of Ophelia, who declares, "I would give you some violets," a flower that serves as an emblem of faithfulness, "but they wither'd all when my father died."[8]

Before moving on to another Grateful Dead song, it is perhaps valuable to give the literary inheritance of "Rosemary" more of its due by briefly considering another strong literary source for some of its imagery, Alfred, Lord Tennyson's "The Lady of Shalott." This poem relates the tale of a figure from Arthurian legend who lives alone on an island full of flowers. Encircling the island's watery verge are (in the words of the 1832–33 version of the poem) "The yellow-leaved waterlily" and "The green-sheathed daffodilly," while

> The little isle is all inrail'd
> With a rose-fence, and overtrail'd
> With roses.[9]

The lady spends her time weaving and singing in isolation, seeing the world outside her bower only as it is reflected in a mirror. Christopher Ricks notes that it is not unusual for a weaver of a tapestry to have a mirror, as the tool enables an artisan to have a view of both sides of the product simultaneously; in any case, as the Grateful Dead song phrases the idea, "Her mirror was a window / She sat quite alone."[10] Eventually she becomes curious about life beyond her hermetic isle and turns away from both the weaving and the mirror. At that moment, the mirror cracks, a curse is unleashed, she boards a boat and floats off—dying as she drifts downstream. Tennyson's first version of the poem suggests that she is a suicide.

The combination of the lady's initial unwillingness to engage with the world and her curiosity about it is more reminiscent of Dylan's Ophelia than of Shakespeare's, although her watery death does echo the fate met by the original character. Too, the poem's staging of a tension between the rarefied purity of art, emblematized by the mirror and the weaving, and the dangers of the real world is reminiscent of Prince Hamlet's own concerns regarding artifice and dissemblance—a topic explored further below. Hunter's lyrics, which overlay elements of "The Lady of Shalott" onto aspects of *Hamlet*, especially the characters of Ophelia and Prince Hamlet, are rightly not mired in the question of consistency—an avoidance that helps the evocative ambiguities of "Rosemary" to arise. Furthermore, the song's interplay between material borrowed from Tennyson and Shakespeare demonstrates the degree to which the Grateful Dead's compositions—much like Dylan's, in such instances as "Desolation Row"—treat literary works as reservoirs of imagery and dramatic attitude, from which songs emerge. Consequently, the piece indicates the ephemerality of any performance in relation to that reservoir. Ophelia and the Lady of Shalott are drawn into the light, commingled, and eventually recede together. Just as Garcia's and Constanten's senses that the music produced by the band on a given night was the temporal manifestation of a purer, endlessly unfolding version of that music in eternity, so "Rosemary" presents itself as a Romantic fragment—a manifestation of the literary absolute, the figurative space from which texts emerge as local manifestations of a foundational creativity—even as it gestures toward a more profound space of potential.

"Rosemary" is not the only song among those recorded for *Aoxomoxoa* that is deeply indebted to Shakespeare and that illustrates the band's engagement with the aesthetics of the literary fragment. "Mountains of the Moon," which received its first of only twelve live performances in Los Angeles on December 20, 1968, likewise finds inspiration in Shakespeare's tragedies. Few Grateful Dead songs have such a high number of evident sources in both the literary and the folk traditions: Gary Snyder's translations of Han-Shan's poetry, Edgar Allan Poe's "Eldorado," the many ancient Greek poems that tell the story of Electra, the ballad "The Two Sisters," the nursery rhyme "The Carrion Crow," and Hans Christian Andersen's fairy tale "The Marsh King" are among the prior texts that have left a mark on the song. Added to the influence of these sources are materials from Shakespeare's *King Lear*, most of which evoke one or more of a handful of themes, including natural loyalty, the tribulations of loss, and the right relations among family members.

One of the many questions *King Lear* asks its audience to consider is how the text's dynamics shape familial bonds. In this play and others, intergenerational conflicts within the royal family are particularly fraught, for they bear not only on domestic matters, but also the gravest political ones. Furthermore, given the belief that a king's authority is both secular and divinely appointed, an affront to royal authority in one of Shakespeare's plays—perhaps especially within the royal family—is an offense not merely to convention, but also to the divinely wrought natural order. In this sense, the obedience of a prince or princess is more than virtuous filial compliance—it signifies insight into the universal truths that govern earthly existence. The mention of

Electra in "Mountains of the Moon" situates these sorts of concerns about succession, treachery, and familial loyalty in relation to tragic poetry in general, and the *Oresteia* in particular. *King Lear* follows Aeschylus and other ancient tragedians who relate the Electra tale in the presentation of a loyal daughter whose moral compass guides her and stands as an implicit rule against which the surrounding less-virtuous characters are measured. At the start of the play, Lear asks his three daughters, Goneril, Regan, and Cordelia, to profess their love for him. Cordelia refrains, for although she loves him best, she regards the event as an exercise in base flattery. Her two sisters are effusive, however, and Lear divides his kingdom between the two of them as he enters semiretirement. Goneril and Regan immediately begin plotting means to disenfranchise their father even further, and soon find themselves at odds with each other, as well. Too, their treachery infects their marriages. The disarray into which the royal house is thrown by this scheming is mirrored in the noble family of Lord Gloucester, as his illegitimate and disloyal son Edmund works to destroy the bonds between Gloucester and his legitimate and virtuous son, as well as rightful heir, Edgar. Act 3 of the play finds Lear near madness, spending a cold, windy, and rainy night on a barren heath. One need not be an experienced reader of Shakespeare to see in the natural violence a mirror image of the social disorder that shapes the play's action.

Among those who remain loyal to Lear is his Fool, who stays beside him throughout the dark night of act 3—one of the most harrowing portions of any of Shakespeare's texts—offering wisdom in the form of veiled arguments and songs that lend themselves to allegorical readings. One set of his lines offers the following:

> He that has and a little tine wit—
> With heigh-ho, the wind and the rain—
> Must make content with his fortunes fit,
> Though the rain it raineth every day.[11]

As is typical with Lear's Fool, the seeming scrap of folk song carries a heavy load. The weather of the song is one that the characters experience, and the "tine wit" Lear displayed in dispensing with his authority indeed means he must make himself "content" with his diminished "fortunes." More to the point here, the "heigh-ho" and "the rain" of the passage open the door to thinking about the play in relation to "Mountains of the Moon," for the Fool's song anticipates the Grateful Dead's

> Hey, the laurel
> Hey, the city
> In the rain

The laurel is certainly a more noble plant than the weeds and flowers with which Lear is dressed later in the act. But to think of the Shakespearean scene when hearing these lines from "Mountains of the Moon" lends some gravity to the verse, which otherwise has the tone of a sort of melancholy pastoral.

Into the midst of Lear's night passed in the elements comes Edgar, who has disguised himself as a mad beggar, bearing the common name of such types: Tom. In this guise of mad Tom, Edgar is central to several passages that are echoed in "Mountains of the Moon." The first develops soon after Edgar's father walks onto the scene. Edgar begins complaining of being tormented by a devil named Flibbertigibbet, who "begins at curfew, and walks [till the] first cock; he gives the web and the pin, [squinies] the eye, and makes the hare-lip; mildews the white wheat, and hurts the poor creature of earth."[12] Flibbertigibbet's power to ruin otherwise healthy "white wheat" recurs in "the white wheat / Wavin' in the wind" in "Mountains of the Moon," while the sense that he is an opponent of Tom, a "poor creature of earth," would seem to underlie Hunter's

> Hey, Tom Banjo
> It's time to matter
> The Earth will see you
> on through this time.

To look at the placement of these various *King Lear*–inflected lyrics within "Mountains of the Moon" is to see that Hunter has woven them throughout the fabric of the song. But one also sees that he resists the possibility that they dominate the text. This resistance to allowing any one source to control the whole composition makes for a more dynamic lyric. Among other points, it leaves room for approaching "Mountains of the Moon" not only as a work inflected by Shakespeare, but also, in part, as an autobiographical statement about the Grateful Dead. From the latter perspective, those dancing in the hall may be viewed as the band's audience. Likewise, "Tom Banjo," in addition to standing in for "poor Tom" of *King Lear*, can be read in terms of the nickname of Tom Azarian, a New England–based banjo player with some connections to the Grateful Dead's world. Azarian was awarded his nickname by students at the University of Connecticut in the late 1950s, the same period during which Robert Hunter was attending the school and was involved with its Folk Music Club.[13] Although Azarian asserts that he did not know

Hunter, they were listening to and playing with a wide variety of performers in the context of the club's events.[14] Among others on the scene at the time was David Grisman, who would go on to meet Jerry Garcia outside a Bill Monroe concert in 1964, play mandolin on two tracks on *American Beauty*, and, eventually, join Garcia for several recordings and performances outside of the Grateful Dead proper.[15] Thus, as is the case with "Rosemary," the Shakespearean content of "Mountains of the Moon" intersects with a wide array of other allusions and borrowings—intertextual components that allow the lyric to register as an evocative fragment of the whole, enriching our hearing of the piece—all without falling into any strict prescription.

That said, the similarities between song and play are sharpened when one accounts for the end of the sixth scene of *King Lear*'s third act, which touches directly on matters of filial loyalty. At this point in the play, Edgar stands alone on the stage, briefly setting aside his disguise of madness for a soliloquy. Among his lines are a reflection on the degree to which Lear is beset by difficulties physical, mental, and familial:

> How light and portable my pain seems now,
> When that which makes me bend makes the King bow:
> He childed as I fathered! Tom, away![16]

Edgar's observation that he and Lear are alike in being betrayed by family is supported by, among other features, their similar dress. Lear, in giving up his kingdom to his disloyal daughters, has figuratively stripped himself of authority, just as Edgar has been stripped of his inheritance by his brother's plotting. Too, Edgar, as mad Tom, is literally unclothed, for Lear describes him as having an "uncover'd body," a state of dress Lear himself adopts soon after first meeting Edgar in disguise as Tom.[17] These variations on nakedness reach Grateful Dead listeners via the lyric "Clothed in tatters / Always will be" from "Mountains of the Moon," where they are used in an ambiguous fashion that may be heard as describing either "Tom Banjo" or "The Marsh King's Daughter"—or both.

Additional contributions to the imagery of "Mountains of the Moon" in Edgar's soliloquy derive from his comparison between "bend" and "bow," which he both summarizes as representing the battered and exhausted condition of himself and Lear, while also anticipating the line "Bow and bend to me," which recurs throughout the Grateful Dead song. Indeed, the bending and bowing of the song grounds a tremendously rich number of readings, including not only the bowing and curtseying that may well be occurring among the various partners of the song's "dancing kings and wives," but also the bending of the bow that fires the poorly aimed arrow in the traditional song "The Carrion Crow"; several lines from various versions of the ballad "The Two Sisters," including "boughs" that are "bent," "bow and balance to me," and

Bow down, bow down,

. . . .
And thou hast bent to me

and the bowing and bending of the knee that are traditional actions performed in recognition of social authority.[18] Furthermore, Edgar's words anticipate Lear's assertion later in the play, "That fellow handles his bow like a crow-keeper," a line that indirectly praises Edgar's and Gloucester's efforts to preserve Lear's fortunes, just as a crow-keeper chases birds away from crops. The several rich valences of "Bow and bend to me" bring Shakespeare's text into closer communion with the "Carrion Crow" of the Grateful Dead song and remind listeners of "the white wheat / Wavin' in the wind" that the hungry crow may threaten.[19] As the above points make evident, hearing the song in relation to Edgar's lines demonstrates just how enriched it is by the context of *King Lear*. No simple ballad, "Mountains of the Moon" dances between virtue and corruption, loyalty and betrayal, as well as appearance and truth.

Perhaps more than anything else, the words and imagery that "Mountains of the Moon" seem to have imported from *King Lear* encourage a hearing of the song in terms of an oblique meditation on moral virtue, especially the bonds of natural loyalty. Intriguingly, the change the song demands when we listen to it on these terms allows us to undergo the same sort of experience as do Lear and Gloucester during the course of Shakespeare's play. Among the revelations that derive from the chaos of the third act are Lear's insight regarding the degree to which material wealth and social advantage can obscure corruption: "Thorough tatter'd clothes [small] vices do appear; / Robes and furr'd gowns hide all."[20] Such realizations of true moral virtue are not something Edgar's remarks while in disguise offer only to Lear, but they are also extended to his own father, whose final words, spoken before his attempted suicide, confirm his belated understanding of Edgar's relative worth: "If Edgar live, O bless him! / Now, fellow, fare thee well."[21] "Mountains of the Moon," with its final line of "Bend to me," confirms for listeners the lessons that the play's characters learn the hard way how to recognize virtue and preserve natural authority.

That "Mountains of the Moon" follows *King Lear* in openness to and recombinations of material manifest in numerous early songs and literary texts allows it to join "Rosemary" in illustrating the Grateful Dead's tendency to the fragmentary. The allusions bring to the fore and then allow the melting away of one or another prior source. Perhaps the best figure for the process is that of a kaleidoscope in motion. Patterns and conjunctions are brought into being and as quickly are transformed or evaporate. The potential for multiplication of significance as these literary and folk materials interact is effectively endless, and the apparent limitlessness of those successive variations points to the very eternality of the literary absolute Lacoue-Labarthe and Nancy joined the German Romantics in describing.

While the preceding examples indicate something of the degree to which Shakespeare's works enrich our hearing of the Grateful Dead's lyrics, I do not mean to suggest that the band's earlier works bear more of his mark than do the later ones. For example, "Black Muddy River," which joined the repertoire only in the band's final decade, not only owes its title to the Irish Romantic poet Thomas Moore, but also the line "And stones fall from my eyes instead of tears" to Shakespeare's *Richard III*. Richard, before his ascension to the throne, praises the assassins he hires by observing, "Your eyes drop millstones, while fools' eyes fall tears."[22]

The most striking instance of the Grateful Dead's lyrical engagement with Shakespeare is its song "Althea." The band began performing this composition in 1979 and first released a recording of it on the 1980 studio album *Go to Heaven*. The song stands in the tradition of the poetic dialogue, presenting a conversation between the titular Althea and a male interlocutor, although it also departs from that tradition in some important ways. The opening verses present an exchange in which the male speaker asks Althea for advice, for he feels adrift and betrayed:

> I told Althea I was feeling lost
> Lacking in some direction
> Althea told me upon scrutiny
> my back might need protection
>
> I told Althea that treachery
> was tearing me limb from limb

While the space given to each speaker in this opening of the exchange is fairly well-balanced, Althea's response to this complaint about treachery will soon dominate most of the song. Thus, the relatively long third verse is among those entirely given over to her advice, and it begins as follows:

You may be Saturday's child all grown
moving with a pinch of grace
You may be a clown in the burying ground
or just another pretty face.

Lines 3 and 4 evoke the first scene of the final act of *Hamlet*, in which the prince and his friend Horatio visit a cemetery, where two gravediggers are at work on a pit that will accommodate the body of Ophelia. Like a lot of other rough commoners in Shakespeare, the laborers are identified as "clowns." Furthermore, as with other less-educated or fool characters in Shakespeare's plays—one thinks of Touchstone in *As You Like It* or Feste in *Twelfth Night*, but especially of the Fool in *King Lear*—the talk of the gravedigging rustics wins our attention, not least because it includes inadvertent insights from which some of the more noble characters could benefit.[23] So, listeners must take care to recognize that Althea's assertion in these lines is not at all a claim that her interlocutor is the bumbling fool our contemporary sense of "clown" suggests, but that he may already unwittingly know the answers to the questions he poses.

It is possible, however, that Althea alludes not to the clowns digging the grave, but to another clownish figure central to the same scene in Shakespeare's play. While making room for a new interment in the already-crowded cemetery, the gravediggers shovel aside older bones. Hamlet learns that one unearthed skull is that of Yorick, who was the court jester for his father. The prince calls on Yorick to speak from beyond the grave, asking him what profit his good humor has earned him now that he is nothing more than a skeleton: "He hath bore me on his back a thousand times, and now how abhorr'd in my imagination it is! my gorge rises at it. Here hung those lips that I have kiss'd I know not how oft. Where be your gibes now, your gambols, your songs, your flashes of merriment, that were wont to set the table on a roar? Not one now to mock your own grinning—quite chop-fall'n. Now get you to my lady's [chamber], and tell her, let her paint an inch thick, to this favor she must come; make her laugh at that."[24] Yorick, of course, does not answer, but Hamlet carries on, and commands Yorick not only to speak, but also, in the final lines of the immediately preceding quotation, to act ("Now get you to my lady's [chamber], and tell her . . ."). The message Hamlet would have Yorick deliver is, in a sense, a mere truism. We all, even if we have the "pretty face" of an ornamented lady of the court, will look like Yorick in the end. Nevertheless, if one assumes the "clown" of the third line of the third verse of "Althea" is indeed Yorick, this Shakespearean context shapes a hearing of the verse's next line in a particular way: Althea's assertion that the listener may be "just another pretty face" is not a thoughtless dismissal, but a remark of real weight, one that recalls Prince Hamlet's reflections on the folly of human vanity. The contentions of this paragraph do not mean to propose that the initial interpretation of those lines considered above—that the clown of the song is a Shakespearean gravedigger—should be supplanted by one focused on Yorick. What they instead submit is that both readings are entangled in the play, and both obtain at once in the song as well. Hunter thereby follows Shakespeare in interweaving intimations of wisdom uncovered in unexpected places with a sense of urgency and dread.

Those ambiguities that proliferate alongside these hints of surprise and obscured sources of wisdom are manifest in a narrative episode that stages a character's confrontation with his own mortality in a burial ground—serving as telling spurs to interpretive exercise. Yorick's skull is for Hamlet not only Yorick's skull, but also the death of Hamlet's father, the fault of his mother, the destruction of Ophelia, the murder of Polonius, and so forth. The skull and its viewer walk the line between the ephemeral and the eternal, as does the text. The plurality of meanings that arise from the contemplation of the skull suggest a living productivity so powerful that even Death's task is frustrated, left incomplete. In this sense, Yorick's skull is not only a relic or a memento mori for Hamlet, but an emblem of the creative power to which the literary fragment gestures. A mere part of the living human, it becomes a richer speaker when disrobed of its flesh. It is perpetually subject to re-engagement, and in their presentations of such incompletions, *Hamlet* and "Althea" both offer a model of closure's resolutions yielding to the inexhaustibility of evocations.

Later portions of the song continue this tendency. The second half of the third verse continues mining the Shakespearean vein, with Althea proposing to her listener:

> You may be the fate of Ophelia
> sleeping and perchance to dream—
> honest to the point of recklessness
> self-centered to the extreme.

It is important to note that Althea does not establish a neat parallel. She does not say, "Your fate may be the fate of Ophelia." If she had, it would suggest an equivalence between Ophelia's destiny and that of the song's initial speaker. Instead, Althea says, "You may be the fate of Ophelia." One could hear this as Althea's declaration that a figurative Ophelia will somehow end up tied, romantically or otherwise, to the song's initial speaker, making him her fate in the sense that she is destined to be with him. Another interpretation is perhaps richer, as it accommodates not only what is in the song, but also what it excludes. Because Hunter's lyric resists a strict parallelism, a sort of off-kilter one emerges—distorting the relationship between the song's initial speaker and Ophelia's fate into a more uncanny dynamic. To wit, the song's initial speaker may himself somehow be an incarnation of Ophelia's destiny.

As the song tells us, that destiny is to be "sleeping and perchance to dream." The line is, of course, an almost-verbatim borrowing from *Hamlet*'s most famous soliloquy, and it reminds us of a particular point with which Prince Hamlet struggles—as death is like sleep, there is a chance the next world will be nightmarish, a fact that leaves us tied to inaction. Here are the most relevant lines:

> To die, to sleep—
> No more, and by a sleep to say we end
> The heartache and the thousand natural shocks
> That flesh is heir to; 'tis a consummation
> Devoutly to be wished. To die, to sleep—
> To sleep, perchance to dream—ay, there's the rub,
> For in that sleep of death what dreams may come,
> When we have shuffled off this mortal coil,
> Must give us pause.[25]

For Hamlet, meditation on this point is multifaceted. Most overtly, the fear of eternal suffering encourages him not to commit suicide, but it also speaks to his general tendency to hesitation. The qualities mentioned in the final lines of the third verse of "Althea"—reckless honesty and extreme self-centeredness—likewise could describe Hamlet, who consistently treads the territory between truth and deception, and who most forcefully embodies a position of destructive self-absorption. At this point, Hunter's lyrics reveal to what degree the Grateful Dead will refashion the Shakespearean original, for while we can recognize that the aforementioned qualities describe Hamlet, we risk forgetting, in doing so, that Althea is describing Ophelia's fate, rather than Hamlet's character. Yet, the songwriter, in allowing the characters of Hamlet, Ophelia, and Althea's interlocutor to bleed into one another, as does Dylan with Romeo and Ophelia in "Desolation Row," clearly employs Shakespearean material to stage advice that will spur the song's first speaker from dreamlike hesitation into action.

When discussing "Althea" in an interview, Hunter points our attention to the ancient origins of the name, positing that she is an incarnation of the goddess Athena.[26] His remarks are helpful in several ways, not least in fleshing out our sense of the character as a figure of wisdom. They also remind us of Althea's ancient literary ancestry. We meet the classical Althaea in a Greco-Roman myth that tells of a woman who was both mother and murderer of Meleager. The extant ancient sources for this story are several, but most, including Aeschylus's *Libation Bearers*, are rather spotty on the details. This deficiency is not the case for Ovid's *Metamorphoses*, which offers a version of the tale that runs roughly as follows: When Althaea gives birth to Meleager, she learns that the Fates have decreed that he will live until a particular piece of wood is burned completely by fire, so she stores the wood in a safe place. Years later, Calydon is terrorized by a monstrous wild boar. Meleager calls a hunt for the beast, a challenge that brings together several of the great heroes of the day. Among the assembled is the nymph Atalanta, who both charms Meleager and draws first blood in battle with the creature. When Meleager finally deals it a fatal wound, he pins it to the ground and yields to Atalanta the trophy of its head, in accord with the rules of the hunt, which presumably have the authority of the goddess Diana. At this point, Meleager's maternal uncles interrupt, arguing that Atalanta should not be awarded the prize. Outraged by this affront against Atalanta, and possibly also the sacrilegious position it implies, Meleager kills his uncles. When Althaea hears of the identity of the murderer, she throws the piece of wood that preserves Meleager's life into a fire. It burns, and he dies in great pain and with disappointment at his relatively ignoble end.[27] Although Hunter did not mention Meleager in his remarks on the song, the tale seems to inform several of its lines, from the fourth verse's "Maybe it's your fire / but baby . . . don't get burned" to the fifth's "When the smoke has cleared" and "This space is getting hot— / you know this space is getting hot." In each of these cases, the literary allusions are part of a warning, one reinforced by the repetition in the final instance—choose quickly, yet wisely.

While the preceding paragraphs have suggested just how extensive the Shakespearean and classical sources for the literary context of "Althea" are individually, they are even more remarkable in combination. Shakespeare's own works are deeply indebted to Ovid's poetry, and Althaea is mentioned in two plays by Shakespeare, *2 Henry VI* and *2 Henry IV*.[28] This chapter now turns to these convergences of ancient and Renaissance sources informing "Althea."

The three plays Shakespeare wrote about Henry VI concern the collapse of England's rule of French territories and the initiation of the War of the Roses, which was the contest between the Houses of York and Lancaster for the throne of England. As the middle play of the trilogy, 2 *Henry VI* shows a kingdom in discord, with various noble families bickering under the eyes of an ineffectual ruler. It also includes, in a passage spoken by Richard Plantagenet, a reference to the myth of Althaea. The most relevant context for the passage containing the allusion concerns England's ceding of several of its provinces on the continent to the French crown in exchange for the hand of Margaret of Anjou. These political and marital arrangements were delineated in the Treaty of Tours, which ended the Hundred Years War. Prior to the marriage of Henry and Margaret, Richard Plantagenet, the third Duke of York, and father of future King Richard III, had served as Lord Protector during periods when Henry was incapable of rule due to his periodic madness. With many friends in the court, and a legitimate, if somewhat indirect, ancestral claim to royal authority, Richard is a justified aspirant to the throne, and it is in his complaint regarding England's loss of territories to the French that we encounter an allusion to Althaea and the burning log that was Meleager's destruction:

> Methinks the realms of England, France, and Ireland
> Bear that proportion to my flesh and blood
> As did the fatal brand Althaea burnt
> Unto the Prince's heart of Calydon.[29]

Here, Shakespeare focuses attention on the destructive, rather than maternal, side of the ancient Althaea as a way of developing our understanding of Richard's perception of Margaret. Just as Althaea destroyed Meleager, so Margaret's appearance in England puts an end to Richard's plans to ascend to royal power. His comment observes, however, the important role of destruction in the turmoil that brings change to the royal house; however he individually experiences the pain, his allusion to Meleager and Althaea acknowledges the intimate connection between dissolution and production, which the German Romantics would later recognize as characterizing the border of the literary absolute. Furthermore, one notes that the third line of the quoted passage, which unites the character of Althaea with fate and fiery threats, leaves a strong mark on Hunter's lyrics, which likewise combine remarks about fate and fire.

Richard's reference to Althaea in 2 *Henry VI* is relatively straightforward, but the reference in 2 *Henry IV* is more complicated. Much of the play is preoccupied with the possible moral corruption of Prince Hal (the future Henry V), who spends a lot of his time carousing and very little preparing for the responsibilities of the throne. At the center of the social demimonde with which he riots is Falstaff, a roguish knight who appears in several of Shakespeare's plays. Falstaff's entourage includes his ensign Ancient Pistol, a pageboy, the prostitute Doll Tearsheet, and the thief Bardolph. The Calydonian boar of the Althaea myth is a background presence to Falstaff and his cronies at several points in the play—one of the public houses they frequent is the Boar's Head Inn; Prince Hal refers to Falstaff as an "old boar"; and Doll Tearsheet calls Pistol a "whoreson little tidy Bartholomew boar-pig."[30] The setting of the Boar's Head Inn may alone have been enough to earn the attention of Hunter and Garcia. Prior to the formation of the Grateful Dead, the two played music, sometimes together, in a variety of folk clubs in the Bay Area. Among these early-1960s venues was "a small coffeehouse called the Boar's Head," which was founded in San Carlos in 1961 by George Howell and Rodney Albin—Rodney is the older brother of Peter Albin, who would go on to fame as a founding member of the band Big Brother and the Holding Company.[31] The very name of the venue implies another Shakespearean connection, for the Boar's Head Festival after which both the London tavern and Bay-Area folk club were named is a celebration on the final night of the Christmas season, an evening that lent its popular name to Shakespeare's *Twelfth Night*.

The allusions to Althaea in *2 Henry IV* are reinforced by the robust intertextual presence of the myth throughout the play. The first explicit reference to Althaea appears in the second scene of the second act, at a moment when a number of Falstaff's crowd are half-playfully arguing with one another. Amid their ribbing, Falstaff's Page declares Bardolph to be "Althaea's dream." When Prince Hal asks the boy what he means by this, the Page declares, "Althaea dreamt she was deliver'd of a firebrand."[32] Falstaff's Page is confused—the woman in ancient Greco-Roman literature who dreams she gives birth to a firebrand is Hecuba, queen of Troy—but he is correct in recalling that a firebrand is affiliated with Althaea and her son. This indirect merging of Hecuba and Althaea results in a figure of some complexity. Hecuba is characterized as embodying maternal excellence in several ancient works, including the *Iliad* by Homer and *The Trojan Women* and *Hecuba* by Euripides. In Homer's epic, she offers both her children and her husband wise advice, and she mourns their deaths in a socially approved fashion in both the poem and the plays. Hecuba is invoked by characters in several of Shakespeare's texts, including *Troilus and Cressida*, *Titus Andronicus*, *Coriolanus*, *Cymbeline*, and

The Rape of Lucrece. She is also a presence in *Hamlet,* during the second act of which Prince Hamlet asks an actor to recite a speech that culminates in a description of Hecuba's mourning for Priam. The lines portray a woman in profound distress, one whose expressions of deep loss stand in strong contrast to those of Hamlet's own, less virtuous mother, whose grief appears rather tepid by comparison. Too, the madness that afflicts and transforms the bereaved Hecuba as she is portrayed in Ovid's *Metamorphoses* anticipates the changes in Hamlet's character.[33] As a consequence of the Page's fumbling intermingling of Althaea and Hecuba, we can read the Althaea invoked in his remarks as less harsh than the vindictive one we meet in some classical sources, although she remains closely tied to the dangerous fire that lends urgency to her decisions. Cumulatively, the references to Althaea in 2 *Henry IV* anticipate the seriousness of the problems Prince Hal faces, particularly his obligation to trade the careless fun of dissipation with Falstaff for royal duty. In these senses, the Althaea of this play is an illuminating predecessor to that of the Grateful Dead song, which features an Althea who likewise offers wisdom regarding the course of future action and insights about the dangers that can come with delay.

The following final remarks regarding 2 *Henry IV* and "Althea" pertain to the play's closing scene, in which Prince Hal, having been crowned King Henry V, repudiates Falstaff. During the coronation parade, Falstaff approaches his old friend, whom he addresses as "thy Grace," but the king's response to this overture is utterly dismissive:

> *Fal.* God save thy Grace, King Hal! my royal Hal!
> . . . .
> *King.* I know thee not, old man, fall to thy prayers.
> How ill white hairs becomes a fool and jester!
> I have long dreamt of such a kind of man,
> So surfeit-swell'd, so old, and so profane;
> But being awak'd, I do despise my dream.
> Make less thy body (hence) and more thy grace,
> Leave gormandizing; know the grave doth gape
> For thee thrice wider than for other men.
> Reply not to me with a fool-born jest,
> Presume not that I am the thing I was.[34]

These lines are at once fiercely biting and stately, delivering a message in a fashion that particularly drew Garcia's attention. In a 1981 interview, for instance, he says of one Dylan song:

It tells that person who's lame that they're lame, why they're lame, which is a very satisfying thing to do.... "Positively Fourth Street" has this way of doing it where it's beautiful, too. And "It's All Over Now, Baby Blue" is basically a putdown, too. It's one of those things like "you're losing bad—dig yourself."

Being able to say that and say it beautifully—it was the beautiful sound of "Positively Fourth Street" that got to me more than the bitterness of the lyric. The combination of the beauty and the bitterness, to me, is wonderful.[35]

The songs that Garcia mentions make clear that he shares with Dylan an appreciation of the sort of simultaneously bitter and beautiful lines that Shakespeare offers, among other places, in the final scene of 2 *Henry IV*.

In addition, the particulars of the newly crowned Henry V's remarks return us to the parts of *Hamlet* most germane to "Althea." In repudiating Falstaff, Henry positions the man as a fool—not as a wise fool like the one in *King Lear*, but as a gluttonous and irresponsible figure. In rejecting his youthful recklessness and self-centered pleasure-seeking, which is embodied in the figure of Falstaff, the king condemns that earlier part of his life as nothing more than a "dream," then points to the wide grave that awaits the corpulent knight. This "dream" evokes the "perchance to dream" of *Hamlet*'s most famous soliloquy, while the imagery of the gaping "grave" recalls the first scene of the final act, in which the prince, Horatio, and the diggers of Ophelia's grave ponder Yorick's skull. Another result is that we encounter, within these fifteen lines of 2 *Henry IV*, a child grown into a man (Prince Hal, having matured into a king), a clown (Falstaff as "jester"), a burying ground (the "grave" that "doth gape"), "grace" (both as Hal's new title and as a term for "soul" in his response to his former friend), and dreams (in the third line of Hal's remark). Consider again the first six lines of the third verse of "Althea," which follow this passage from late in 2 *Henry IV* quite closely:

> You may be Saturday's *child all grown*
> moving with a pinch of *grace*
> You may be *a clown in the burying ground*
> or just another pretty face
> You may be the fate of Ophelia
> sleeping and perchance to *dream* [italics mine]

The similarities between this verse of the song and the final exchange between Falstaff and Henry V are remarkable. Althea presents to her listener a variety of identities, defined on the same terms as those the young monarch uses in his rejection of all the corrupt knight embodies.

The literary context of "Althea" sketched above highlights several points for listeners. First, the song serves as an outstanding example of Hunter's ability to interweave disparate sources from the literary tradition, uniting and refashioning elements of classical mythology, Renaissance drama, and the songs of Bob Dylan within the context of a new creation. Moreover, he does so successfully enough that we can see Hunter's lyrics not just as deriving from the literary tradition but also as participating in it—and in two distinct fashions. On the one hand, just as Shakespeare's texts are not for us what they were to Elizabethan or Jacobean audiences, but rather what they are as filtered through Ben Jonson, Goethe, and Eliot—the latter of whom is mentioned by name in "Desolation Row"—so Hunter's lyrics retroactively influence how we read the poems and plays that are their ancestors. This phenomenon reminds us that the folk tradition transmits in a fashion akin to the literary tradition. The Grateful Dead's reshaping of the centuries-old ballad "The Lady of Carlisle" in its own "Terrapin Station," for example, very much relies on folk music's tendency to rework earlier material for particular performers and audiences, a nonlinear process echoed in the way the Grateful Dead's Ophelia has been mediated by works like Eliot's *The Waste Land* (the "goodnight, sweet ladies / good night, good night" lines of which are drawn from Shakespeare's *Hamlet*) and Dylan's "Desolation Row."[36] On the other hand, such examples of the Grateful Dead's engagement with literary tradition help us understand why the band has appeared, as the conclusion of this book explains, in works by contemporary literary figures.

A second concluding observation is that the literary context of "Althea" enriches our hearing of the piece, not only in the ways so far delineated, but also as a foothold for thinking about the possible metafunction of the lyrics. Indeed, the literary context leads me to propose that we regard "Althea" as a self-referential song, one that encourages listeners to reflect on the potential opportunities and certain challenges fostered by the shape of the Grateful Dead's career at a transitional point in its development. I am not the first to suggest we hear the song as speaking to matters germane to the band itself. Anecdotal evidence suggests that some fans hear "Althea" as one of Hunter's attempts to caution Garcia off hard drugs. But the literary context points us in the direction of a more general and richer meditation on the interchanges between creation and destruction—as embodied in the classical Althaea, who is both mother and killer of her child—and between hesitation and action, as Hamlet, Prince Hal, and Dylan's Ophelia remind us. With this context in mind, we might consider that point at which the band seemed most drawn to the song. It debuted "Althea" in 1979 and performed the piece more in 1980 than in any other year. This was a somewhat uncertain time, in the sense that the Grateful Dead was figuring out how to move forward without the talents of the husband-wife team of Keith and Donna Jean Godchaux while incorporating the new possibilities keyboardist and singer Brent Mydland brought to the stage. There is also evidence that songwriting may have become more challenging for them during this period; at the very least, this is suggested by the scarcity of new songs by Hunter and Garcia at the time. After "Althea" and "Alabama Getaway," both from 1979, we find nothing in 1980 or 1981, only three new compositions in 1982 ("West L.A. Fadeaway," the unpopular "Keep Your Day Job," and the acclaimed "Touch of Grey"), and nothing again in 1983, 1984, and 1985.[37] There were, of course, many reasons for productivity to have slowed, but it is not unreasonable to hear, in Althea's call to action and her recommendation for wise reflection on what is most valuable, a sentiment that would have been particularly appealing to the band during a transitional period, serving as a means to comment on the complexity of creative exercise at a moment in its career when its reputation and performances hovered between the near full-stop of its mid-1970s hiatus and the astronomical popularity it found in the late 1980s.

In addition, the improvisatory transitions between incarnation and loss that are the dynamic forces driving much of the song are, as noted briefly at several points above, entirely in keeping with the literary fragment as celebrated by the German Romantics. The exchanges in "Althea" between form and dissolution, chaos and system, betrayal and fulfillment, and birth and death are central to their understanding of the potential of the fragment. Its powers are evocative, but this is an evocation not limited to the facile sense of encouraging speculation. Instead, the fragments drawn from Shakespeare point to what Nancy follows the Romantics in calling the literary absolute: a reservoir of potential from which creative works emerge. The Grateful Dead's engagement with Shakespeare thus ultimately brings listeners back to this point at which the inexhaustible generative process unfolds—a point to which the band returned listeners repeatedly across its thirty-year career.

Finally, because study of Shakespeare is endless and because erstwhile Grateful Dead keyboardist Tom Constanten asserted that the band's signature improvisational vehicle, "Dark Star," never stops playing, this chapter will offer, as a last point, something of an open-ended variation on what it has discussed so far.[38] As fans will recall, the Grateful Dead's repertoire includes a song entitled "Jack Straw," a violent revenge tale set in America's desert Southwest. Among the scenes in Shakespeare's *2 Henry VI* are several related to the fifteenth-century popular uprising led by Jack Cade. That rebellion is often read by historians as a resurgence of class troubles that earlier manifested in the fourteenth-century peasant revolt led by the historical figure Jack Straw, whose personality and story were made theatrical in an Elizabethan play titled *The Life and Death of Jack Straw*.[39] This work is of unclear authorship, but it appears, like Shakespeare's *Henry VI* plays, likely to have enjoyed some popularity on the English stage in the 1590s.[40] In this sense, the historical Jack Straw's story is one with that of the historical Henry VI, and the dramatization of Straw's life on stage is likewise united with the performance history of Shakespeare's texts about that monarch. The Grateful Dead's "Jack Straw," therefore, not only brings together the English historical record and murderous tales of the American frontier but also taps into the same realm of Elizabethan theater and the literary tradition that it has shaped, just as "Althea" does. Taken together as a measure of the Shakespearean influence on the Grateful Dead, these and other pieces by the band offer us a picture of rock musicians as wise clowns who dig through Elsinore's cemetery, unearthing the oddities of our cultural heritage while reminding us, as does Yorick, not to overestimate the worth of our ambitions.

On the Heels of Rimbaud

BOB DYLAN, THE GRATEFUL
DEAD, AND THE NATURE
OF THE LITERARY

In early 1991, Blair Jackson conducted a joint interview with Jerry Garcia and Robert Hunter. They were more than usually forthcoming about their songwriting practices and sensibilities, and the conversation eventually turned to the importance of Bob Dylan. Hunter commended Dylan as an innovator, stating, "We've got to give Dylan credit for being the guy who really opened the door to being literate in music." Garcia continued the point: "He gave rock 'n' roll the thing I'd wished it had when I was a kid—respectability; some authority. He took it out of the realm of ignorant guys banging away on electric instruments and put it somewhere else altogether." He added, "Dylan is the guy who allowed the music to become what some of us hoped it could be."[1] Hunter and Garcia are hardly alone in recognizing Dylan's exceptional talent as a songwriter. Dylan's work is much lauded, and claims for his greatness as a lyricist began early and grew fairly steadily for decades. The most distinguished recognition of his exceptional talent and affirmation that his work answered to the highest standards of literary writing came when he was awarded the Nobel Prize in Literature in 2016.

This chapter explores what Hunter means by "literate in music," which the concurrence of remarks suggests is the same as, or at least near kin to, Garcia's point that Dylan gifted rock and roll with "respectability" and "authority." The following exploration of these qualities as manifest in the music of the Grateful Dead, and particularly at moments when the band's career most clearly intersected with Dylan's, proceeds with an eye to three components. First among these are the biographical connections between Dylan and the Dead that are a matter of historical record. Second are the exchanges of practice and perception between the Dead and Dylan fostered by those biographical connections and evident in their remarks on their own and each other's songwriting and performance histories, including song selection, performances on given nights, and rhythms of public engagement across months and years. The final, and most important, component is the similarity between the literary identity of the Grateful Dead and that of Dylan, particularly in terms of their poetics and the ways they position themselves in relation to literary predecessors. This final consideration is especially illuminated by consideration of both in relation to the work of the French Symbolist poet Arthur Rimbaud. While the opening two sections of this chapter pursue historical factors necessary to a fuller picture of the relations between the Grateful Dead and Dylan, and thus turn away somewhat from the literary fragment, Rimbaud's sensibilities as a poet will pull the inquiry strongly back in that direction, particularly insofar as his work illustrates the degree to which the interplay between dissolution and production informs both the terms of creative potential and the birth of the subject. This three-pronged inquiry demonstrates not just points of bio-historical congruity between Dylan and the Grateful Dead, but also a shared appreciation for songwriting so exceptionally strong that it demanded recognition from the literary establishment.

"Fuck, They're Damned Good": Shared Histories

While one might speculate about their paths crossing earlier than the documentation supports, Dylan's first recorded exposure to the Grateful Dead dates to 1971. Tom Constanten, who sat in for a show with his old bandmates on April 28, 1971, confirms Dylan's presence at the prior night's concert.² A more elaborate description of the evening comes via a *Rolling Stone* article that discusses that April 27 Grateful Dead concert: "'I want you to meet another famous California group,' said Jerry Garcia, late in a Grateful Dead set at the Fillmore East.... And who appeared but the Beach Boys. They did four numbers ... then jammed with the Dead for a good 45 minutes.... Bob Dylan watched from the sound booth commenting, 'Fuck, they're damned good.' Then the light show flashed the word 'Dylan' for an instant, and Bob, his privacy jeopardized again, split out the door."³ According to John Glatt, Dylan's presence at New York City's Fillmore East on that night in April was engineered in part by Bill Graham, who had hoped to get the two acts to perform together.⁴ While the *Rolling Stone* paragraph is somewhat ambiguous in terms of whether Dylan's praise is directed at the Beach Boys or the Grateful Dead, subsequent events suggest the latter was the object of his attention. That attention was not merely appreciative fandom, either, as eight months later, following the Band's New Year's Eve show, he told Levon Helm, "I'm thinking of touring with the Dead."⁵ Another nine months on found him still on the scene: Patrick Carr describes spotting Dylan at the rainy September 19, 1972, Grateful Dead show at Roosevelt Stadium in Jersey City, New Jersey, where he was "picking his way around under" the stage "in the dark."⁶

That Dylan's interest in the Grateful Dead was mirrored by the band is suggested not only by his presence backstage at shows, but also by their performances of his songs, which included "She Belongs to Me" and "It's All Over Now, Baby Blue" as early as 1966 and "It Takes a Lot to Laugh, It Takes a Train to Cry" starting in 1973. Despite their mutual enthusiasm and near misses in the early 1970s, the Grateful Dead and Dylan would not share a billing until March 23, 1975. On that date, a charity concert organized by Bill Graham saw a late-morning performance by a band advertised as Jerry Garcia and Friends. This group included all of the Grateful Dead's mid-1970s members, with the exception of Donna Jean Godchaux, as well as Ned Lagin and Merl Saunders. Closing out the event was Neil Young, whose performance featured Dylan as a special guest. So, Dylan and the Grateful Dead performed on the same stage on the same day, although they did not share time in front of the crowd.

While the 1975 date is premature in terms of joint performances, the 1980s would see significant changes. The first hints of more productive cross-fertilization occurred in 1980. At that point, Dylan's setlists were dominated by the Christian music that filled most of a trilogy of albums he released in the late 1970s and early 1980s. Fan reception of this material was not always enthusiastic, and this meant that attendance figures for Dylan's 1980 tour were relatively low. On the night of November 16, at the Fox Warfield Theatre in San Francisco, Bill Graham encouraged Garcia to join Dylan on stage, partly to generate excitement about Dylan's concerts.[7] Garcia accommodated the request, performing with Dylan for eleven songs.[8] Curiously, while this is the first documented instance of Dylan playing with a member of the Grateful Dead, bootleg recordings of Dylan's introduction of Garcia suggest an as-yet unearthed performance history, as he says, in part, "Here's a young man, I know you know who he is. I've played with him a few times before. I'm a great admirer and fan of his and support his group all the way: Jerry Garcia. He gonna play with us." When and where Dylan "played with" Garcia "a few times before" remains unclear. Perhaps these were casual, private sessions. The phrasing could be a somewhat misleading reference to the 1975 date, or maybe Dylan was uncharacteristically at a loss for words, or, more characteristically, he was simply improvising a bit with the facts. In any case, Garcia would go on to join Dylan at least twice more on his own, on May 5, 1992, and (as your author can confirm, as he was in attendance) June 25, 1995.

Though Garcia's occasional performances with Dylan were noteworthy, they were not collaborations with the full Grateful Dead. More substantial interactions would develop in the mid-1980s, first in 1986, when the Grateful Dead coheadlined a handful of dates with Dylan, whose concerts at the time entailed his performance of some numbers solo and others backed by Tom Petty and the Heartbreakers. Dylan and Petty were on an extended tour, one that saw overseas and domestic dates stretching from February to August. The Grateful Dead, after a three-night run at the Greek Theatre at UC Berkeley as spring closed and summer opened, were also on the road, albeit on a more modest, eight-show jaunt. On five nights (June 26 and July 2, 4, 6, and 7), the Dylan and the Grateful Dead tours coincided, with the performers trading opening and closing sets. Some of the dates on this joint tour stand out for being Dylan's first public appearances with the full Grateful Dead ensemble: Dylan joined the band for three songs on July 2 and two on July 7. The pieces performed were mostly Dylan's ("Don't Think Twice, It's All Right," "It's All Over Now, Baby Blue" [both nights], and "Desolation Row"), but also included a nod to their shared folk-blues ancestry in the form of Robert Johnson's "Little Red Rooster." The song titles and performance histories of these moments of collaborative interaction between the Grateful Dead and Dylan may at first glance seem like fairly mundane points, but they are key nodes on the map of the initially somewhat cautious, but mutually engaged, exploration of common ground between the two. Once that ground was settled, the stage was set for rich developments in the coming years, developments marked not only by collaboration, but also by reinvigorated songwriting and performance.

The 1986 summer tour led to more robust collaborations in 1987. Between July 4 and 26 of that year, the Grateful Dead performed nine shows, six of which were coheadlined by Dylan. The arrangement differed from the previous year, and it also varied a bit for the first few concerts. On July 4, the show involved a set by the Grateful Dead followed by a set by Dylan with the Grateful Dead as his backing band, culminating in a jointly performed encore. July 10 worked in a similar fashion, although Dylan did not appear for the encore. The remaining four shows were quite long, as each included two sets by the Grateful Dead, followed by a third set during which it served as Dylan's backing band, culminating in a jointly performed encore. Across the six shows, the Grateful Dead performed twenty-seven songs new to its repertoire, in addition to returning to "It's All Over Now, Baby Blue" and at least two other Dylan songs that it had already covered on its own prior to these shared dates, "When I Paint My Masterpiece" and "All Along the Watchtower."

Later intersections between Dylan and the Grateful Dead were less concentrated than the 1987 dates. On February 12, 1989, Dylan joined the Grateful Dead on the stage for eight songs, all of which were already part of the Grateful Dead's repertoire: two were Dylan's, three—"Alabama Getaway," "Dire Wolf," and "Cassidy"—were Grateful Dead originals, and three were covers of songs by others. According to Howard Sounes, Dylan phoned the Grateful Dead's office the next day and asked if he could join the band. The band took a vote, presumably under its usual rule requiring unanimity, and Lesh shot down the idea.[9] The fact that Dylan's call to join the Grateful Dead came in early 1989 is worth noting, given that it places the request just a few months after the stability of the Traveling Wilburys—an all-star group that had allowed Dylan to perform as something other than a headlining solo artist and bandleader—was shaken by the death of member Roy Orbison. Although the plan of Dylan and the Grateful Dead joining forces on a more permanent basis did not work out, they also did not rule out future opportunities. At the October 17, 1994, Grateful Dead show, the band aired "All Along the Watchtower," and Dylan joined for an encore of "Rainy Day Women #12 & 35." Furthermore, Dylan would open for the Grateful Dead five times in June 1995. These many collaborations, coheadlined shows, guest appearances, and general shared direction make evident the extent to which Dylan and the Grateful Dead worked either together or in parallel for a substantial part of the band's career.

A Lot of Spaces and Advances: Songwriting, Performance, and Touring

Taken together, the performance histories of Dylan and the Grateful Dead described above suggest a strong and mutually appreciative relationship. From Dylan's positive comment in 1971 and the band's early performances of his songs through to the joint concerts of 1987 and the final shared billings of 1995, it is evident that Dylan and the Grateful Dead were amenable to collaboration and recognized that it promised something otherwise unavailable. The bare facts of the shared history suggest a strong connection, but they may also make one wonder what specifically drew the two performing entities together. The next several pages explore Dylan's connection to the Grateful Dead, examining what initially drew him to the band and why he continued to return to its stage periodically throughout the last decade of its career. As the following paragraphs argue, the shared dates with Dylan certainly had an impact on the Grateful Dead, but the more significant influence was felt in the opposite direction, as Dylan found in the band's approach perspectives on songwriting, performance, and touring that helped him reconnect with his career and creative vision at a time of disillusionment. While this book has largely avoided discussions of performance or the mechanics of touring as a component of the Grateful Dead's literary identity, the case of at least this one Nobel Prize in Literature recipient suggests that these aspects of its career are an integral context shaping its attitudes toward songwriting.

Dylan did not initially make a strongly positive impression on members of the Grateful Dead. The first time any of them saw him play predated the formation of the band by two years, and it resulted from Garcia and Hunter's participation in the 1963 Monterey Folk Music Festival. The two were present at that event not only as fans of other musicians, but also in their capacity as the banjo picker and bass player in the Wildwood Boys, who took the stage on May 19. That was a somewhat successful day from their perspective. The ensemble won the Best Group award in the amateur division, and Dennis McNally further claims that Garcia won the prize for Best Banjo Player, although Jackson indicates otherwise.[10] Dylan offered his own solo set the preceding day, and, in addition, he and Joan Baez came out together for a performance of one of his songs. Garcia's take on those performances was less than positive. McNally reports that "Dylan had scandalized the purist Garcia by writing new songs outside the folk canon," and while Hunter suggests poor sound equipment played a role in their reaction, the pair left while Dylan was still on stage.[11] Of course, Garcia would not be the only folk purist to bristle at Dylan's career decisions. Most readers will know that Dylan's early years saw him uncomfortably pigeonholed by fans, the industry, and the press as a topical folk singer, and that his decision to perform with electric instruments and in a rock and roll style provoked a strongly negative reaction from many. This transition to electric instrumentation and a new mode of songwriting inspired booing from the audience and fretting on the part of organizers during his July 25, 1965, appearance at the Newport Folk Festival, and such reactions continued for many months, including, perhaps most famously, the May 17, 1966, concert in Manchester during which an irritated fan catcalled Dylan "Judas."

The electric-guitar-slinging Garcia of 1965 and 1966, however, was no longer 1963's folkie purist pursuing perfection on the banjo. Instead of bemoaning further developments in Dylan's work, Garcia found himself appreciative of Dylan's turn to rock. "I never used to like Bob Dylan until he came out with electric music. . . . I sure liked that a lot more," he stated, adding, "Dylan was getting a little less heavy, he was having a little more fun. That was a nice change."[12] Garcia made a similar point about Dylan numerous times, including the following remarks during a 1972 interview: "Back in the folk music days I couldn't really dig this stuff but on *Bringing It All Back Home* he was really saying something that I could dig."[13] In the same piece, he mentions one track in particular: "'It's All Over Now, Baby Blue,' we did that from the very beginning because it was such a pretty song."[14] Hunter also focused on Dylan's mid-1960s recordings as special in this way, stating, "I first started waking up to the possibilities of rock lyrics being serious with *Blonde on Blonde*." He continued, "It opened up everything; it said it was okay to be as serious as you wanted in rock."[15] The fact that the band played pieces like "She Belongs to Me" when they did suggests that the Grateful Dead's interest in Dylan emerged not during the members' early folk revival phase—when Garcia, Hunter, Bob Weir, and McKernan were steeped in traditional music and developing as writers and performers—but when the band transitioned to electric guitar and rock.

Setlists make clear that Garcia and Hunter were hardly alone among members of the Grateful Dead in their continued appreciation for Dylan's songwriting. As previously mentioned, the band played a handful of Dylan tunes prior to the collaborative shows of 1987, but sharing the stage prompted an explosion of Dylan covers in the Grateful Dead's later years. Dylan pieces were so entrenched in the period's repertoire that fans talk about setlists with reference to the "Dylan slot," which, Shenk and Silberman explain, is "the point about five or six songs into the first set where . . . Weir has frequently 'pulled out' a cover of a multiverse Bob Dylan ballad."[16] The trend was born immediately following the shared 1987 dates, with the first set appearance on August 11 of "When I Paint My Masterpiece" and the same night's second set airing of "All Along the Watchtower." The phenomenon continued until the end, with "When I Paint My Masterpiece" closing the first set on the band's July 9, 1995, swan song. Weir's first-set Dylan slot, the fact that Garcia often opted for a Dylan song for an encore, and the likelihood that the Grateful Dead would play a traditional or cover song that Dylan had also performed or recorded—like "Peggy-O"—helped preserve, for fans' ears, the sympathetic connections between Dylan and the Grateful Dead in the years between their shared performances. In this way, Dylan exerted an impact on the final decade of Grateful Dead concerts that was possibly more profound than that of any other single person outside the band and its immediate concert and stage crew, as the band's setlists reflected a deep appreciation for his compositions.

While Dylan clearly affected the Grateful Dead's repertoire, the Grateful Dead also left its mark on Dylan, and in a manner that reshaped his attitudes toward touring and songwriting, activities that for him were rooted in his feelings about his own music. For both Dylan and the Grateful Dead, tours were more than excursions to play for audiences, in large part because both Dylan and Garcia were expected by many fans to be much more than musicians. As Jackson writes with reference to the coheadlined 1986 tour:

> Garcia had attended a Dylan-Petty show . . . that spring and had spent considerable time chatting with Dylan. . . . It was this night . . . and . . . the following summer tour that cemented their close personal relationship. They were mutual admirers who shared similar roots in American folk and blues. And they had both carried heavy loads since the '60s—Dylan as the de facto poet laureate of American music; Garcia as the embodiment of the libertine Haight-Ashbury ethos—and had attracted more than their share of fanatics and devoted followers who placed them on uncomfortable pedestals.[17]

The strong attitudes toward Dylan and his work meant that his career had been marked by serious controversy at several stages. As explained above, his composition of original songs was not exactly laudable in the eyes of early folkies like the young Garcia, and his turn to rock was, to many of the same crowd, nothing short of a betrayal of the cause. The pressure on him during the first half decade of his career was so great that a motorcycle accident in 1966 was used as an excuse to take a break from touring, and, with a handful of notable exceptions, that break led to a moratorium on public performances between May 1966 and January 1974. Dylan was at first cautious in his return to the stage after that extended hiatus. A much-celebrated comeback tour with the Band in 1974 was followed by the well-regarded Rolling Thunder Revue performances of 1975 and 1976, which saw Dylan and a host of fellow travelers performing in smaller venues. One appeal of the Rolling Thunder Revue tour for Dylan was doubtless its format, which featured a rotating cast of performers whose presence allowed Dylan to manage his own time in front of audiences. Sounes writes, "Although the show ran very long—up to four hours some nights—Bob was usually on stage less than an hour."[18] The massive world tour of 1978 reintroduced the pressures of extended touring in the traditional superstar format, a condition that made the poorly received gospel tour of 1979–80 even more difficult than it otherwise might have been. The difficulties with audience reception of his studio and live work in the late 1970s carried over into the 1980s. Such ups and downs were neatly summarized by the first part of the stage introduction Dylan started using in 2002, which this author has heard numerous times: "Ladies and gentlemen, please welcome the poet laureate of rock and roll. The voice of the promise of the sixties counterculture. The guy who forced folk into bed with rock. Who donned makeup in the seventies and disappeared into a haze of substance abuse. Who emerged to find Jesus. Who was written off as a has-been by the end of the eighties." The final sentence makes clear that both Dylan's career and his artistic sensibilities were at their nadir when he joined with the Grateful Dead in the late 1980s. In his memoir, he acknowledges as much, writing of his attitude in 1986, "I had no connection to any kind of inspiration. . . . My own songs had become strangers to me, I didn't have the skill to touch their raw nerves."[19] In short, the Dylan of the mid-1980s was out of touch with his music and himself, and in a manner that affected both his attitudes to performance and his sense of himself as a songwriter.

The situation had not improved by 1987, when Dylan arrived at the Grateful Dead's property on Front Street in San Rafael. Dylan's struggles were apparent to the band; as Garcia remarked, "He wasn't writing too much then. . . . I think he was looking for a new direction in which to take his songs."[20] At one point, the troubled Dylan left the building and wandered about in the rain, then entered a bar, where he listened to a jazz singer who awakened something in him.[21] The tale is extraordinary, but so were the results. When he "played these shows with The Dead," he, by his own account, "never had to think twice about it." He adds, "Maybe they dropped something in my drink, I can't say, but anything they wanted to do was fine with me."[22] Dylan particularly singled out Garcia as having helped him turn a corner. As had been the case earlier in Dylan's career, inspiration grew from a return to roots. Garcia explains, "We talked about people like Elizabeth Cotten, Mississippi Sheiks, Earl Scruggs, Bill Monroe, Gus Cannon, Hank Williams. We tried a few of those things out at rehearsal. I showed Bob some of those songs: 'Two Soldiers,' 'Jack-a-Roe,' 'John Hardy,' and some others."[23] Dylan doubtless profited from a return to folk material, but he also recovered something of the spirit behind his own songs with which he had lost touch. Paul Williams reports that Dylan told a journalist in 1997 that Garcia used to "say, 'Come on, man, you know, this is the way it goes, let's play it, it goes like this.' And I'd say, 'Man, he's right, you know? How's he getting there and I can't get there?' And I had to go through a lot of red tape in my mind to get back there."[24] The transformation in Dylan's perspective on his own songs, which he acknowledges was rooted in his time with the Grateful Dead, set the stage for the remarkable work he would begin producing over the following decade, work that he stumbled toward on *Down in the Groove* (which included two songs written by Hunter and backing vocals on one track by Garcia, Weir, and Brent Mydland), began to realize with *Oh Mercy*, presented somewhat less apparently on *Under a Red Sky*, reinforced by a deeper return to musical roots on *Good As I Been to You* and *World Gone Wrong*, and has made consistently present since the release of *Time Out of Mind*.

As Dylan's approaches to songwriting and performance evolved, so, too, did his touring schedule. Aside from a late 1987 run with Tom Petty and the Heartbreakers, Dylan's live performances since his time with the Grateful Dead in July 1987 unfolded almost entirely in the context of his Never Ending Tour, which ran from 1988 to the outbreak of the COVID-19 pandemic. The sheer number of performances over the years clearly suggests Dylan has been less troubled by the pressures of the road than he had been before, and he has attributed some of this transformation to his time with the Grateful Dead: "It didn't really occur to me until we did those shows with the Grateful Dead. . . . If you just go out every three years or so, like I was doing for a while, that's when you lose touch. If you are going to be a performer, you've got to give it your all."[25] The Grateful Dead, then, not only encouraged Dylan's rediscovery of his own songs, but in their steady touring modeled for him a means to keep that rediscovery alive.

While Dylan came to the Grateful Dead at a low point, the band's situation during the shared dates was rather different. Not only Garcia's health, which had been poor, but also their record-selling profile improved dramatically as the tour unfolded. Its album *In the Dark* was released on July 6, 1987, just a couple of days after the shared dates with Dylan got underway. As one concert followed another, the album and its lead single, "Touch of Grey," steadily, and somewhat surprisingly, climbed the *Billboard* charts, eventually earning the band its first Top 40 hit, more than two decades into its career. The moment was in many ways a curse in disguise. The popularity helped bank accounts and attracted support for side projects and pet causes, but the increased finances also magnified bad habits. Mydland died of an overdose in 1990. Garcia struggled with persistent problems with addictions that exacerbated the health problems that would send him into a coma and then lead to his death in 1995. Tensions in general grew among the band members, staff, and crew, extending beyond the immediate group. Garcia had been worried about this sort of situation and feeling the pressures of public attention for decades, stating as early as the late 1960s, "In the old days . . . nobody was famous; it was just us . . . heads . . . , and it was a celebration and everybody was getting together and getting stoned together . . . and having a great time of it. The fame thing is really insidious, it[']s like a nasty temptation. . . . And the things that happen as a result of that are things that don't in any way make you play better or make you more conscious."[26] By 1991, Garcia was talking about taking another hiatus, but the Grateful Dead was a train without a brake at that point.[27] Much of that darkness was, however, all in the future during the months when "Touch of Grey" was becoming a hit, and the Dylan concerts therefore bring into sharp relief the gulf between Dylan's struggles and the upward swing of the Grateful Dead's fortunes.

The problems that arose with the increased attention that success garnered for the band, and for Garcia in particular, are well-documented and, of course, reached their climax with his death, which brought an end to the Grateful Dead as a performing unit. That event evoked a statement from Dylan that remains perhaps the best encapsulation of all that listeners could find in Garcia's music:

> There's no way to measure his greatness or magnitude as a person or as a player. I don't think any eulogizing will do him justice. He was that great, much more than a superb musician, with an uncanny ear and

dexterity. He's the very spirit personified of whatever is Muddy River country at its core and screams up into the spheres. He really had no equal. To me he wasn't only a musician and friend, he was more like a big brother who taught and showed me more than he'll ever know. There's a lot of spaces and advances between The Carter Family, Buddy Holly and, say, Ornette Coleman, a lot of universes, but he filled them all without being a member of any school. His playing was moody, awesome, sophisticated, hypnotic and subtle. There's no way to convey the loss. It just digs down really deep.[28]

Perhaps just as illuminating, in terms of Dylan's appreciation for Garcia as a friend and as a man, are two remarks Dylan uttered as he left Garcia's funeral. One was addressed to John Scher: "That man back there is the only one who knew what it's like to be me."[29] Sandy Rothman mentions a second: "He was there for me when nobody was."[30]

While Garcia's death meant the end of the Grateful Dead as a band, it was by no means the end of the story of the cross-pollination of its music with Dylan's. Shared performances, recordings, and songwriting collaborations between Dylan and members of the Grateful Dead are all part of the post-Garcia world. Hunter distinguished himself as Dylan's preferred collaborator, adding to the two songs he contributed to *Down in the Groove* ("Silvio" and "Ugliest Girl in the World") eight on *Together Through Life* and one on *Tempest* ("Duquesne Whistle"). Hunter was appreciative of the attention, stating, "As far as I'm concerned, Bob Dylan has done . . . my songs, and . . . other things are far away, distant and not very interesting."[31] The evidence of these eleven tracks supports Dylan's explanation of the congruity between the two: "Hunter is an old buddy, we could probably write a hundred songs together if we thought it was important or the right reasons were there. . . . He's got a way with words and I do too. We both write a different type of song than what passes today for songwriting."[32]

Dylan and the Grateful Dead's mutual appreciation has also been enshrined on several albums and continues to shape Dylan's performances. *Postcards from the Hanging* collects strong Grateful Dead versions of many Dylan tunes, while *Garcia Plays Dylan* presents more such material by the Grateful Dead and similar tracks by several of Garcia's other bands. Dylan's March 1, 1999, performance of "Friend of the Devil," released on the tribute album *Stolen Roses*, returns the attention. In 2006, Dylan reflected on his time performing with the Grateful Dead in a manner that speaks to its ongoing significance to him as a model for performance and devotion to the craft:

"The Dead did a lot of my songs . . . better than me. Jerry Garcia could hear the song in all my bad recordings, the song that was buried there."[33] Dylan shared related observations at other times, explaining that the Grateful Dead "taught me to look inside these songs I was singing that, actually . . . I couldn't even sing. . . . I had a hard time grasping the meaning of them, although the Dead didn't. They found great meaning in them."[34] He adds, "They understood these songs better than I did."[35] Dylan carried some of the inspiration and vitality he found in the Grateful Dead's approach to performance into the workings of his own band. For example, in a profile of Larry Campbell, who served as guitarist in Bob Dylan's band for most of a decade, Patrick Doyle notes that Dylan "had [his] band listen to Dead bootlegs as an example of how to cover a song."[36] In yet another intriguing instance of the wheel turning around, Dylan's band has also covered several Grateful Dead songs, including not only "Friend of the Devil" but also six others frequently featured in concerts: "Alabama Getaway," "West L.A. Fadeaway," "Truckin'," "Stella Blue," "Black Muddy River," and "Brokedown Palace." The fact that Dylan hired former Jerry Garcia Band drummer David Kemper in 1996 and performed "Only a River," a song cowritten by Weir, reinforces the point that Dylan has continued to look to the world of the Grateful Dead.[37]

Furthermore, shared performances between Dylan and members of the Grateful Dead did not end in 1995 and have unfolded largely during two periods in the years since. Dylan first coheadlined seventeen shows with Phil Lesh and Friends in October and November 1999. On three of those dates, Lesh joined Dylan for a mix of Dylan originals, Grateful Dead songs, and covers. July and August 2003 saw Dylan opening for the Dead, a performing group that included Weir, Lesh, Hart, and Kreutzmann, at eight shows. At seven of those concerts, Dylan sat in with the band for a few songs.

Of the Grateful Dead songs to which Dylan has paid special attention, "Truckin'" stands out for being featured in Dylan's book *The Philosophy of Modern Song*. The essay on "Truckin'" opens with a statement few might dispute: "The Grateful Dead are not your usual rock and roll band."[38] The remainder of the piece is in many ways a clarification of the terms of that assertion. Some portion of it focuses on the crowd: "When you go to a Dead concert you are right there in Pirate Alley on the Barbary Coast"; the female fans are "free floating . . . like in a typical daydream," and the audience as a whole "is part of the band."[39] The Grateful Dead stand out as a dance band, a point reiterated several times, and they have in Kreutzmann and Lesh a rhythm section that is "hard to beat."[40] Weir's unorthodox rhythm playing, with its "strange, augmented chords and half chords at unpredictable intervals," is noted, and

Garcia gets special attention, being described as a combination of Charlie Christian and Doc Watson. Finally, though by no means neglected, is the "writer-poet" Hunter, in whom Dylan finds a synthesis of Stephen Foster, Rilke, and Kerouac.[41] These are all points Dylan makes before he even turns to the song that is the ostensible subject of the chapter, and it serves as a reminder of the degree to which the context for performance is repeatedly an aspect of Dylan's appreciation of the Grateful Dead. Yes, Garcia may have reminded Dylan that relations between a singer and his art are born from certain intuitions about what drives the song, but so, too, are all the other elements rolled into "Truckin'," including the personalities of musicians and hangers-on, the space of the performance, the audience, and the rhythm of the tour.

In discussing "Truckin'" as a song, Dylan makes several points. First, the song name-checks various cities, even as it advances the broader truth that they are "all on the same street." In this sense, one attraction of the song is that it describes a dynamic tension between specificity in space, which draws places into view via relief, and a flattening of perspective that erases distinctions among those places. There is a similar tension on the temporal axis. The song presents snapshots of people and places in discrete moments, as when one is "sitting and staring out of a hotel window" or when one hears that "sweet Jane" has "lost her sparkle," but those snapshots accumulate into a statement that is timeless: "This could easily be a Dead song from one hundred years earlier," Dylan writes.[42] That complex temporal framework is reflected in the pace of the playing, as the tempo is medium, but the song seems to accelerate. The impression of acceleration is not so much a matter of urgency as one of compositional accretion. Each verse is strong, yet the lyrics "pile up on top of each other" in an undifferentiated heap. Nevertheless, this happens without sacrificing any meaning, which "is understandable and clear."[43] It is a song about hard traveling, but listening to it is not hard work.

Dylan's closing point is made briefly but powerfully, and it is most suggestive in relation to the question of why he is drawn to this song even more than others. He claims that the "guy singing the song"—whom Dylan reasonably reads not as Garcia but as a persona, even though it is, in many ways, the most autobiographical of Grateful Dead songs—"acts and talks like who he is, and not the way others would want him to talk and act."[44] Such qualities are the hallmarks of authenticity and independence, but the point demands more than that facile gloss, given that it is Dylan's closing assertion. Any statement about the noble difficulty of speaking and behaving as one truly is, rather than just being "the way others would want," cannot be a mere truism to Dylan. He asserts that "what a long strange trip it's been" is a "thought that anybody can relate to," but few have brought it to life and confronted its challenges as persistently as have Dylan and the Grateful Dead.[45] The often ill-formulated expectations that audiences brought to Dylan and Garcia, and media attempts to pigeonhole Dylan as the voice of a generation or the Grateful Dead as emblems of the 1960s, demand consistent confrontation, and stepping on stage, into the strong and at least occasionally clear-sighted persona of "Truckin'," is a means of taking that stand. Dylan's remarks on the song are in these senses a summary of much that he seems to have found in the Grateful Dead. "Truckin'" is a study of the performer on tour, a song that speaks its mind while accepting contradiction, a recognition that challenging work need not be grueling, and a timeless expression of American space and sound.

The Ghost Too Was More Than One Person: Dylan, the Grateful Dead, and Literature

The two preceding sections of this chapter describe points of congruity between the Grateful Dead and Dylan in terms, first, of the bare facts of when and where they converged as performers and, second, of what their comments and actions in that context suggest about how they perceived the personal, artistic, and professional values of those intersections. When and where they played together, what inspiration and perspectives they found in one another's works, and what they most admired about one another are all framing conditions for the music they made and the songs they shared. This final section of the chapter turns more directly to the nature of those songs, particularly as they can be understood as a measure or component of what I have been calling the literary imagination of the Grateful Dead. Among its other intentions, the following argument demonstrates the degree to which the Romantic fragment offers an illuminating view of lyrics in songs by both Dylan and the Grateful Dead. This effort is abetted not only by the situation of the Grateful Dead in relation to Dylan, but also by the broader contextualization of both in relation to their literary predecessors. Dylan and the Grateful Dead shared several such touchstones, with works by authors discussed in earlier chapters, such as Burns and the Beats, among their many points of common ground.

One can discern the helpfulness and even necessity of such contextualization by considering the diverse natures of the thirty-seven songs by Dylan that the Grateful Dead performed. Thirty Dylan compositions were aired during the shared concerts of 1987; eight of those thirty pieces were also performed at least once by the Grateful Dead without Dylan, while seven other songs were part of the Grateful Dead's repertoire but never played with Dylan at any point. In the following paragraphs, I consider three of the Dylan songs most performed by the Grateful Dead. "Queen Jane Approximately," which I do not discuss here, was also played very frequently (129 instances), but unlike the songs to which I devote more attention, was not in the Grateful Dead repertoire prior to the shared dates of 1987, suggesting it is possibly less powerful as an illustration of the band's longer-term interest in Dylan's work. The three remaining pieces are, considered together, notable for being quite different from one another in content, tone, and structure. "It's All Over Now, Baby Blue" (145 performances) is an address to someone whose world is crumbling, expressed in a rather callous or even caustic tone across four six-line verses, each of which closes with the titular sentence. "When I Paint My Masterpiece" (144 performances) offers a collage of images concerned with a frenetic rejection of stagnation and perhaps unreasonably positive ambition, balanced against the solidity of personal ("back of my memory") and collective ("ancient footprints are everywhere") pasts, expressed via two eight-line verses followed by a rhyming couplet and a third eight-line verse. "All Along the Watchtower" (123 performances) is a dialogue about destiny and authenticity, framed by imagery that rings apocalyptic tones and appears on the page as two four-line stanzas, followed by two couplets. Intriguingly, both Dylan songs most played by the Grateful Dead were not played when they performed with Dylan.

Taken together on the terms foregrounded so far, these three Dylan songs so often covered by the Grateful Dead would seem to share relatively little beyond their period of composition, a fact made evident even when one considers only how diverse the songs are in terms of such rudimentary structural features as verse length and chorus repetition. To that consideration, one may add changes in perspective, which shifts from first to third person across the three songs. Furthermore, the subject matter and tone of each piece are rather different—listeners move from the personal tension of "It's All Over Now, Baby Blue," to the almost cartoonish and geographically rich misadventures of "When I Paint My Masterpiece," to the challenges of moral and spiritual rectitude described in "All Along the Watchtower." The point here is not that these three songs in particular share qualities that we can declare Dylan's mark on the Grateful Dead. Rather, their differences speak to the diversity of material that the discussion entails, as well as the need for perspectives that will help consideration of points more complex than the superficial incongruities in that material noted above. One interpretive lens that is particularly helpful in this regard is shaped by the life and works of Arthur Rimbaud, which offer themselves as a means to recognize commonalities between the Grateful Dead and Dylan even where similarities might otherwise seem lacking. To put that otherwise, there is a winding pathway that begins near Rimbaud's poem "After the Flood," passes through the Grateful Dead's *Wake of the Flood*, and points in the direction of Dylan and the Band's *Before the Flood*. The scenery and side routes one encounters on that journey are many and wonderful.

Dylan's own debt to Rimbaud has long been recognized, with Dylan himself acknowledging it. At a 1965 news conference, Dylan was asked what poets he appreciates. First named in his response is Rimbaud.[46] More importantly, the singer's familiarity with the French poet's work is on tacit display in many of his song lyrics, and explicit acknowledgement is offered in "You're Gonna Make Me Lonesome When You Go." There, Dylan sings:

> Situations have ended sad
> Relationships have all been bad
> Mine've been like Verlaine's and Rimbaud

One year later, on his 1976 album *Desire*, Dylan's liner notes offered additional evidence of his interest in the French poet, opening with, "Where do I begin?" before answering himself, "on the heels of Rimbaud moving like a dancing bullet."[47] Robert Shelton describes approaching Dylan about reading Rimbaud as early as 1961, although he reports that Dylan's response to that initial recommendation was noncommittal. Shelton continues, "I raised Rimbaud with him a couple of times after that. Much later, I was up at his place.... On his shelf I discovered a book of translations of French symbolist poets that had obviously been thumbed through over a period of years! I think he probably knew Rimbaud backward and forward before I even mentioned him."[48] One notes that Dylan's writing, including both song lyrics and liner notes, sometimes focuses on the biography of Rimbaud, who had a stormy romantic relationship with Paul Verlaine and spent much of his life on the move, not only within France, but also in Java, Yemen, Ethiopia, and Cyprus. This point serves as a reminder that it is not only Rimbaud's poetry, but Rimbaud as a figure of the artist, that warrants attention in discussing the works of Dylan and those of the Grateful Dead.

For its part, the Grateful Dead, and Hunter in particular, joined Dylan in explicitly acknowledging Rimbaud. In his foreword to fellow Grateful Dead lyricist Robert M. Petersen's *Alleys of the Heart*, Hunter quotes a passage from a letter by Rimbaud that is worth reproducing in full:

> The task of a man who wants to be a visionary poet is to study his own awareness of himself. He must seek out his soul, inspect it, test it . . . learn all forms of love and suffering; search until he exhausts within himself all poisons and preserves their quintessences. He must endure unspeakable torment, where he will need the greatest faith and superhuman strength, where he becomes among all men the great invalid, the great criminal, the great outcast—and the Supreme Scientist! For he attains the unknown! And if he finally loses the understanding of his visions, he will at least have seen them![49]

Hunter's appreciation for this passage as a statement and celebration of Petersen's spirit speaks not only to the mind behind such Grateful Dead songs as "New Potato Caboose" and "Unbroken Chain," but also to Hunter's own sensibilities. Those listening to the Grateful Dead, then, must recognize the presence—either direct or in spirit—of Rimbaud in works by two of the band's most accomplished lyricists. At the same time, one must recall that while Hunter, as well as Petersen and perhaps John Perry Barlow, were spending time with Rimbaud's work, his techniques, preoccupations, and attitudes were simultaneously reaching them as filtered through the works of Dylan.

In considering the degree to which both the Grateful Dead and Dylan honored the example of Rimbaud, the Dylan critic is on familiar ground, for a not insignificant amount of scholarly prose has been directed toward examining the place of Rimbaud in his lyrics. Consequently, some focus can be lent to the consideration of Dylan's importance to the Grateful Dead by looking through a Rimbaud-inflected lens at the songs by Dylan to which the Grateful Dead were most drawn, those of the mid- and late 1960s. Three paths of inquiry stand out as particularly promising, each illustrating central qualities of the Romantic fragment. First, Rimbaud offers a view of the poet as a visionary. In Rimbaud's case, this sort of poetic identity means adoption of a mode of seeing and being that prioritizes the intense, revelatory moment. This aspect of the poet is eminently amenable to the Romantic notion that the fragment unsettles traditional assumptions and perceptions in a manner that opens the way to the emergence of beauty and truth. Secondly, Rimbaud presents a disclosure of inauthenticity in the self and other that makes of them legitimate targets for critique in any number of registers, from the abuse of erotic power in private life to the frustrations of broad political or social complexities in the public sphere. The failures of authenticity Rimbaud presents serve not only as descriptions of faults in psychological, spiritual, or social identity, but also as illustrations of the failures that can frustrate processes of self-definition on what the Romantic fragment describes as the border between creation and death. Finally, the preceding characteristics stage the possibility for strong shifts in character and setting that result in a kaleidoscopic montage of often incongruously juxtaposed images. The dynamism and complexity of these shifts serve to illustrate the power of the open freedom that the German Romantics declare necessary for the play between creation and destruction, that generative play to which a true literary fragment will point.

The passage by Rimbaud that Hunter chose to discuss in relation to Petersen is also intriguing in terms of what Hunter's translation leaves out: the wildest sense of Rimbaud's writing, which is, in many ways, among the most sympathetic points of contact between Rimbaud, Dylan, and the Grateful Dead. The passage comes originally from a letter of May 15, 1871, and Rimbaud's opening lines may otherwise be translated with an emphasis on disorientation, as they read, "Le Poète se fait *voyant* par un long, immense et raisonné *dérèglement* de *tous les sens*. Toutes les forms d'amour, de souffrance, de folie; il cherche lui-même."[50] This might strictly be translated as follows: "The poet makes himself a visionary by a long, immense, and deliberate disordering of the senses. All forms of love, of suffering, of folly; he searches for himself."[51] One may stumble a bit over the notion that being a visionary is a matter of any sort of "deliberate" activity, but the sense persists: This is a project of redefining the artist as something other than what he was, of systematically and intentionally pursuing radical and strong experience—just as *règle* is "rule" in the sense of both management and measurement, in tune with accepted practice or in line with familiar hierarchies of power, *dérèglement* is not only mental or spiritual disorientation, but also the transgression of boundaries in general—as a means to see more, and to see it more capably and incisively. Hunter's translation certainly moves to this point, but it also implicitly retains the initial assertion of the need for transgression as a component of freedom, as if he recognizes that this much can go without saying. And perhaps, in the world of the Grateful Dead, the rejection of rule, the death of the ego, and the valorization of serious fun are so reliably woven into the fabric of the music and its performance that they can be left unstated.

A common example of Dylan's lyrics that present a rejection of the norm, like that for which Rimbaud calls, is his "Mr. Tambourine Man." This piece may not be among the most-performed by the Grateful Dead—they aired it only once, during the 1987 tour with Dylan—but it comes from and is consistent with other Dylan songs from the mid-1960s to which the Grateful Dead were most drawn. The following verse illustrates the point:

> Take me on a trip upon your magic swirlin' ship
> My senses have been stripped, my hands can't feel to grip
> My toes too numb to step
> Wait only for my boot heels to be wanderin'
> I'm ready to go anywhere, I'm ready for to fade
> Into my own parade, cast your dancing spell my way
> I promise to go under it

As Anne-Marie Mai argues, Dylan's "swirlin' ship" would seem to be a descendant of Rimbaud's "The Drunken Boat," which recounts the adventures of a small craft that sails not under control of a helmsman or captain, but rather only by the accidents of wind and tide.[52] After its crew is killed, the boat drifts aimlessly across the seas, passing waterspouts, icebergs, marshes, and storms, as well as creatures familiar and fantastic on distant shores. While the boat takes on water and occasionally feels nostalgia for the days of a guiding hand on its rudder, it far more often revels in its freedom, under which conditions it "Light as a cork . . . danced upon the waves."[53] Like "Mr. Tambourine Man," "The Drunken Boat" offers a vision of freedom in adventure as one with freedom from control, even as the dancing of the song's speaker mirrors that of the poem's craft. The abandonment of everyday experience in favor of aimless wandering on the seas (as with the boat) or the "dancing" and "magic" spell of the tambourine in Dylan's song, advances similar varieties of the "disordering of the senses" that Rimbaud declares central to the visionary task of the poet. In terms of the perspective of the German Romantics, the conflation in both Rimbaud and Dylan of the poet's work and the disordering of experience can be seen as highlighting the freedom that is the necessary condition of creation.

In the songs of the Grateful Dead, the discovery of freedom via experience beyond the normal limits features prominently in many pieces, from the bus ride of "That's It for the Other One" and the quest for Terrapin in "Terrapin Station" to the flight of the song's speaker across the Rio Grande in "Mississippi Half-Step Uptown Toodleloo" and the wanderings of the "drifting and dreaming" mariner, who hears the tempting calls of "sea birds" and "a ghost wind," in "Lost Sailor." The freedom of Rimbaud's poems and Dylan's songs is not, however, a matter only of extreme or unusual adventure, but rather tied to art, and particularly to the rhythms of poetry and music. The boat of Rimbaud, for example, notes that the ocean on which it drifts is an instance of poetry itself: "I've been bathing," it declares, "in the Poem / of the star-infused and milky sea."[54] The boat's adventures on these poetic waters evoke a rocking motion akin to the loss of self-control in "Mr. Tambourine Man," in which the speaker becomes so overwhelmed that her hands and toes have become unruly. Too, like the boat, the dancing and music of the Tambourine Man call the speaker of the verses out of herself, a yielding to rhythms like that of the boat floating on the swells and troughs of the sea. In this manner, Rimbaud and Dylan suggest, the artist's profit becomes that of the audience. The poem is the result of a program of disordering the senses undertaken by the artist, who then has the technical and visionary experience needed to invite the audience to share in it.

This corollary quality, found in both Rimbaud and Dylan—namely the centrality of art to the process of salutary disorientation—is likewise essential to the Grateful Dead's lyrics. Such a condition is foregrounded strongly in pieces like "The Music Never Stopped," which begins with vague hints of structured sound: "it might have been a fiddle" and "it could have been the wind" yield to "there seems to be a beat." After that point, we are in the realm where the self is given over to the tune:

> There's a band out on the highway,
> they're high-steppin' into town
> It's a rainbow full of sound
> It's fireworks, calliopes, and clowns
> Everybody's dancin'

The song unfolds with images of the self and world disordered, with the "Stars . . . spinnin' dizzy" and the dancers who "forgot about the time." The natural world, too, seems to have been overturned, with "balls of lightning" that "roll along" and a "Crazy rooster crowin' midnight." It is nevertheless fertile, with corn that's "a bumper crop" and "fields . . . full of dancin', / full of singin' and romancin'" that validate the generative power of the artists. While examples of this sort abound, the Grateful Dead's celebration of Rimbaud's disordering of the senses, as conjoined with the power of his poem of the sea and the music of Dylan's Tambourine Man, is perhaps most pithily summarized in "Franklin's Tower," which promises wisdom for those willing to fall under the spell of the music, even while offering relief without subjection to control: "If you get confused listen to the music play." In the case of pieces such as "The Music Never Stopped" and "Franklin's Tower," then, the Grateful Dead join Dylan in recognizing that experience beyond the pale is tied to the power of art, and that the artist—whether figured as a boat, the Tambourine Man, or a musician in "a band out on the highway"—both profits from extraordinary conditions and encourages others to share them.

Furthermore, to have faced the sort of disorienting trials illustrated by Rimbaud's drunken boat is not only to have become unmoored from familiar places and faces but also to have become productively disoriented as a self. It is on the basis of such experiences that Rimbaud can declare, "I is an other," a fragmented formulation of the self that cannot be understood in terms of prior descriptions of the philosophical subject.[55] Rimbaud's declaration that the self has become foreign coincides with the Romantic view that the poetic fragment is not only an entrance into the space of literary productivity, but also an opening to the interplay between the dissolution of the former self and the recognition of possible selves. This limen is the point at which exchanges transpire between creation and death, and it is the point from which the subject creates itself. To recognize that the self emerges from these exchanges between destruction and creative power allows one to register the internal and external constraints to self-realization. This perspective can be that which affords the grounds for critique, whether of others or oneself. In the case of Rimbaud, the outwardly directed critique was aimed at nineteenth-century provincial mores, an overbearing mother, and the Catholic Church. For Dylan and the Grateful Dead, the external critical light was typically directed at points of stagnation in American culture, while the internal one was a critical mirror turned on the self.

As Timothy Hampton notes, Dylan's listeners encounter a shift in focus from external to internal critiques when turning from one of the mid-1960s albums to the next. The songs of *Highway 61 Revisited* typically direct vitriol at people who are not hip enough to keep up with changing times, while those of *Blonde on Blonde* more often take reflexive aim at the song's speaker or even the performer.[56] The former mode is clearly presented in pieces like "Ballad of a Thin Man," which repeatedly takes a Mr. Jones to task for his cluelessness via the chorus:

> something is happening here
> But you don't know what it is
> Do you, Mister Jones?

The songs of this sort take particular delight in attacking the veil of inauthenticity, as is the case in the Dylan song the Grateful Dead played more often than any other, "It's All Over Now, Baby Blue." Here, the words are directed at a figure whose world is crumbling. The sky is "folding," and the carpet is "moving"; the armies, the sailors, and a lover have all abandoned their posts; and the garments that once projected a seemingly genuine self-definition have been taken over by "The vagabond who's rapping at your door." The only hints of sympathy are the cold comforts of "Take what you have gathered from coincidence" and "whatever you wish to keep, you better grab it fast." A song such as this might employ images that evoke the collapse of any number of things, from Macbeth's reign to the Jim Crow South, but the tone here is entirely personal. The inauthentic self that was projected has been swept aside, and what remains is defined more by absence and insufficiency than fullness of presence.

The Grateful Dead, despite its resistance to topical songs, join Dylan and Rimbaud in articulating externally directed critiques of inauthenticity. A very early example is "Cream Puff War," which takes a bickering couple to task for being a drag. Garcia sings, "Your constant battles are getting to be a bore / So go somewhere else and continue your cream puff war." As is the case in many of Dylan's most biting pieces, "Cream Puff War" directs its criticism more pointedly against the woman in the dyad, although the man is subjected to criticism in terms of his lack of awareness: "No, no, she can't take your mind and leave / I know it's just another trick she's got up her sleeve." While the tone of the piece is Dylanesque as a whole, several lines are particularly reminiscent of his mid-1960s output. "You're both out in the streets and you got no place to go" brings together a sense of the directionless, exilic world of "Positively 4th Street" and "It's All Over Now, Baby Blue," while "all the endless ruins of the past must stay behind" is not so far in spirit or image from Dylan's "Leave your stepping stones behind, something calls for you / Forget the dead you've left, they will not follow you."

As these lines from "Cream Puff War" demonstrate, the Grateful Dead could certainly offer critiques of others, but its repertoire as a whole tends much more toward the introspective self-examination that Dylan explored on *Blonde on Blonde*. Many Grateful Dead songs of this sort grapple with questions of change: How can the self be altered or improved? How can one meet the stasis that sometimes prevents change? What becomes of the self either in the wake of change or, perhaps, following frustrated opportunities? In other words, there is a subset of Grateful Dead songs that proffer to listeners a tension between development and stagnation, or movement and stasis, and these songs follow the example of such Rimbaldian pieces from *Blonde on Blonde* as "Visions of Johanna."

Many Grateful Dead songs that explore stagnation and transformation are drawn from, or penned under, the aegis of the road-song genre. The band brought several of these to the stage, including such traditional and cover tunes as "Beat It on Down the Line" and "Goin' Down the Road Feeling Bad" in addition to originals like "Truckin'." "Black-Throated Wind," and "So Many Roads." Dylan, too, has long been drawn to such material, although its usefulness to him has shifted over time. In his reading of Dylan's "Visions of Johanna," Hampton notes that the value of the road changes as Dylan matures as a songwriter. In the early protest songs, "stepping to the road" is one with the "rambling" of Dylan's idols such as Woody Guthrie. In such cases, hitting the road is a means to uncover and even experience for oneself those abuses of justice that inspire topical songwriting. The road is, in this sense, potentially a sourcebook for the sorts of moral outrage and rectitude that define the work of the artist-as-protest-singer. In Dylan's lyrics of the later 1960s, however, the mobility of the road has come to seem less than satisfactory, and songs such as "Visions of Johanna" instead lead listeners to an encounter with a voice that is divided against itself, a split subjectivity that feels impelled to change but is forced to confront the point that it cannot escape what change leaves behind. Hampton regards this as "nothing less than the splitting of Dylan's own subjectivity in song."[57] On the one hand is a figure identified as "The fiddler," who "now steps to the road," escaping the situation. On the other is the song's speaker at a point of crisis. This half of Dylan's persona recognizes that he will be haunted by Johanna no matter where he hangs his hat, suggesting that the fiddler's seeming escape is no escape at all. Immobilized emotionally, he is distressed ethically—his "conscience explodes." Because he cannot escape his preoccupations with what is absent, the past is never past, and "these visions of Johanna are now all that remain." The moral center of the song, then, is not about working up the bravery to take to the road, but instead a matter of confronting the fact that the road is no real means of escape. The song's speaker has failed to realize the terms of the self-creative powers that the fragment allows, as the contextual framework denies the freedom necessary for that recognition.

A similar tension between motion and paralysis, overlaid with emblems of authenticity and betrayal, is one of the dynamics driving songs like "Truckin'." As suggested earlier in this chapter, the lyrics of that song present a panoply of visions, yet recognize, at the same time, that all the cities it describes are fundamentally similar: "Chicago, New York, Detroit, it's all on the same street." Journeying on the road is, from this perspective, perhaps necessary as a tool for realization, and even a means to shift the ethical framework from social to personal and back again, but it is not always a solution to whatever challenges spurred one to take to the road in the first place. Just as the drunken boat of Rimbaud finds that the liberty in which it has reveled courts not only adventurous freedom, but also the dark pull of self-destructive disaster ("O let my keel burst! Let me go to the sea!"), and just as the speaker of Dylan's song is drawn to change even as he recognizes its false promises, and thus experiences a crisis of subjectivity ("my conscience explodes"), so the central voice of "Truckin'" is split between two incompatible alternatives, concluding, "I'm goin' home / . . . back where I belong," while simultaneously declaring the return home a means to "get back Truckin' on."[58] The crisis of self as intimately connected to vision emerges in lines that are perhaps the best known in the Grateful Dead songbook:

> Sometimes the light's all shining on me
> Other times I can barely see
> Lately it occurs to me
> What a long strange trip it's been

In the end, "Truckin'" is in many ways a study of the Grateful Dead as motion or momentum, but that study is one in which the vacillations of the speaker regarding personal/domestic versus collective/social crises complicate easy readings of its ethical and subjective center. More importantly, here, the elusive but very powerful revelatory experience—"the light's all shining on me"—keeps those disorientations of the self in the mode of Rimbaldian vision.

Grateful Dead songs such as "Wharf Rat" and "Black-Throated Wind" dramatize crises of subjectivity even more markedly than does "Truckin'." In the case of "Wharf Rat," the band offers a piece that reverses the terms of a song like "Visions of Johanna." In the latter, Dylan sketches the crisis of disoriented subjectivity. In "Wharf Rat," the fragmented self first appears as two distinct voices, only later drawn into an approximation of congruence. In other words, the lyrics are not about the dissolution of a unified self, but instead the revelation of an already disunified one. The song unfolds as a dialogue between an unnamed speaker and "August West." The latter is a "blind," indigent man panhandling

> down
> way down
> down, down by the docks of the city

Although the other character in the song has no money to share with West, he has time, offering himself as an audience for West's recounting of a personal narrative. West summarizes his past as one of betrayal and despair:

> Half of my life
> I spent doing time for
> some other fucker's crime

Meanwhile, the "Other half found me stumbling around / drunk on burgundy wine." Balanced against the pain of this existence is an undying love for "Pearly Baker," along with the conviction that "Pearly's been true." West remains convinced that he will, with the help of "the good Lord," "get up and fly away" one day. The persistence of such optimism, however uplifting, is based on a series of self-contradictions that make fulfillment of the promise of escape seem even less convincing than it already was. West's mention of the helpfulness to him of the "good Lord" is undercut by his earlier claim that "my maker" is "no friend of mine"; too, Pearly's belief that West would "come to no good" is not only the result of Pearly's believing others, but also part of the speaker's appraisal of himself, expressed as "I'd come to no good / I knew I would." These self-contradictions on West's part are intriguing, but his intoxication lacks the sort of systematic methodology that would make of it something properly Rimbaldian.

More promising than West as evidence of an ego struggling with questions of its own coherence is the original first-person speaker of "Wharf Rat." Following the relation of West's "story," the nameless character leaves him and wanders "downtown." When weighed against West's stagnation, that motion first speaks to a point of genuine distinction between the two characters, but the wandering is revealed as aimless, for the listener has "nowhere to go" and will "just . . . hang around." Furthermore, his own "girl," who is "named Bonny Lee," is missing from his life, although the song closes with his repeated assertions of her faithfulness. While we may not initially see the primary speaker of the song as being in such desperate conditions as West, his lack of "a dime," his missing beloved, his repetition of unsupported assertions of loyalty and affection, and the absence of any goal all speak to the same sort of situation that characterizes West. In this way, "Wharf Rat" issues a challenge to the boundaries of discrete identities, as West and his listeners within the song seem to merge with the audience hearing it. Both characters are haunted by loss in the present and unable to let go of what seem expired hopes. What reason could the original speaker in the song have for being

> down
> way down
> down, down by the docks

without money, with no need to be anywhere else, and with no one by his side, if not a desperation similar to West's? The unnamed speaker, in recounting his own tale in the song's latter part, replicates the narrative he first experienced as a listener. In a remarkably well-executed meta-lyrical move, this condition situates listeners themselves in that unnamed character's former position. This structural maneuver brings the Grateful Dead's audience member into a new and nearer relation with the characters of the piece, prompting a moral exercise in empathy by reconfiguring the interpretive subject's position in relation to the world described in the song. Hunter's decision to present West's story in the context of the partially sketched frame narrative thus makes it demand not just by virtue of its content, but also by its structure, a rethinking of the self. As the line between storyteller/performers and listener/audiences becomes more porous, characters and listeners both are led to reformulation of their own positions, which simultaneously are rooted in the realm of performance and reception.

While "Wharf Rat" is a study of foreclosed futures, it still extends to the listener a hope, however desperate, that both of the song's speakers express. "Black-Throated Wind" offers a view of the subject that is at points darker and more powerful, in that it collapses the divide that had been dramatized as a dialogue in "Wharf Rat" into the voice of a single disoriented person.[59] The opening verses of the song reveal that the speaker is hitchhiking, and in less than entirely desirable conditions, as he is (like August West) "blind," "bound" to an emotional "load," and "alone." His hitchhiking is unsuccessful, and his lack of motion leaves space for the song to unfold a vision that connects the lonely earth to the heavens at the close of each of the opening verses, with "The buses and semis / Plunging like stones from a slingshot on Mars" and "Alone with the rush of the drivers who won't pick me up / The highway, the moon, the clouds, and the stars." The decision to end both of the opening verses with this spatial—even astronomical—orientation allows Barlow to highlight the isolation of the song's primary character, even as it compresses the vastness of outer space into the soul of an individual. That compression creates a tension between expansiveness and constriction that will increasingly serve as an illustration of the self as the song progresses, making manifest a figure of the self that is foreign to itself.

As the song unfolds, it maintains a balance between personal and more generalized crises. The former is presented in terms of a failed romance, with lines such as "you weren't the woman I thought I once met" and "Capture a glance and make it a dance / Of looking at you looking at me." In another register, the expansiveness of the song's opening verses clears the stage for the development of mythic resonances. The third verse sees the emergence of the titular "black-throated wind," which offers a bleak but false vision of stasis in "a life where nothing is new," "a life that passes like dew," and "a lie that could almost be true." One with, or at least working in sequence with, the wind is a mythic Magna Mater known as "Mother American Night," in which the speaker is "drowning," even as he formulates a petition: "I give you my eyes, and all of their lies / Please help them to learn as well as to see." These mythic terms transform a song that might otherwise only ever be heard as a piece about a failed romance into an interrogation of the American self. Listeners learn that a bad experience drove the speaker to the road, but much like the characters of "Wharf Rat," or "Visions of Johanna," little changes for him as settings shift:

> What's to be found, racing around
> You carry your pain wherever you go
> Full of the blues and trying to lose
> You ain't gonna learn what you don't want to know

Faced with the bleakness of the lonely American night, and then granted a sudden burst of insight eminently in keeping with the Rimbaldian visionary experience, as evident in "Ah, Mother American Night, here comes the light," the central character reconceives his plans:

> Goin back home that's what I'm gonna do
> Turnin' around
> That's what I'm gonna do

The song thus advances a sense of open possibilities on the road, only to illustrate that the pain of the past is inescapable. No matter what sort of geographic relocation is effected, the city of blues is ever-present.

The conclusion of "Black-Throated Wind" leaves several compelling but incompatible interpretations hanging in balance, most of which depend on how one hears the closing "you've done better by me / Than I've done by you." These lines may be the acknowledgment of responsibility for damaging the song's romantic relationship, an explanation of the wrong the speaker has perpetrated, and the terms of the motivation he feels to abandon his flight and set things right. Alternately, they could be addressed to the Mother American Night. Heard in this sense, the generalization of private pain, universalized in the song as the black-throated wind, demands an assumption of responsibility for previous disregard for the pain that is part of the American past. To go home with this knowledge is neither to return home as the self who left, nor to find that the home one left behind remains unchanged. Instead, it is a recognition and an expansion of the responsibility of, and for, American life and American community. When framed in this fashion, conclusions multiply. The message blown on the wind and the light, evident when confronted by the incarnation of America as a dark maternal presence, are one. To be in American places is not to be unfairly burdened as an individual, but to confront the fact that one is "bound" inescapably "to the load" of the national past. The speaker's initial conception of self in relation to this American vision is false insofar as he believes he can disburden himself entirely of pain. While the notion of the self as disconnected from some collective is only ever false, it is also the case—as the rapid shifts in scale at the start of the song suggest—that the song's American self is at once singular and collective.

The preceding point is made not as a means to declare the speaker of "Black-Throated Wind" entirely misguided in setting out on the highway. That action exposed him to the black-throated wind and Mother American Night, and the internal disorientation that was required to reach that point, and to move beyond it, can be read as one with that which Rimbaud described as essential to the work of poets, and which the German Romantics found in the poetic fragment, identifying it as the first step in the reformulation of the self. Lacking that profound risk, the truths revealed as a result of the song's encounters in the mythic register could never have unfolded. Given its presence, however, the song is a strong example of the challenges to the consistency of the self that Rimbaud calls for in his statements about the nature and method of the poet, and likewise it follows not only the German Romantics, but also Pöhlmann in their efforts to come to terms with its power and to extend its reach beyond dissolution to both subjective creation and political futures.

Accompanying Rimbaud's understanding of the artist as one who uncovers truth via the disorientation of the self and pursuit of the visionary experience are his radical experiments with language. These experiments find him shifting his voice mid-poem with little indication of any change in the speaker, widely ignoring conventions of poetic form, and juxtaposing images of very different natures in the interest not of sensory coherence, but instead, like a montage, of a cumulative and combinatory effect. Wallace Fowlie explains that this aspect of Rimbaud's works "has to do with what the poet brings back with him from the unknown, or from the source to which he gained access by means of sensuous derangements. . . . If what he brings back has form, he gives it form. . . . But if originally, at the source, it had no form, he gives to it a formlessness. . . . The poet is the translator of his own truth, of what has been vouchsafed to him from universal truth and universal language."[60] In practice, this sort of poetic language approaches the limits of rational articulation, as in a stanza like this one from "The Drunken Boat":

> Who, spotted with electric crescents ran,
> Mad plank with escort of black hypocamps,
> While Augusts with their hammer blows tore down
> The sea-blue, spiral-flaming skies.[61]

Rimbaud's imagery is striking, and cumulatively it produces a surrealist text that very much anticipates both the strong imagery that Dylan would offer in the mid-1960s, as well as the formal strategies he used to provide some cohesion to those collections of images.

Dylan's approach was not entirely hermetic. Songs of that era offered listeners at least occasional insights into the sensibility that governed the nature and arrangement of their material. For example, "Desolation Row" declares of the song's characters that Dylan "had to rearrange their faces / And give them all another name." The assertion that the rearrangement has compositional justification brings cohesion to a montage-like cluster of images that otherwise lack unity. In this way, a portrait like

> Dr. Filth, he keeps his world
> Inside of a leather cup
> But all his sexless patients
> They're trying to blow it up

can stand alongside an episode like the following:

> they bring them to the factory
> Where the heart-attack machine
> Is strapped across their shoulders
> And then the kerosene

Is brought down from the castles
By insurance men

The powerfully surreal imagery is even more pronounced in certain other selections, such as "The ghost of 'lectricity howls in the bones of her face" in "Visions of Johanna," "A question in your nerves is lit" from "It's Alright, Ma (I'm Only Bleeding)," and the "When all of your advisers heave their plastic / At your feet..." of "Queen Jane Approximately." Again, the material is powerful as images, but the images' even stronger effects emerge from Dylan's use of Rimbaldian montage and accumulation rather than from the terms familiar in earlier folk and pop music, such as causal narrative development, simple lyricism, or topical exposition.

One may regard the approach as driven in part by construction of a dynamic relationship between coherence and incoherence, or form and disorder. When the Grateful Dead build on the innovations Dylan brought to his lyrics in its own pieces, the lines often take shape in terms entirely amenable to that Rimbaldian dynamism between order and fragmentation. "Dark Star" offers several striking examples, as in

> Reason tatters
> the forces tear loose
> from the axis

as well as

> Mirror shatters
> in formless reflections
> of matter
>
> Glass hand dissolving
> to ice-petal flowers
> revolving

Even songs that were rarely performed by the Grateful Dead participate in this effort. "What's Become of the Baby?" is a satisfying example. It begins:

> Waves of violet go crashing and laughing
> Rainbow-winged singing birds fly 'round the sun
> Sunbells rain down in a liquid profusion
> Mermaids on porpoises draw up the dawn

"What's Become of the Baby?" is particularly intriguing in terms of its relation to the legacy of Rimbaud because it follows his tendency to stage the visionary experience as a textual and literary one. This song turns, in its latter half, to the narrative and poetic, especially in the following lines:

> Sheherazade gathering stories to tell
> from primal gold fantasy petals that fall
> But where is the child
> who played with the sun chimes
> and chased the cloud sheep
> to the regions of rhyme?

The strong but elusive imagery of songs like "Dark Star" and "What's Become of the Baby?" can be read simply as examples of Rimbaldian poetic practice at the edge of comprehensibility, but at least some of the Grateful Dead's songs also partake of the tradition of Rimbaud-inflected montages that resemble Dylan's "Desolation Row." In the latter cases, relations among images and portraits are governed by the logic of accretion. "China Cat Sunflower" is perhaps the strongest instance, as it brings together a "Copperdome Bodhi" that drips "a silver kimono" with "A leaf of all colors" that "plays / a golden string fiddle" and "Comic book colors" that cry "Leonardo words / from out a silk trombone." Taken on their own, each image is challenging; collectively, they may boggle the mind. Such concatenations of words are not only textual challenges but also artifacts that call familiar modes of understanding into question. The unsettling of conventional cogency effected by the lyrics runs parallel to the dispersal of subjective coherence that the post-Kantian German Romantics saw as part of the playful exchange between destructive and generative powers from which the potential for both poetic creation and subjective reformulation—as well as the potential for both art and philosophy—can emerge. Furthermore, "China Cat Sunflower" not only gestures in the direction of such possibilities but also reintroduces interpretive possibilities via the suggestion of new orders of world and self, for the song employs its unconventional images within the bounds of just a few discursive fields: the metals of copper, silver, and gold; descriptions of music (fiddle and trombone); and the range of visual arts, from comic books to Leonardo. In other words, the piece may be surreal in simple terms, but it is by no means entirely nonsensical, encouraging as it does a surprising and delightful, but not impenetrable, recategorization of its imagery. Here, language has become its own other. Fans seem to have realized as much, as Hunter writes of "China Cat Sunflower," "Nobody ever asked me the meaning of this song. People seem to know exactly what I'm talking about. It's good that a few things in this world are clear to all of us."[62] The comment suggests to what extent the Grateful Dead, and its fans, display a comfort with the more challenging tendencies of Rimbaud's poetry, which Dylan found invaluable in his evolution as a songwriter beyond folk.

Dylan's engagement with Rimbaud's example in the mid-1960s shaped his lyrics in profound ways, and his innovations led Hunter and Garcia to praise him for showing that popular music's lyrics could be less about vapid bubblegum adolescence and more about a creative endeavor that displayed and could accommodate a much greater measure of literacy, authority, and respectability. The features in Dylan's work that they appreciated were, as described above, challenging to many members of his audience. The barbs directed at him from critics and the booing from former fans alike were, in many ways, confrontations with the question of whether popular music could—and how it should—take itself seriously. Decades later, when Dylan was awarded the Nobel Prize for Literature, a similar reaction was evident. He certainly had notable fans both within and beyond the worlds of critics and poets, but the reactions evoked and provoked by the awarding of the prize to Dylan reflect concerns that, in many ways, persist in framing the work of this book: Is one justified in treating popular music lyrics as literary texts? What is lost, and what is gained, when we do so? Is the application to popular music of critical practices and theoretical frameworks, which were conceived and refined in relation to traditional literary exercise, misguided—either because the material is not robust enough to justify the work or because it is simply of a different sort from that for which those interpretive tools were designed? While each reader will have to answer these questions for herself, the questions as applied to the Grateful Dead demand an answer that accounts for, among many other concerns, the band's ongoing conversation with Dylan's oeuvre.

It is tempting to ask what Rimbaud's later works may have contributed to the composition of lyrics in popular music, but the query would be pointless. In 1873, after roughly a half decade of innovative and profound production, Rimbaud stopped writing poetry. He was only nineteen. Robert Hunter's book *Sentinel* includes a poem, "Rimbaud at Twenty," that proffers a glimpse of the French poet at the time of his retirement from literature. It reads, in part:

> I seek climes with
> gods whose names
> I shall not study
> to learn[63]

Hunter's lines acknowledge that, while Rimbaud abandoned writing, he was only reaching the opening of his adventurous life. It is intriguing that Hunter notes this shift in Rimbaud's practice. While Hunter hardly stopped being a songwriter, his own career changed remarkably around the time this poem was published, as the next chapter will show.

5

Like an Angel

JAMES JOYCE, RAINER MARIA RILKE, AND ROBERT HUNTER'S MODERNIST INHERITANCE

The late 1980s were marked by a renaissance for the Grateful Dead. The success of the single "Touch of Grey" and the album *In the Dark* made the band members rock stars in a way they had never been before, and Garcia's recovery from a 1986 diabetic coma led, within a few years, to acclaimed tours in the summer of 1989 and the spring of 1990, during which both individual musicians and the band as a whole delivered performances that were remarkably strong.[1] However, when histories reach the second half of the band's third decade, the tale usually becomes one of sharp decline, starting with the death of keyboardist Brent Mydland in 1990 and proceeding to Garcia's renewed serious health problems, an increase in audience injuries, and even death threats against band members.² Unruly crowds could be added to this list of issues, and the band's response included something that would have seemed inconceivable a decade earlier: the issuance of strongly worded statements interrogating fans' actions and supporting the efforts of security staff and police officers at concerts.³

Despite the darkness on which many histories of the band focus when discussing the later years of the Grateful Dead, the band's ongoing popularity meant that the music and lyrics were reaching more ears than ever before. In addition, the repertoire continued to grow. Several cover songs entered the rotation, and everyone in the band except Kreutzmann continued to write new material, with additional compositional input from Hunter, as well as bassist Rob Wasserman, Caribbean musician Andrew Charles, sound technician Bob Bralove, and blues legend Willie Dixon. However, while a healthy number of original pieces were composed and performed after Mydland's death, fewer than half came from the familiar songwriting team of Hunter and Garcia; the band abandoned several of the newer pieces before they had a chance to mature on stage—a proven part of the Grateful Dead's successful composition process—and attempts to produce studio recordings failed.⁴ So, although the repertoire was healthy in some senses, and there was enough material for another studio record, nothing of the sort materialized. One result of the lack of a studio album and the relatively brief stage life of much of the new material was a sense that compositional productivity had declined sharply; perhaps curiously, this impression of stagnation found some compensation in the lyricists' increasing presence in the world of print media, a trend particularly evident in the publication of several volumes of poetry by Hunter.

Although not all the Grateful Dead's lyricists had remained entirely invisible in the world of print prior to the 1990s, none had actively sought the limelight. John Perry Barlow, Peter "Monk" Richard Zimels, Eric Andersen, and Gerrit Graham had little to no presence in published literature. Robert M. Petersen was for some time the most celebrated poet among them, although even he reached audiences primarily via the fugitive publications of the underground press. Aside from his privately printed 1980 volume, *Far Away Radios*, he had previously placed poems in *The Willie*, *The San Francisco Phoenix*, *Georgia Straight*, and *Desperado*. Too, it was Petersen's work that Alan Trist saw fit to collect posthumously, in 1988, as *Alleys of the Heart*. In the case of Hunter, short pieces appeared here and there beginning in 1969, but only infrequently; the venues that offered the closest thing to semiregular publication were the *Dead Heads* newsletters, to which Hunter contributed poems, sketches, and often absurd or satirical writings about the homegrown pseudophilosophy of Hypnocracy. Yet, these newsletters did not appear on any rigorous schedule, and Hunter's works in them are generally unsigned, so many early readers must have remained ignorant of the author's identity. The situation changed significantly in 1987, with Hunter's most substantial publication of the first two and a half decades of the Grateful Dead's career: his translation of Rainer Maria Rilke's *Duino Elegies*. This was an auspicious event, not only because it was the longest piece to have emerged from behind Hunter's veil of authorial privacy, but also because he had apparently chosen such an intimidating effort for his belated debut.

However, the Rilke translation broke the floodgates, and the 1990s saw a tremendous increase in Hunter's published work, including two editions of his collected song lyrics under the title *Box of Rain*; the small-press, book-length poem *Idiot's Delight*; a special issue of the magazine *Spike* given over entirely to a clutch of new poems titled *Infinity Minus Eleven*; republication of his translation of the *Duino Elegies*, now paired with his translation of Rilke's *The Sonnets to Orpheus*, in 1993; the graphic novel *Dog Moon*, with artist Timothy Truman; several fugitive pieces that remain uncollected; and three major-press volumes of poetry: *Night Cadre*, *Sentinel*, and *Glass Lunch*. Hunter's online archive offers a remarkable number of additional writings dated to the 1990s that are still available only electronically. These productions include short poems, journal entries, and correspondence, as well as such substantial efforts as *A Strange Music*, a book-length poem written in response to media coverage of the Gulf War; *Visions of the Dead*, an unfinished film script; the short fictions gathered under the title *Red Sky Fishing*; and a novel, *The Giant's Harp*.

The nature of Hunter's catalog of audio recordings changed somewhat during this time as well, and in a fashion that indicated some partial turn of attention away from songwriting and toward more traditional poetic composition and recitation. While singer-songwriter albums in the folk-rock mode had always been at the heart of his solo career, he had also tested the ground between recorded music and traditional print literature in several ways, as with the 1984 "rock novel" *Amagamalin Street* and, in 1985, a narrative poem set to music, *Flight of the Marie Helena*. Hunter ceded to that latter inclination again in 1988, when initial publication of his translation of the *Duino Elegies* was accompanied by a recording of his reading of the translations set to music provided by Tom Constanten, while a later and expanded version of the cassette added the recitation of his translations of *The Sonnets to Orpheus*. Yet, it was not until 1993 that audiences encountered Hunter's first release of a spoken word album that eschewed musical context entirely. *Sentinel*, the record in question, included his readings of several poems from his book of the same name, as well as selections from some of his other volumes.

Setting aside the observation that he may have found fewer opportunities to compose with Garcia during the later years of the Grateful Dead's career, one might wonder what it was about the task of translating and publishing Rilke's *Duino Elegies* that motivated Hunter's output as a writer for the public page to shift into high gear. There are, of course, many ways of approaching the question, but one less speculative response might take the shape of a consideration of what Rilke offered to Hunter as a poet. What did Hunter find in Rilke, and what impact did the Austrian poet have on Hunter's work? This chapter pursues these and related questions, first by considering the nature of the Modernist fragment and the Grateful Dead's debt to literary Modernism in general, and then by turning to a consideration of specific aspects of Rilke's poems in relation to Hunter's, particularly those published after the Rilke translations.

The Grateful Dead, Robert Hunter, and Literary Modernism

Literary Modernism has undergone significant reconsideration in the past few decades, and many recent remarks on the movement have revised traditional understandings of its coherence, its cultural politics, and its hallmark characteristics. Among these revisions are points that bear on the Modernist uses of the fragment, which resembles but is by no means entirely congruent with the Romantic conception thereof. This chapter is making its way to a close consideration of Hunter in relation to Rilke, but that movement will be helped by a preliminary defense of the view of Rilke as a Modernist and some remarks on the nature of the Modernist fragment. Traditional readings of Rilke's poetry offer a view of the poet as unquestionably Modernist, as Andreas Huyssen explains: "If ever there was a German poet said to embody the essence of high modernism, it surely must be Rainer Maria Rilke. And if literary modernism found its ultimate manifestation in lyric poetry, then Rilke's *Sonette an Orpheus* and his *Duineser Elegien* had to be full-fledged embodiments of this privileged art form of the twentieth century."[5] The many qualifications in this passage make evident Huyssen's skepticism regarding Rilke's consistency as a Modernist, and that skepticism is generally warranted, as many of Rilke's early poems and the novel *The Notebooks of Malte Laurids Brigge* fall somewhat short of the Modernist mark. Nevertheless, Huyssen offers no reason to disqualify the poetic sequence of the *Duino Elegies*—which are the poems by Rilke to which Hunter was most powerfully drawn—from consideration as an exemplary Modernist work.

Even in the cases where criticism significantly extends Huyssen's points, there is no strong challenge to the notions that the *Duino Elegies* remain a definitive example of a Modernist text, and that fragmentation is a key element of Modernist aesthetics. For instance, even as Ihor Junyk joins Huyssen in rethinking *The Notebooks of Malte Laurids Brigge* as something other than a Modernist novel, he affirms the close relations between Modernism and fragmentation, declaring that Rilke "provides a radical rereading of the antique as fragmentation and lack, and posits this . . . as the ideal form for a Baudelairean modernity defined by 'the ephemeral, the fugitive, [and] the contingent.'"[6] Likewise, Amie Elizabeth Parry, who presents an illuminating study of Modernism's "exclusionary cultural politics," finds that even the minor Modernisms she uncovers share with High Modernism an interest in "fragmented form."[7]

While the Modernist fragment is not identical to that of the German Romantics, there are nevertheless similarities between the two, and those similarities are perhaps especially apparent in Rilke's poetry, given the latent Romanticism evident in so much of his work. As Parry explains, Modernist fragmentation is generally either a registration of a variety of crises at the level of representation—including the decay of the unified subject and a concomitant sense of loss or alienation—or a response to those crises that foregrounds itself as a formal critique of the dominant cultural paradigm.[8] Neither of these promises, on a superficial level, that evocative signposting of the literary absolute that Nancy finds in the German Romantics' celebration of the fragment. Nevertheless, the fragment was central to Modernism, and it could evoke the possibility of recuperation and extension, as when the speaker of T. S. Eliot's *The Waste Land* responds to the horrors of the poem by making a bulwark of those fragments of earlier texts, which compose so much of the poem, while declaring, "These fragments I have shored against my ruins."[9] In other words, although it is essential to note that the Modernists reconceived the role of the fragment as a sign of corruption, the persistence of the fragment as key to their practice signals some points of compatibility between Romantic and Modernist aesthetics. Furthermore, that Rilke had until fairly late in his career latent Romantic tendencies suggests, as later sections of this chapter will confirm, that even his most steadily Modernist works engaged more than one variety of fragmentation.

In the background of Hunter's mid-1980s decision to translate Rilke are decades of engagement with other aspects of Modernism by members of the Grateful Dead. One notes in this regard such instances as Weir's appropriations from Béla Bartók in "Victim or the Crime" and his use of Pablo Picasso's surname for "Picasso Moon."[10] Likewise, Lesh and Constanten have displayed an interest in a wide variety of Modernist composers, with Lesh's constellation featuring Charles Ives prominently.[11] Too, there is Garcia's fondness for Modernist painters like Picasso, Max Ernst, and Paul Klee.[12]

In terms of literary Modernism, band members evince interest in several figures. Bill Kreutzmann, for instance, mentions that he "read a bunch of" William Faulkner.[13] Too, Nicholas Meriwether has explored the connections between "It Must Have Been the Roses" and Faulkner's short story "A Rose for Emily" in depth, illuminating such similarities between Faulkner and Hunter as their eclectic sources, dense symbolism, focus on characterization, and compositional tension between inspiration and revision.[14] One notes also the title of the track "Silver Apples of the Moon" and the mention of "silver apples in the sun" in "Pride of Cucamonga," which phrases recall (in addition to Morton Subotnick's *Silver Apples of the Moon*) the closing lines of W. B. Yeats's "The Song of Wandering Aengus," which measure the days' passage with reference to "The silver apples of the moon, / The golden apples of the sun."[15] Furthermore, Hunter, in an interview by Mary Eisenhart, speaks with familiarity of Thomas Mann's novels and discusses reading Marcel Proust's *In Search of Lost Time*.[16] Too, one must recall the many lines of literary Modernism that reached the Grateful Dead via their interest in and friendships with the Beat writers, some of whom were in direct contact with the leading figures of American Modernism. Allen Ginsberg and Michael McClure, for instance, met at a party in San Francisco at which W. H. Auden was the guest of honor, and Ginsberg later corresponded with, and in some cases personally visited, such titans of the movement as Ezra Pound, Marianne Moore, and William Carlos Williams.[17]

More apparent evidence of the Grateful Dead's interest in the literary Modernists are the band's lyrical echoes of Eliot's poetry. Among these is the similarity between the "Shall we go, / you and I / while we can / Through / the transitive nightfall / of diamonds" of "Dark Star" and the opening lines of Eliot's "The Love Song of J. Alfred Prufrock," "Let us go then, you and I, / When the evening is spread out against the sky."[18] There is, as well, the echo in the "I've stayed in every blue-light cheap hotel" of "Stella Blue" of another line from the same poem by Eliot, which mentions "restless nights in one-night cheap hotels."[19] Too, as discussed in the introduction to this book, "Weather Report Suite, Part 2 (Let It Grow)" also borrows from Eliot, in that case from the closing section of *The Waste Land*. Finally, one might note that Hunter's stepfather, who worked as a sales manager and editor for such publishers as McGraw-Hill and Harcourt Brace, had something of a professional connection on this front, as he "could recall seeing . . . Eliot in the office."[20]

One literary Modernist perhaps stands out even in comparison to Eliot as a strong inspiration for the band from its earliest days: James Joyce. In a 1992 interview by Steve Silberman for *Poetry Flash* magazine, which remains by a fair margin the most informative source regarding Hunter's own sense of his identity as a poet, Hunter states, "Before I was writing songs, I was a stoned James Joyce head, *Finnegan's* [sic] *Wake* head. I can still recite the first page and last couple of pages of that thing. There was something in the way those words socketed together, and the wonderful feel of reciting them, that very, very deeply influenced me."[21] Constanten confirms Hunter's interest in the text, as evidenced during the recording sessions for *Anthem of the Sun*: "Instead of hearing 'testing . . . one . . . two . . . three' for sound checks, there'd be Robert Hunter reciting the opening pages of *Finnegan's* [sic] *Wake*—by heart."[22] Joyce has also long been of interest to Lesh, whose early enthusiasm led him to compose a piece called "Finnegan's Awake" for the San Mateo College Jazz Band. At least one 1959 performance of that band playing the piece was recorded and circulates among fans.[23] Too, stage chatter between David Nelson and Lesh at the February 16, 2014, David Nelson Band concert not only recounted for audiences Nelson's memories of Lesh's fondness for *Finnegans Wake* in their youth but also included Lesh's apparently impromptu recitation from memory of a few lines from the text. Constanten and Lesh's shared interest in Joyce was doubtless reinforced by their time studying with Luciano Berio, whose own works were inspired in several ways by the writer, including the early composition *Omaggio a Joyce* and a reliance on the water motifs of *Finnegans Wake* as a means to generate unity in his *Sinfonia*, which also draws substantially on the writing of Joyce's protégé Samuel Beckett.[24] Garcia was likewise a confirmed Joyce fan early in life, and the Irish author's works remained a touchstone for him, even when describing the confusions he suffered in the wake of his 1986 coma: "It was as though in my whole library of information, all the books had fallen off the shelves and all the pages had fallen out of the books. . . . For the first few days it was mostly sort of Joycean inversions of language."[25] A few years later, Joyce provided one of the links in the mutually appreciative relationship that developed between mythographer Joseph Campbell and the Grateful Dead, for Garcia "had been a Campbell fan since reading" *A Skeleton Key to Finnegans Wake*, which Campbell had written with Henry Morton Robinson.[26]

Joyce's texts, and especially his third novel, *Finnegans Wake*, inform the lyrics of the Grateful Dead and offer instructive insight into how literary Modernism informed the words the band sang. As with so many of the other canonical literary sources related to those lyrics, we must take the measure of Joyce's influence on the band indirectly. There is little evidence to support a claim that the band's songwriting was an intentional effort to transmute the words and works of the Irish writer into an American setting, to recast their collected lyrics as a hippie-Haight day in the life of Leopold Bloom. In this regard, they are distinct from such friends as the Jefferson Airplane, whose song "Rejoyce," from *After Bathing at Baxter's*, was laden with allusions to Joyce's second novel, *Ulysses*. Nevertheless, Garcia, Hunter, and Lesh all spoke to the powerful influence of their encounter with Joyce's prose, and his work left a strong mark on much of theirs.

The Joycean presence is most on display in the 1973 album *Wake of the Flood*. One may initially be inclined to regard the coincidence of the word "wake" in the titles *Finnegans Wake* and *Wake of the Flood* as inconsequential, but connections between the album and the novel are numerous, as a closer look at the lyrics reveals. Listeners will recall that the album's title appears as the initial phrase of the song "Here Comes Sunshine," which opens the second side of the original record with the following lines:

Wake of the flood
laughing water
'49

According to a note by Hunter, this song is devoted to "remembering the great Vanport, Washington flood of 1949, living in other people's homes, a family abandoned by father; second grade."[27] So, while the title of the album, as viewed on its own, foregrounds what are primarily biblical references, Hunter's lyrics were inspired by a particular historical moment: a flood in the town of Vanport in the mid-twentieth century. Hunter's note, however, presents errors, both spatial and temporal: Vanport is in Oregon, not Washington, and it was famously flooded in 1948, not 1949. Yet, sometimes mistakes are more revealing than successes, and thus Hunter's indication in both his note on the song and in the lyrics of "Here Comes Sunshine" that the year was "'49" is perhaps worthy of some additional consideration. Among the effects of the song's shortening of the year to only its final two digits is the potential expansion of the song's resonances to any century's "'49," including the most active year of that flood of West Coast–bound hopefuls whose migration is known as the California Gold Rush. A supposition that 1849 is within the discursive field allowed by the song is reinforced by the immediately succeeding lines,

> Get out the pans
> don't just stand there dreaming
> get out the way.

The "pans" of these lines could be heard as those grabbed, along with other trappings of the kitchen, as one flees a flooding house. Alternately, they could be understood as the tools of miners panning for gold in the nineteenth century, belonging to those workers whose presence on the West Coast led to the rapid instantiation of California as a state and the rise of San Francisco as a town of national significance. The latter consideration foregrounds the forty-niners as part of the Grateful Dead's Bay Area social ancestry, and their risk-taking for gold serves admirably as a model of the band's own adventurous spirit.

Hunter's comment that "Here Comes Sunshine" is, in part, about an absent father bears attention, not only in relation to Hunter, but also to Garcia and Joyce. Absent fathers marked the lives of all three men: Garcia's father, the musician Joe Garcia, drowned while trout fishing on the Trinity River when Jerry was only five years old; Hunter's father deserted his family when the lyricist was seven, an age that aligns well with Hunter's claim that "Here Comes Sunshine" was about an absent father during the second year of primary school.[28] Although Joyce's father neither died during the novelist's youth nor entirely abandoned his family, he was nonetheless not an entirely conscientious lord of his castle, even if, in some respects, he embodied masculine energy for James Joyce. As Richard Ellmann writes, "John Joyce filled his house with children and with debts," and later "became increasingly difficult to handle as his drinking caught up with the pace of" his wife's long illness, a tendency that would, by 1904, leave "the furniture mostly pawned or sold" and the family home lost.[29] James Joyce's response to his father's delinquency was, in part, artistic. As Joyce's semi-autobiographical character, Stephen Dedalus, moves through the world of his youth in Joyce's first novel, *A Portrait of the Artist as a Young Man*, and into the independent young adulthood of the second, *Ulysses*, where he also appears, he casts about in search of a father figure more attractive to him than his biological one, Simon Dedalus. Hugh Kenner even goes so far as to declare the effort a defining feature of the first novel, asserting, "*Portrait* is unified by Stephen's twenty years' effort to substitute one father for another."[30]

Joyce suggests, in *Ulysses*, that the opening for Stephen's father may be filled by that novel's protagonist, Leopold Bloom, who sees in Stephen a replacement for his own son, who had died in his infancy.[31] One particularly striking moment in this regard is when Bloom attempts to comfort Stephen after the latter is shaken by a peal of thunder: "A black crack of noise in the street here, alack, bawled back. Loud on left Thor thundered: in anger awful the hammerhurler. Came now the storm that hirst his heart.... And he... waxed wan... and shrank together and his pitch that was before so haught uplift was now of a sudden quite plucked down and his heart shook within the cage of his breast as he tasted the rumor of that storm.... And Master Bloom... spoke to him calming words to slumber his great fear."[32] Stephen blusters a bit, keeping up appearances before his friends, dismissively assigning to the god who would send thunder in anger William Blake's construction, "Nobodaddy," a portmanteau name we could unpack not only in the usual sense followed by Blake's readers, as "nobody's daddy," but also as Stephen's roundabout suggestion that his biological father, like the heavenly one he has renounced, has likewise gone missing.[33] In the end, Bloom is unable to soothe Stephen, whose fear of thunder is entangled with hesitations about his renunciation of his faith, and especially the implications of his atheism for the afterlife. Yet, the irresolution takes nothing away from the surrogate father-son relationship growing between the two characters, one that is especially poignant in light of Bloom's persistent sadness regarding his deceased son. Stephen's association with Bloom and his ongoing search for a satisfactory father figure are in, an additional sense, intriguing in relation to Hunter's biography, for just as Joyce unites Stephen with a figure with whom he feels some connection, so Hunter found another, and in almost every way better, father when his mother remarried. As McNally explains, Norman Hunter was a true boon for the boy, who was already fascinated by books and undertaking his own writing projects. Norman's work in the publishing industry enabled him to offer the aspiring Robert help developing his artistic sensibilities, primarily via editorial advice regarding his work.[34]

"Nobodaddy" also brings one, in a roundabout fashion, back to the town of Vanport, the name of which is also a portmanteau, combining in this case the nearby cities of Vancouver (Washington) and Portland (Oregon). That aspect of the town's identity suggests a connection in "Here Comes Sunshine" not only to the aforementioned thunder passage from *Ulysses*, but also, and much more strongly, to *Finnegans Wake*. As anyone who has looked even casually at the latter novel knows, the portmanteau is a definitive stylistic feature of the text. Joyce's use of words combined and recombined across the boundaries that usually proscribe the limits of individual languages creates a profoundly resonant discursive field, one in which words and even individual syllables exist within a wide associative network defined by their neighbors near and far. A consequence of Joyce's puns and portmanteaux is the generation of fields of indeterminate meaning, and it is with this point that one can recognize a similarity between the power of Joyce's wordplay and the Romantic fragment. The indeterminacies allow every sentence to perform multiple narrative functions, each of which gains additional meanings when it is considered in relation to its nearby and distant neighbors. In failing to mean one definite thing, every part of a given sentence is allowed to carry many interpretations; multiplicity and ambiguity are not at all frustrations of meaning, but instead paths to a surfeit of significances. This explosive proliferation of meanings speaks to a significant productivity born from the playful ambiguities that obtain at the granular level of the word, a process that resembles in most every particular the effects that the German Romantics attributed to the literary fragment. It is in light of such multilayered fields of association offered by *Finnegans Wake* that we can return to "Here Comes Sunshine" and *Wake of the Flood*. Like Joyce's portmanteaux, the songs of the album foreground a number of rich connections that enliven individual passages and unify the record as a whole.

Among similarities between the Grateful Dead's album and Joyce's novel is their shared dependence on water imagery. One of the most prominent unifying elements of *Finnegans Wake* is the River Liffey, which flows through the heart of Dublin on its path to the sea and serves as an emblem of a number of components of the text. That Ireland's most remarkable river serves as a unifying force in *Finnegans Wake* is most obvious in the circularity indicated by the sentence fragments that close ("A way a lone a last a loved a long the") and open ("riverrun, past Eve and Adam's, from swerve of shore to bend of bay, brings us by a commodious vicus of recirculation back to Howth Castle and Environs") the novel.[35] It is not unusual that the fluctuant meanings that derive from the ambiguities of Joyce's work lead critics to call it a "fluid" book, but, as the preceding example demonstrates, the term is more apt than a casual reading might register—water unites and provides an important dynamic force driving the entire novel. Furthermore, this element of the text pertains not only to waterways per se, but to other facets of the narrative, including characterization. Joyce's techniques in this regard are as unconventional as the pun- and portmanteau-laden style of his sentences, and his characters therefore take shape not as narrowly delineated personalities, but as multifaceted ciphers who manifest in a variety of guises. As a consequence, the River Liffey is both a body of water and, in another register,

Anna Livia Plurabelle, the central female character in the text. Anna Livia's name alone suggests her close ties to the river. Not only does "Livia" resemble "Liffey," but her given names are especially resonant in light of the Irish-language name for the Liffey, "An Life." Furthermore, her watery identity is indicated by the French word for rain, *la pluie*, which begins her surname. In this way, the character of Anna Livia emerges as a manifestation of the River Liffey, sharing and multiplying its unifying power.

Like *Finnegans Wake*, *Wake of the Flood*, from its title onward, finds unity in water imagery. The opening piece, "Mississippi Half-Step Uptown Toodleloo," contains the name of the mother river of the United States in its title, manifests the ill fortunes of the song's opening in the watery tears of the father ("Daddy sat down and cried"), and closes with the speaker's later crossing of another river central to the national imagination: "Across the Rio Grand-eo / Across the lazy river." The Mississippi and Rio Grande both appear in *Finnegans Wake*, the first as "missus, seepy" and the second, without modification, close to a portmanteau of "lazy."[36] Elsewhere on the first side of the album, the "levee doin the do-pas-o" of "Row Jimmy" suggests the bulwarks of the levee are on the brink of collapse, thus anticipating the flood of "Here Comes Sunshine" and explaining the need for Jimmy to "row" in the first place. In this fashion, watery imagery connects the songs of the first side of the record and prepares readers for the magnification of the motif in the remainder. Along the way, rivers accrue meaning: familial distress, imminent disaster, the difficulty of exile and displacement, and so forth.

As suggested above, the watery motif is strongly reinforced at the opening of the album's second side with the flood described in "Here Comes Sunshine." Even when songs turn somewhat away from watery motifs, bodies of water typically remain implicit in the mention of water-related features, such as the "beaches" of the heart in "Eyes of the World" (which song also repeatedly reminds us to "wake up"). Tellingly, while there are some exceptions to the prominence of water in the lyrics of songs on *Wake of the Flood* ("Let Me Sing Your Blues Away" and "Stella Blue"), of the several compositions that debuted live and, in some cases, were even attempted in the studio during the album's recording sessions, those lacking water imagery were more often excluded than not: "China Doll," "Loose Lucy," and "They Love Each Other" are examples. Even in the case of "Stella Blue," however, certain lines offer oblique hints of water. "[I]t seems like all this life / was just a dream," for example, finds a partner in the "row, row, row" of "Row Jimmy." Taken together, these two songs provide the opening and closing lines of a one-verse song about being on the water that everyone knows:

Row, row, row your boat
. . . .
Life is but a dream

The culmination of the water motifs appears in the one composition on the album for which Hunter did not write the lyrics, "Weather Report Suite." This piece offers not only a "river shore," but also "Winter rain," "a desert spring," "silver beads" that "pass into the sea," water-gathering, a "wide and clear" river that can "greatly flow," and advice to "stand inside the rain" to hear "the thunder shout." That final phrase also stages another strong similarity to *Finnegans Wake*.

While water may be the strongest unifying element of *Finnegans Wake*, thunder is also a recurrent motif, although it largely serves to represent discontinuity rather than unity. Ten onomatopoetic representations of thunder are scattered throughout the book; in nine of these instances, the thunder word has one hundred letters and emblematizes an apocalyptic moment, usually one in which a heroic father figure crashes to his doom, as a prelude to some sort of renewal or revitalization. The first of these thunder words, "bababadalgharaghtakamminarronnkonnbronntonnerronntuonnthunntrovarrhounawnskawntoohoohoordenenthurnuk," appears on the novel's first page, effectively serving as the narrative's big bang.[37] Thunder likewise has the last word at the end of a cycle in the Grateful Dead's work, for the lyrics of *Wake of the Flood* end with a repetition of thunder's shout. But, as is also the case in *Finnegans Wake*, the thunder is not just an emblem of ruin, but more truly apocalyptic. From its destructive power emerges the revelatory and epiphanic moment that calls for a return to the beginning, fully in keeping with the many images of natural cycles and circular motion that "Weather Report Suite" offers. In this way, the recursive and cyclical view of the human condition presented in *Finnegans Wake*, transmuted to the experience of listening to *Wake of the Flood*, moves the audience from the record's closing declaration of existence, "I am," to its opening one, "On the day that I was born." The return reinitiates consideration of the father figure and the originary moment, just as the fatherly Bloom comforted Stephen when the thunder roared in *Ulysses*. More broadly, the circularity of the album sends listeners back to the two rivers that control its opening, the Mississippi and the Rio Grande, just as Joyce's novel returns readers to the "riverrun" of Dublin's Liffey.[38]

With some of the above context in hand, we can also undertake another return, in this case to Hunter's assertion that "Here Comes Sunshine" is about an absent father. In critical discussion of *Finnegans Wake*, the novel's father figure is typically referred to with the shorthand "HCE." Among other things, HCE lends his initials to phrases and names scattered through the text. Such a formulation appears in the opening passage quoted above, as "Howth Castle and Environs," but is also famously realized in the novel's second episode as "Here Comes Everybody," a phrase that anticipates the Grateful Dead's "Here Comes Sunshine."[39] Too, like Anna Livia Plurabelle (ALP), HCE is a cipher for many identities. Among the more mundane and developed of these personae is that of a tavern-keeper named Humphrey Chimpden Earwicker, in which capacity he is Anna Livia's husband and the father of two sons. In the novel's fourth chapter, Anna Livia attempts to calm one of these boys, who has had a nightmare. This son, like his parents, appears in numerous guises and under various names throughout the novel, yet in this most quotidian of situations, he is H. C. Earwicker's child, and he bears a name that must resonate strongly with anyone with any knowledge of the Grateful Dead: Jerry. Ruth von Phul's remarks on the character of Jerry ascribe to him a remarkable power, that of dreaming the action of the book, and she additionally asserts, "The dream occurs shortly after the death of Jerry's father. . . . Jerry is the only character in the book possessing both the artist's insight and the encyclopedic learning needed to evolve a dream of such fantastic richness."[40] Von Phul also offers a remark that brings Jerry Earwicker together with Joyce, declaring Jerry's "dream-self Shem . . . Joyce's self-portrait."[41] The character of Shem-as-Jerry might thus be regarded as a figure of the novelist-artist, and I suspect it would be difficult for anyone who listens to the Grateful Dead not to see in this fatherless boy named Jerry an additional connection between Garcia and the author of *Finnegans Wake* himself. This provocative confluence of names is further reinforced when one hears Garcia sing "Row Jimmy," given that Jimmy is a diminutive of our Irish novelist's first name.

 The dreaming of Jerry demands more consideration, but before moving into this point more fully, it may be helpful to linger for a moment on the character of Jerry in one of his other incarnations, that of Cain. Cain, of course, figures not only in *Finnegans Wake*, but also in "Mississippi Half-Step Uptown Toodleloo." In the song, as in the Bible, Cain embodies a rift between parent and child, as "Daddy sat down and cried," and between siblings, as "Cain caught Abel / rolling loaded dice." In *Finnegans Wake*, the figure of Jerry/Shem directly declares his own affiliation with Cain.[42] Too, like the biblical Cain, Joyce's Jerry/Shem has a fraternal antagonist, in the figure of his brother Shaun, or Kevin, whom Shem circuitously aligns with Abel, humorously asking him at one point, "I cain but are you able?"[43] Furthermore, Joyce's Shaun is a figure who is perhaps not above the sort of cheating that Hunter's song ascribes to Abel; the novel's second chapter concludes with a ballad, the final lines of which declare, "For there's no true spell in Connacht or hell / (bis) That's able to raise a Cain."[44] As J. Mitchell Morse has argued, the "'true spell' is a *Treuspiel* or confidence game."[45] So, like Hunter's Cain, Joyce's can detect and enact revenge for Abel's cheating, even when it is veiled by the more sanctimonious brother's good reputation. The biblical Cain's fratricide is, of course, the act that condemns him to exile and wandering, a point that would make him a most sympathetic character to Joyce, for whom the figure of the exile is a central one. His biography and works alike testify in countless ways to a sense of the wanderer as a figure of admirable independence. This, too, is Hunter's image of Cain: he who walks so much that his boots have become nothing more than a "pile of smoking leather"; who enters and departs in the same line of the lyric, with "Hello baby I'm gone, good-bye"; and who leaves familiar ground to wander the territory beyond the pale, "Across the lazy river." So, Hunter follows Joyce's lead in the sympathetic presentation of Cain, aligning him with both the artist and the exile.

As the pairings of Jerry and Kevin, Shem and Shaun, and Cain and Abel make evident, Joyce's novel relies heavily, for much of its conceptual and narrative dynamics, on the relationship between mutually supportive opposites—or, to use the language Campbell and Robinson employ when they attempt a brief description of the subject of the novel, on *"mutually supplementary antagonisms."*[46] Such rather fluid interactions between contrary poles of significance have been, with an eye also to the text's stylistic complexities, the basis for numerous critical assertions that the action of *Finnegans Wake* is that of a dreamer's night, such as the one by von Phul cited above. A similar, if more modest, claim might be advanced about *Wake of the Flood*. While the entirety of the album may not be the dream of one sleeper, references to dreams do contribute to the collection of songs by adding some additional coherence. The opening lines of the record's second side, which include the request that the listener not "just stand there dreaming," are echoes of the close of the first side, which ends with "Stella Blue." This latter piece not only offers two lines about "broken dreams," but finds in them, as does *Finnegans Wake*, a valuable motif. It opens with "All the years combine / they melt into a dream," and closes, "it seems like all this life / was just a dream." If we align ourselves with the Joyceans who would see in the dream not only an aspect of *Finnegans Wake*, but also a unifying element that controls the manner in which the whole unfolds, the dream-laden "Stella Blue" comes into its own as a track governing the album, reminding listeners that all that precedes and follows it is subject to the logic of dreams—which, to return to the point made above, with reference to von Phul, positions Jerry in control of the action.

One final point regarding *Finnegans Wake* and the Grateful Dead concerns the relation of the book to the folk song that, with only a very slight alteration, provides the novel with its name. "Finnegan's Wake" is an old vaudeville number that Campbell and Robinson succinctly summarize as follows: "Tim Finnegan . . . is an Irish hod carrier who gets drunk, falls off a ladder, and is apparently killed. His friends hold a deathwatch over his coffin; during the festivities someone splashes him with whisky, at which Finnegan comes to life again and joins in the general dance."[47] Tim Finnegan, in other words, did not die, but is only fractured from the fall and brought fully back to life by his encounter with whiskey, or usquebaugh, the water of life. The origins of the vaudeville song are somewhat vague, with Norman Cazden, Herbert Haufrecht, and Norman Studer explaining that Edwin Ford Piper dates it to 1884, while other collectors trace it back an additional two decades—or more.[48] Whatever the date of its original composition, variations on the air and the traditional lyrics are numerous, and it is difficult to imagine that Pigpen and Garcia, who both had Irish Catholic ancestry and some familiarity with the stage and taverns, could have avoided encountering it—even if one ignores the fact that Garcia was a devoted student of folk music.

The question of whether Garcia or anyone else in the Grateful Dead knew "Finnegan's Wake" is perhaps less interesting than the fact that the song offers a folk workingman's version of the cycle of downfall and rebirth that is central to both Joyce's *Finnegans Wake* and the Grateful Dead, the latter embodying this theme both locally, as realized in the self-renewing song cycle of *Wake of the Flood*, and as an architectonic experience for band and fans alike. Attempts to describe this part of the Grateful Dead experience have been made numerous times across the years, using a wide variety of terms: Mickey Hart and Fredric Lieberman follow Garcia's claims that the band's name signals a kind of ego death and thus discuss the music as an evocation of spiritual trance, "a form of egolessness that is the ground for any sacred exploration"; Jim Tuedio and Stan Spector draw attention to Nietzsche's *The Gay Science*, which declares, "What is living is just a subset of what is dead"; while Robert H. Trudeau approaches the process via the lens of Victor Turner's work, in light of which both individual songs and setlist decisions as a whole can be viewed as arcs that begin with a separation from quotidian life, followed by an adventure defined by a transgressive liminality, before culminating in an ultimate reintegration of self and world.[49] Readers at all familiar with the literature on the Grateful Dead can doubtless point to countless other articulations of the idea, many of which deploy other sorts of popular or academic language or models for explanation. But in nearly every instance, the music and the experience of listening to it answer to the pattern of Tim Finnegan's death and return to life that undergirds the structure of Joyce's *Finnegans Wake*. In sum, *Finnegans Wake* clearly offers a rich intertext for *Wake of the Flood*, displaying both broad and local semantic and structural similarities that enliven and illuminate an album created in the months during which the Grateful Dead pondered its own loss and revitalization in the wake of Pigpen's death.

Rilke

As the example of *Finnegans Wake* read in relation to *Wake of the Flood* indicates, literary Modernism informed the aesthetics of the Grateful Dead in numerous ways, from enriching images to modeling means to structure engagement with concepts and themes. With this example in mind, one can turn to Rilke's significance to Hunter with not only a sense of his specific interest in the *Duino Elegies*, but also a more general appreciation of Modernist aesthetics. Two short narratives might provide those less familiar with Rilke's poetry some insight into the compositional history of the *Duino Elegies* and the literary reputation that the collection and its author have earned.

In 1912, Rilke was a guest, courtesy of Princess Marie von Thurn und Taxis, at Duino Castle, near the Adriatic Sea. He began composing the sequence that would become the *Duino Elegies* at that time, but both World War I and psychological turmoil prevented him from completing the work. Most of the following decade saw the poet besieged by one state of distress or another, until, in early 1922, he experienced a burst of inspiration and composed the entirety of his other great late poetic sequence, *The Sonnets to Orpheus*, as well as the remainder of the *Duino Elegies*, within a few short weeks. The story is a strong example of nigh-supernatural artistic inspiration, and it anticipates Hunter's remarks about the role of the muse as a key component of his own writing of songs and poems. In the case of Hunter, the phenomenon perhaps appears most famously in "Terrapin Station," but he discussed the nature of inspiration numerous times.[50]

In addition to serving as a famed instance of poetic inspiration, the history of the composition of the *Duino Elegies* indicates the profound divide in Rilke's poetry between the typical life of the mind, beset by difficulty and confusion engendered by the experience of worldly necessity and transience, and the artistic one, which opens itself to the good and ill of the world via an artistic process of transformative internalization that unveils significances of and grants permanency to what otherwise remain accidental confusions. At its most extensive, this process of opening oneself to external things on their own terms led to famed poems like "The Panther," in which Rilke imaginatively inhabits a beast in a zoo, writing from its perspective rather than that of a human visitor to the menagerie. As presented by Rilke, this union of foreign externality and human interiority is a metamorphic process, one that creates a sort of preternatural beauty that continues to shine long after the work is complete and the artist in her grave. The process itself is the subject of many of Rilke's works, including another of his most widely read poems, "Archaic Torso of Apollo." As that work demonstrates, a confrontation with an embodiment of beauty, in this case the fragment of an ancient sculpture, stands as a challenge to the viewer, judging her and demanding that any encountering the work must strive to be as perfect in their way as it is on its own terms. Consequently, the poem concludes with a forceful call to action, "You must change your life!"[51] In the *Duino Elegies*, the much-discussed figures of the angels occupy something of the same realm as the spirit embodied in ancient sculpture. Thus, in addition to understanding the burst of inspiration that led to the completion of the *Duino Elegies* as an example of muse-like intervention from outside the poet's normal capacities, one may add the sense that Rilke's astonishingly fast completion of his late poems indicates that he reached a moment in his career that allowed him to enact at least a partial response to an imperative he saw as definitive of the artistic work, specifically that described in "Archaic Torso of Apollo."

Perhaps even better known than the history of the composition of the *Duino Elegies* and *The Sonnets to Orpheus* is the story of Rilke's death. Popular memory tells us that the poet, gathering roses from his garden for a beautiful woman, accidentally pricked his finger on a thorn. The wound did not heal, infection spread rapidly, and he soon died in agony. The fairy-tale nature of the narrative tells us that it cannot be literally true, and Rilke's biographers support the suppositions of our common sense. Ralph Freedman, for example, explains that, while the pricked-finger incident did happen, it was not contemporaneous with the sufferings that immediately preceded Rilke's death, which were instead due to the sudden onset of symptoms caused by leukemia.[52] On the other hand, the imaginative conflation of the actualities of Rilke's death and the incident with the rose speak to the degree to which the flower informed his poetic life. Rilke returns to images of the rose repeatedly—most famously in "The Bowl of Roses," which is the closing poem of his first major collection; again in several of the late poems, written in French rather than his native German; and, finally, in his epitaph. While the symbol serves somewhat different purposes at different times, the fact that Rilke returned to it so often speaks to what William Gass calls Rilke's "life of recurrent symbols," which includes the mirror and the rose.[53] Anyone familiar with the lyrics of the Grateful Dead will recognize that Hunter, too, returned repeatedly to a set of emblematic items and situations that are both familiar from the popular songwriting tradition and also material he made his own, such as the card game and the locomotive. Indeed, the Grateful Dead as a whole is marked by a recurrent iconography, of skulls and roses especially, that serves as a sort of symbolic shorthand.

"The Bowl of Roses" demands a bit more comment, even though it is immature in relation to the *Duino Elegies*. The poem progresses, in part, via the speaker's speculations about roses of different sorts. A yellow one reminds him of the rind of a fruit; a white one, revealing its interior, presents itself like Botticelli's Venus; another open one offers only further layers of petals, as if trying to shield an all-seeing eye at its center. Finally, one contains "nothing but itself." The poem approaches its end with a meditation on this recognition:

> And aren't they all that way, simply self-containing,
> if self-containing means: to transform the world outside
> and the wind and rain and patience of Spring
> and guilt and restlessness and muffled fate
> and the darkness of the evening earth
> out to the roaming and flying and fleeing of the clouds
> and the vague influence of distant stars
> into a handful of inwardness.[54]

The movement is first one of expansion, seeing in the small rose blossom all the world, from guilt to stars, and then one of powerful contraction, condensing everything into the space contained within a few flower petals. The flower is, in this way, like the bower of Tennyson's "The Lady of Shalott," which brings the world to the lady via a mirror, while simultaneously preserving her inviolate space. This is, too, the garden of the Grateful Dead's "Rosemary," which cannot be permanent for us ("no one may stay"), except insofar as we internalize it via memory before the "flowers decay." The movement between inner and outer, and between contraction and expansion, is typical for Rilke, one that effects, as Lawrence Ryan explains, a "dislocation of perspective" that is the work of poetic metaphor serving as a bridge. When more powerful, such a trope not only brings opposites into closer relation, but also reveals the degree to which the object under consideration transforms "the viewing perspective" to which it was initially subject.[55] The mind may impose its order on the world, but Rilke shows us how poetry creates a space within which the reverse may happen—a space in which the world may impose a new order on us.

To the story about the fantastic composition of the *Elegies* and the apocryphal tale about Rilke's own death, one more preliminary element may be added: Rilke would not have been the first to characterize his time as an elegiac one, but he makes this point explicit from the opening lines of the *Duino Elegies*. The Modernists offered a critical reassessment of the elegy, one that interrogated its form and implications in a way that resulted in the rethinking of some of the genre's traditional features. It is useful, in approaching the question of how the Modernists rethought the elegy, to have some sense of its history. The poet Edward Hirsch defines the elegy as "a poem of mortal loss and consolation."[56] This is a good pocket definition, but, as Hirsch acknowledges, it is hardly the whole story. The ancient Greeks, whose term for the funeral lament, *élegos*, gives us our name for the genre, composed *élegoi* about losses of many sorts. Like most ancient Greek poetry, this sort of poem had a musical component—it was affiliated most closely with the flute. Yet, the elegy was distinguished by not only musical accompaniment and thematic content, but also formal qualities. For the Greeks, elegiac poems were any of those written in what we call elegiac distichs, couplets that alternate between lines of dactylic hexameter, which are relatively long, and slightly shorter lines that scan as pentameter.[57] Rilke's elegies sometimes offered such a distich, and a fairly good example in English can be found in Henry Wadsworth Longfellow's "Elegiac Verse": "So the Hexameter, rising and singing, with cadence sonorous, / Falls; and in refluent rhythms back the Pentameter flows."[58] As Longfellow's poem both asserts and displays, there is something of an aural cycle here, with lines alternately extending into new territory and returning home, informed by the excursion. Too, this form offers a complex tonal mix, combining hexameter, which has historically been associated with an elevated tone, with pentameter, which has a wider range. This combination can provide a powerful blend of the highly formal and the deeply personal.

While the Greeks may have crystallized the genre, there are many great elegies in every language. In English, we could point to John Milton's "Lycidas," Thomas Gray's "Elegy Written in a Country Churchyard," Percy Bysshe Shelley's "Adonais," Alfred, Lord Tennyson's *In Memoriam, A. H. H.*, Walt

Whitman's "When Lilacs Last in the Dooryard Bloom'd," and W. H. Auden's "In Memory of W. B. Yeats." Peter M. Sacks points out that, in almost every case, the conventions of the genre follow "ancient rites in the ... passage from grief or darkness to consolation and renewal."[59] In other words, the elegy is not only a poem about a particular topic (death) or in a particular rhythm, but one governed by a thematic convention—following a death, a mourner's grief is mitigated and overcome via reconnection to the world. In this sense, the genre is custom-built to display that same sort of exchange between chaos and order that the Grateful Dead offered on stage just about every night, and which the German Romantics saw as the generative source of artistic achievement and philosophical thought.

Hunter discusses his own efforts to think and write about loss in his foreword to *Alleys of the Heart*. There, he describes his difficulties finding the right words when asked to deliver a eulogy for Robert M. Petersen, his fellow poet and Grateful Dead lyricist, and he writes that his struggle to articulate something about his death eventually led him to turn, as discussed in chapter 4, to the writings of Rimbaud. Rimbaud's words offer us something of the high seriousness of those who regard the work of the wordsmith as a spiritual endeavor, mediating between eternal truths and human languages. Hunter's published work does, indeed, sometimes tread that ground. His chapbook-length poem *Idiot's Delight* is one example, shuttling between the quotidian and weighty meditations on the way in which our culture's cultivation of empty appetites creates a spiritual sickness. Hunter told Steve Silberman that he began the poem as a sequence of Spenserian stanzas, but, over time, that genealogy has melted away entirely.[60] Instead, the text is divided into eleven sections, each of which contains eleven stanzas of eleven lines. There is an echo here of the eleven-syllable lines that Dante uses in his *Commedia*, and of the eleven-line stanzas of Algernon Charles Swinburne's roundels, but Hunter's poem is not governed by strict structural or formal principles. Here is one page of the text:

> Summer sickness
> is followed by
> Autumn sickness
> with a little space
> for the legitimate
> illnesses of Winter.
> There is another
> season, I can't

> remember what,
> stuck between now
> & the day I die[61]

These lines are reminiscent of "Black Peter." What stands out most strikingly is that the speaker refrains from mentioning spring. That season, conventionally viewed as a period of rebirth and recovery, is missing from the litany of ills. A reader may think there is some saving grace here, that the hidden season will be a delight in contrast to the ill winds of its siblings, but the following page of the poem undercuts this assumption, declaring it even worse than they. Spring is the season

> when Nature
> lets fly the
> full battery
> of lascivious
> poisons—wind
> so thick with
> sweet sting it
> clots the eye
> & clings to
> the lungs like
> syrup of sin.[62]

These lines might be read as Hunter's version of the opening of *The Waste Land*, with its assertion that "April is the cruelest month" because it awakens "Memory and desire."[63] Perhaps a truer ancestor is the first poem of Rimbaud's *Une saison en enfer*, which tells us, "Spring brought me the idiot's frightening laugh."[64] Hunter here reminds us of the hard truth of the world—our experience is shaped by the persistence of suffering and delimited by death. *Idiot's Delight* does eventually propose an alternative, one that envisions existence as an ongoing process rather than as the terminus of capitulation to our baser selves. The following lines illustrate the point:

> It seems we
> must learn to
> value the place
> of becoming:
> the almost but
> never quite—
> the sense of

impending as opposed to the consummation of any desire.[65]

While the preceding examples demonstrate that *Idiot's Delight* indeed contains some elegiac passages, the poem is by no means an elegy in its entirety. Nevertheless, its turn away from the genre's conventions suggests something of Hunter's compatibility with those Modernists who found reason to rethink this part of the poetic tradition.

For many literary Modernists, the elegy served admirably to articulate the crisis of cultural skepticism and spiritual pessimism endemic to the decades immediately following the First World War, the era when artistic Modernism flourished. However, while the Modernists were drawn to the elegy for several reasons, many resisted its more consolatory features. As Jahan Ramazani argues, "The modern elegist tends not to achieve but to resist consolation, not to override but to sustain anger, not to heal but to reopen the wounds of loss."[66] In denying the resolution of grief, Modernist poetry turns with distrust on traditional presentations of mortal loss, and consequently the elegy itself becomes subject to critique, especially insofar as it proffers itself as a mechanism for healing.[67] Sandra Gilbert concurs with this argument, recognizing that the point of renewal reached in the traditional pastoral elegy is traded, in the Modernist one, for moments of additional suffering—for the twentieth-century mourner, the dissipation of grief and the transference of mourning to a poem constitutes a betrayal of the dead. Furthermore, Gilbert adds, the turn to landscape and natural cycles of rejuvenation is difficult to celebrate when the meadows and copses of the nineteenth-century landscape have become the wastelands and corpses that World War I revealed as characteristic of machine-age warfare.[68] Consequently, as Patricia Rae asserts, the traditional elegiac intent, which one might express as the working through of grief, is bartered by many poets of the last century for a "resistant mourning," an elegiac poetics that finds, in ongoing attachment to the lost friend, family member, or lover the living's ethical obligation to the dead.[69] While the preceding points are useful as a means to indicate strong inclinations to elegiac poetry on the part of Modernist poets, as well as their tendency to turn something of a critical eye on its mannerisms, they do need some qualification. Revised attitudes to the elegy are by no means a wholesale rejection of the mode; too, as this chapter's remarks on Rilke will demonstrate, not all poets call into question the same aspects of the traditional elegy, nor are those who share similar concerns entirely consistent with one another in their approach.

Rilke's *Duino Elegies* are compatible with the works of other Modernist poets in that they test the limits of the traditional elegy, and in that they express a sense of loss that is congruent with the deep spiritual unease that characterizes much of Modernist literature. Yet, while Rilke's elegies were begun shortly before and completed somewhat after the war years, and are thus very much of that moment, they differ from many elegies of the era in some important ways. Perhaps most evident is that the struggle with which Rilke grapples is not the sort of public mourning familiar from so many poems inspired by the Great War. Neither is the loss Rilke's poems negotiate of the personal sort that such later elegies as Sylvia Plath's "Daddy" or the poems of Donald Hall's *Without* present. These points are helpful in approaching the *Duino Elegies* because they allow one to recognize that the poems might best be described not as a series of elegies proper, but as a sequence of poems in the elegiac mode. As this sequence progresses, it grapples with certain concerns that point to the nature and ambition of the whole: How can we be reconciled to the facts that we are bound in time and that our existence is constrained by death? Can we somehow overcome the world's seeming limits, perhaps reaching a superior state of being? If we are constrained to one mode of being, can we reconcile the increasingly chaotic aspects of experience to produce something whole, or at least something open to productive possibility? What is the role of the artist, and particularly the poet, in approaching these problems?

While the key points will be given more intensive consideration below, and while Rilke's poetry is typically less linear than digressive and recursive, it is still the case that some sense of the overall arc of the *Duino Elegies* can be described, and it is useful in developing a preliminary sense of Rilke's approach to these central questions. Kathleen L. Komar recommends organizational groupings for the poems that lend themselves to an especially lucid explanation of the general shape of the collection. According to her schema, the first six elegies test potential models that allow the poet to reach beyond the typical realm of human existence and into a superior one defined by unification rather than fragmentation. Elegies 7–9 reject the earlier effort, trading transcendence for transformation. Here, the poet turns to the bare physical world, testing whether they have the power to change it into something more lasting. The tenth elegy affirms the wisdom of the reversal presented in the preceding three poems, celebrating the poet as capable of overcoming the dissatisfactions of human existence by reconceiving them as doorways to the eternal.[70] In other words, Rilke's sequence rejects the notion that overcoming life's difficulties is best achieved by turning away from the world, and instead recommends a working through of our condition via art.

An assessment of Hunter's debt to Rilke thus needs to account for more than the features to which I gestured above, such as the sort of symbolic vocabulary evident in Rilke's poetry, or a reading of Rilke's work that relies solely on the rather romanticized notion of poetic process suggested by biographical anecdotes. Instead, we must approach the question of how the *Duino Elegies*, in particular, require us to think carefully about how Hunter's poetry received, expressed, and possibly revised traditional models, and to what extent that reflection on the nature of art accords with the model provided by Rilke's elegies.

Rilke, Hunter, and Hunter's Rilke

While there are numerous intertextual relations between Rilke's poems and Hunter's, the most notable concern the three aforementioned definitive qualities of the Rilkean elegies: the centrality of vatic inspiration; the attraction to, but ultimate rejection of, transcendence; and the presentation of poetry as a project of describing and enacting transformation. Taken together, these components of Rilke's poetry, and of Hunter's, express a preoccupation with some of the definitive components of poetry itself, including its origin, nature, and potential as a mode of thought and articulation.

HUNTER, RILKE, AND THE MUSE

It is difficult to overstate the degree to which inspiration remained a central concern of Rilke's work. As Judith Ryan writes, "Even . . . when he saw hard work as paramount and accepted no excuses for laziness, his poems attempt to force the appearance of inexplicable moments during which the object is illumined or transformed. . . . Something that goes beyond the speaker's sheer willpower is what turns a mundane observation into a work of poetry. During his crisis of 1910–14, inspiration is more overtly at issue. The *Poems to Night*, the poems to the future beloved, and the *Duino Elegies* all circle around this topic."[71] Ryan's claim is certainly justified, although the nature of inspiration in the *Duino Elegies* looks somewhat different from the traditional invocations of the muse familiar from the works of classical poets or even from the "inexplicable moments" central to Rilke's earlier verse. Rather, governing all the elegies is the story of the poem's inception, which Rilke himself related—climbing to the top of a tower in Duino Castle during a terrific storm, the poet heard a voice dictate the opening two lines of the first poem.[72] The tale clearly demonstrates that Rilke has cast his lot with those who assert true art must have its source outside the poet.

The position is immediately problematized, however, by the nature of those opening lines: "Who, though I cry aloud, / would hear me in the angel orders?"[73] In this fashion, and against the implications of Rilke's story about the source of his breakthrough inspiration, the opening of the poem asserts not the sort of communion between the human and the superhuman on which inspiration, as traditionally conceived, relies, but rather a state of disunity, doubt, and lonely despair. These are among the qualities that most strongly demand that the work be viewed as elegiac, and are likewise those that allow readers to regard it as within the tradition of long Modernist poems, such as Ezra Pound's *The Cantos*. Furthermore, the speaker's initial response to the opening plea of the *Elegies* is hindered by the awesome power of the angels, who are so intimidating that the speaker withholds or retracts the question, stating a few lines later, "I constrain myself and / swallow the deep, dark music."[74] As Komar asserts, the aborted initial connection to the muse demands that the poet devote the remainder of the *Elegies* not to the poem's initial question, but rather to "the impulse to ask it."[75] In other words, while inspiration remains central to Rilke's work, the opening lines of the *Elegies* do not allow it to serve as the origin of the text, but transform it into a problem that the poet takes as his subject matter throughout the sequence.

Like Rilke's *Duino Elegies*, Hunter's debut book of poetry opens with a poem that foregrounds disunity and loss, for the speaker and his audience dismantle their bodies to form a container:

> we put what we *did* know
> into something like a basket
> with your *arms* for handles
> & my *feet* to steady it . . . [76]

The second stanza shows the improvised basket running away, leaving the footless (and thus immobilized) speaker with no way to catch it without help from the poem's addressee, who, having just donated her arms, cannot carry him. In this way, the poem works something like a record of the biblical fall—knowledge ("what we *did* know") leads to fragmentation and incapacitation. The concluding line of the poem, "Love is like that in the City," pulls the text toward a particular reading. This is a love poem, a record of the ways we come together with another person under some set of assumptions ("what we *did* know") that are quickly disproven, even as the bond between those involved deepens and the difficulties of life together become a shared burden.

Yet, in terms of the poem's Rilkean motifs, more important than the ratcheting of the text in the direction of a particular genre like the love poem is the appearance of a setting that serves Rilke as a recurrent motif: the "City." Rilke's works, in a rather Romantic fashion, repeatedly present urban landscapes as the home of opportunities for distraction, as places where the most frivolous and tawdry elements of human activity interfere with the nobler aspirations of the soul. As Huyssen argues, Rilke's character of Malte finds in Paris, as does the speaker of Eliot's *The Waste Land* in London, or Franz Biberkopf in Berlin in some portions of *Berlin Alexanderplatz*, a setting that is "disrupting, fragmenting.... One of ... deindividualization, and alienation."[77] The *Duino Elegies* of Rilke follow suit. The Tenth Elegy, for example, describes a "City of Sorrow," wherein sounds are false, emptiness takes on shapes, and a carnivalesque atmosphere caters to a confluence of greed and desire, to what the poem, in Hunter's translation, calls "The sex life of money."[78] Opposed to the rampant falseness is the "real world," where "Children play and lovers touch," these more sincere places and events are "off to the side," rather than at the heart of the City. Hunter's closing line, which brings together lovers in the city, thus situates his speaker and audience in a space defined by the threat of looming corruption, where the search for the missing basket becomes an impossible task. As a consequence, while Hunter may offer a greater measure of levity than does Rilke, and while the love declared in the poem is something of a tonic to the undiluted despair it might otherwise present, it is still the case that Hunter's first book of poetry opens with emblematic landscapes, predicaments, and sentiments familiar to readers of the *Elegies*.

In responding to the fragmentation and loss the opening texts of his first book present, Hunter again follows Rilke. Just as the Austrian poet returns endlessly to the topic of inspiration, so Hunter circles back in one piece after another to the subject. Indeed, considering the importance of the muse to Hunter's work reinforces a sense of the centrality of songs such as "Terrapin Station," even while it suggests we might listen to others as oblique treatments of the topic. In this way, something like "Althea" could be read not only as a love song or a dialogue about wisdom, but also as a meditation on the artist courting—and perhaps being outwitted by—his muse. The topic is one of persistent interest in the poems, as well, and pieces such as "The Door to the Sea," "Holigomena," and "Trapping a Muse" are wholly or partially concerned with it.

"The Door to the Sea" and "Holigomena" both follow Rilke in many regards, not least because they commingle a desire for communion with doubt about its likelihood before turning to a critique of poetry. "The Door to the Sea" begins, like the *Duino Elegies*, with a question that opens in two directions at once. On the one hand is a movement of expansion, with the question echoing to cosmic reaches. The speaker is shown

> sounding an unseen hall
> suggesting great distance
> and lending roundness to
> pronouncements [79]

On the other hand, the poem is driven by a turn inward, as the need for a response calls for an exercise in self-interrogation. The question "we" ask demands "an answer / . . . *from us*."[80] Unlike Rilke's first elegy, however, in which the question is stifled, a muse quickly manifests herself in Hunter's poem:

> You were mute until the gods
> spoke through you making
> the air shiver and shade[81]

The moment is one of potential revelation, but "The Door to the Sea" follows the *Duino Elegies* in looking at expression with suspicion. In the fallen world Hunter's poem describes, even the voices of the gods produce a text warranting some measure of skepticism:

> considering the condition
> of the door to the sea itself,
> the results cannot be expected
> to be particularly everlasting.[82]

The notion presented in these lines—that vatic utterance derives meaning not from supernatural sources of truth, but from context (just as the "door" of the poem frames the sea)—is consistent with other poems by Hunter and with Rilke's tenth elegy.

That tenth elegy is largely devoted to a young man's travels in an underworld, through which he is guided by a woman who is one of those beings whose type, called "Laments," rule and populate the place. The nature of this underworld is perhaps particularly that of the poets. As Judith Ryan argues, "The realm of Laments is a written world, a world that exists only by virtue of the existence of previous textual worlds."[83] As a consequence, the shape of the experience is determined in no small part by the model of three canonical German Romantic elegies: Schiller's "Der Spaziergang," Goethe's "Euphrosyne," and Hölderlin's "Brot und Wein."[84] The Schiller text, in particular, offers Rilke the model of a landscape as a textualized space via which the poet can read and negotiate the legacies of earlier civilizations. In the case of Rilke's *Elegies*, those legacies are not only the great poems of German Romanticism, but also the icons of the ancient Egyptian past, an element lent greater weight in Hunter's hands by the importance of Egypt to the Grateful Dead's history. As Rilke's character passes a monument that is a twin of the Sphinx, an owl bursts from behind it, brushing the youth's face with a wing that is heard rather than felt. The synesthetic sound touch opens realms of sensory experience that the poet describes in particularly textual terms:

> an indescribable outline
> scrawled as thought across
> the leaves of an open book.[85]

The poem's youth cannot read this book, being still too recently dead to fathom the workings of the underworld. Nevertheless, the Lament functions as a mediating figure between his abilities and the textuality of this place, in much the same way Beatrice helped Dante, and very much in the same manner that a muse does for any artist.

In Hunter's poetry, this passage from Rilke, which combines misunderstanding, the feminine guidance of a muse or muse substitute, and loss, returns in numerous forms. To the earlier suggestion that "The Door to the Sea" can be read on these terms, one could add the instance of "Holigomena." That poem begins with a description of fallen people, who are described as "the aftermath" and "the infidels." These are individuals who, like the youth of Rilke's final elegy, find themselves at a loss to comprehend and express their situation. Lacking the capacity to articulate their meanings clearly, this preterite bunch can only reach for

> the meaning of . . . words,
> finding only other words to mark
> the helplessness of longing.[86]

Faced with this dispersal of intention, Hunter's speaker calls for assistance, and the result reminds one of the journey Rilke describes in the tenth elegy, with its owl bursting from behind a Sphinx to come to the aid of a mournful muse in a pseudo-Egyptian land of the dead. The relevant passage from Hunter's text reads:

> Mistress of Mourning,
> in the Valley of Reptiles,
> erupt from some unguarded recess
> of our incoherent souls to conquer us,
> despite reason, as we blunder through
> the sophistries of this and other ages
>
> attempting
> to speak truly
> if not
> truthfully[87]

Recognizing the Rilkean ancestry of the poem makes of it something more than a versified version of Hunter's song "Boys in the Barroom." Instead, it places the speakers in the land of the dead, reaching for help as they strive to articulate their condition with words that are ill-suited to the task. A potential guide, the Mistress of Mourning, may be an explicit object of the appeal, but the poem (and the book, for it closes *Night Cadre*) ends before the prayer is answered, just as Rilke fails to tell us of the conclusion of the youth's journey in the tenth elegy. Consequently, like the ambiguous framing of "The Door to the Sea," the matter of clear communication is left suspended, and the muse's help is both central to the poem and less than entirely certain. One may read the ambiguity of the poems' closing movements as a frustration of its promises, but to read it in the context of the Romantic fragment is to recognize another possibility. The palimpsestic presence of Rilke's inconclusive tenth elegy in the background of Hunter's likewise unresolved "Holigomena" encourages a reading of both in the terms of the Romantic fragment, which likewise prioritizes irresolution, insofar as that quality can signal something that lies beyond the text entirely. From this perspective, Hunter's poem enacts a fragmentary aesthetic, one that finds a muse who resists contributing any facile conclusion and instead gestures toward the space from which creative power emerges.

A final example of Hunter's complex, Rilkean presentation of poetic inspiration might be offered with reference to the third stanza of his poem "Trapping a Muse." The text is much concerned with the mechanisms of creation and literary ancestry: It includes allusions to Sir Walter Scott and Joyce, as well as several Rilkean motifs and a nod to the Egyptian god of creation, Amon-

Ra. The third stanza, however, foregrounds a conflicted relationship with the muse, describing

> How a mild breeze
> can shut a door so that
> you look up wondering
> what she wants of you:
> *nothing and everything.*
> Look to your lines
> and ignore the source.[88]

Here, the poet focuses on the requisites of devotion to his art and concludes that, if one is lucky enough to be listening when the music comes from the goddess, one must not count the cost. As in many of Hunter's other poems, and in many of Rilke's, the muse presented here is a necessary figure, but the exchange between her and the artist is a fraught one; she is demanding, and her messages are not always closed to uncertainty. The poem's title, "Trapping a Muse," is effectively overturned: Hunter, like Rilke, submits his poetic self to external inspiration and declares that the means to win the muse is no snare, but rather unwavering devotional openness. Indeed, in an inversion of the title, it is not the muse but the poet who appears to be the one trapped. Taken together with such other poems as "Like a Basket," "The Door to the Sea," and "Holigomena," "Trapping a Muse" evinces not only a celebration of a vatic poetic identity, but also a problematization of the compositional process, one that reveals the tensions between poetic intentions and the motivating power of inspiration.

HUNTER, RILKE, AND THE TEMPTATION OF TRANSCENDENCE

Hunter's exploration of poetic inspiration is by no means the only aspect of his works that evinces debts to Rilke. The Austrian poet also left his mark on Hunter's poetry in the form of a tension between an attraction to transcendence and a commitment to the foundational importance of everyday things. This aspect of Hunter's development of Rilke's own poetic arguments is perhaps especially striking for the conceptual breadth it displays. Too, it is among the aspects of Hunter's poetry that resemble most directly the Grateful Dead's ability to shuttle quickly between the humble and the exalted, from the earthy wisdom of "Brown-Eyed Women" to the deep space of an extended jam in a second set's "Playing in the Band."

The cry of despair with which the *Duino Elegies* opens (again, "Who, though I cry aloud, / would hear me in the angel orders?") expresses succinctly the poles of the question at hand.[89] Feeling the anguish of earthly existence, the poet calls to a transcendent order, while remaining skeptical about whether communion between such realms is possible. As the sequence progresses, readers find that Rilke tests various models of a less fractured and even more ennobling earthly existence, models that present the familiar not only as something for which we settle, but as something we relish and that offers joy. The poem thus considers lovers, heroes, and children as possible models for the poet's consciousness, because their innocence or devotion to others allows an escape from the solipsism of despair by remaining present in the moment. As Komar asserts, a key formulation for this opening section of the poem is "Denn Bleiben ist nirgends," which Hunter translates as "Nowhere may we remain."[90] *Bleiben* is a temporal word; it contributes to the notion that we cannot stay put in time. *Nirgends* is spatial, and, with the equation of it to *Bleiben*, Rilke turns the temporal into a spatial category. With this verbal innovation, Rilke offers an escape from the anxieties of an existence bound by time to an existence liberated by the openness of space.[91] Many of the most productive points in the poem follow this lead, creating semantic paradoxes that free the speaker from the cage of a confining temporality.

As does Rilke across the *Duino Elegies*, Hunter weighs the appeal of the transcendent against that of the earthly repeatedly in his works, and again like Rilke, he repeatedly finds succor not via an escape from the world, but via a relation to it that is differently tuned. "Warmup," a short poem from *Night Cadre*, is a good illustration of this tendency. The piece describes a musician preparing to perform, and its first two stanzas point out both the unfolding of music "with time" and the "anxiety of" the moment.[92] Hunter confronts this sense of time passing as concomitant with anxiety by following the lead of his Austrian predecessor, making of the temporal problem a spatial fact. The challenge of performance is a matter not of time, so much as the proper disposition of the body in relation to the instrument, with music created like "a hand approaching keys."[93] Hunter thus echoes Rilke in presenting a poetically satisfying recontextualization of the issue, while also acknowledging the conceptual awkwardness it introduces. There is something here of Russell's paradox, perhaps especially as it is filtered through Wittgenstein, as Hunter acknowledges in the following lines:

> like syntax
> there is no
> framing its law
> without its aid[94]

The logical difficulty of musical, lyrical, or poetic expression, the poem asserts, is limited by the fact that only music and poetry can define music and poetry. Put otherwise, the poem's troubling of logic's authority, and its valorization of the poetic, presents Nancy's point regarding literature as the absolute of philosophy. As we are dealing here not with logical propositions, but with poetic truths, there is no point of urgent concern. Still, the very paradoxical nature of the situation motivates a retreat into the physical, a movement away from abstraction and anxiety to the familiar:

> it is a matter of
> some importance
> that thought resolve
> in metaphor
>
> and that the metaphor
> be flesh and that the
> flesh be warm . . . [95]

This shift in the direction of the poetic dynamic mirrors quite well Komar's description of Rilke's development in the first six of the *Duino Elegies*: "The poet comes to understand that it is not the grand gesture . . . that ameliorates self-consciousness, but rather the small, familiar interaction."[96] In turning away from the anxieties of time, Hunter and Rilke recontextualize problems poetically, seeking resolution not via an approach to the transcendent or immersion in the abstractions of thought, but instead via figurative language that returns the artist to the ground of the living, breathing world.

Another poem that offers a concise example of this Rilkean tendency to weigh a transcendent against an earthly experience is Hunter's "A Clatter Like Fine Mist." The piece contrasts the Empyrean and the sublunary realms of sound, ultimately arguing for the virtue of the latter. Representing the former are images of a certain kind of perfect world, one in which the audience will find the elements united as respondents in the form of "the ocean's applause / and clouds for critics."[97] In this sort of ideal realm, in which emblems encompassing all of nature join to sing praises, "silence is memory." When all is united in an eternal present, the distinction between sound and silence falls away, leaving nothing but a recollection of the contrasts between varieties of experience on which our earthly, differentiated reality depends.[98] Against that ideal the poem weighs a different sort of silence, one that is found in the interval between the ringing of "enormous bells."[99] This sort of silence unfolds in time. It is not the eternal calm of the unified whole, but a silence that takes shape in a world in which one has

> sensation and a chance
> to fall far enough to consider
> the possibility of redemption.[100]

While the poem refrains from explicitly aligning itself with the Empyrean or the sublunary, it does conclude with consideration of the everyday world, which is rich with "sensation" and "possibility." With such an ending, Hunter's poem moves beyond its balanced consideration of the transcendent and the mundane to follow Rilke in nudging the reader away from the former in favor of the latter.

A more elaborate example of this tendency may be found in title poem of *Sentinel*, one of several longer pieces that Hunter published. It, too, presents a dynamic tension resolved only in the poetic practice of devotion to the everyday. At the heart of that tension are competing views of the nature of poetry. On the one hand, it presents readers with insights regarding the flux of appearances; on the other, it testifies to the immutability of true beauty. The sentinel in question is the figure of the poet, who begins the sequence watching "from" a "tower beside the sea" and offering reports on what he sees that answer in a circuitous fashion:

> Not to seem to say
> yet to have said: this
> is the measure of saying.[101]

After one day's watch, the sentinel-poet falls asleep, and three strangers he earlier saw approaching the tower write in his journal, declaring him a failure in two senses. In the first place, he cannot maintain any objectivity in his report, falling prey instead to the ways that "desire" and "concept" subjectivize his seeing and saying.[102] Second, his words fall short of the mark in terms of articulating immutable truths, a situation the three visitors seek to address by speaking "only to angels in prime numbers."[103] Bringing the angels into the world will effect a "completion," reaching a state of stable and peaceful conformity.[104] Later in the poem, the sentinel awakens and remarks on the notes left by the three, surprisingly telling readers that "the hand in which the words / were written" is his "own."[105] In sum, the poem presents the work of the poet as a saying that dances between an impulse to present a totalizing view of the world and a sincere effort to articulate the fluctuant terms of quotidian existence.

"Sentinel" ultimately unites these two controlling tendencies of the poet in the image of a flower, the beauty of which outshines but is utterly dependent on the unremarkable seed from which it grew and the relatively ugly stem on which it relies. The image first appears in the following lines:

> A stem twists in my hand,
> seeking after its flower but
> the flower knows not the stem,
> acknowledges no kinship
> to the stalk of its arising.
>
> I have a message: Beware!
> The stem knows not the root
> and the flower presents no seed.
> Yet there is perfume in the air
> of a phantom blossom blooming.[106]

The flower that does not know or acknowledge its dependence on the other parts of the plant on which it grows can also be found in Rilke's fifth elegy, especially the passage that reads:

> Around this center
> the Rose of Looking
> blossoms and sheds.
> Around this pounding pestle,
> this self pollinating pistle [sic]
> producing petals of ennui,
> blooms of customary apathy
> speciously shine with
> superfluous smiles.[107]

The lines are sonically a strong translation in Hunter's hands. The alliterative *Stampfer*, *Stempel*, and *Staub* of Rilke's original are echoed in the "pestle," "pistle," and "petals" of Hunter's translation and seem to lurk behind the "stem," "seed," and "stalk" of Hunter's "Sentinel." As Judith Ryan argues, these and other alliterative components of Rilke's original suggest that any beauty offered by a self-pollinating and self-absorbed flower such as the

LIKE AN ANGEL   189

one the poems describe will be imperfect, monotonous in its monovocality.[108] This monotony is subjected to critique by both Rilke and Hunter, and Hunter's poem does so in part by returning to images of plants in its final pages:

> If Beauty is to be,
> it must root in what
> is less than beautiful;
> allow itself to sprout
> shabby foliage serving
> as a rough protective
> cover for its seed.[109]

In aligning beauty with potential, and in turning partially away from flowers that exhibit stasis and containment and more toward those that exemplify fluidity and change, Hunter indeed follows the lead of Rilke's fifth elegy, which valorizes poetry as an art that is particularly well equipped to represent both stability and its opposite. The fifth elegy's unfolding of this theme begins with a consideration of acrobats as presented in Picasso's *La Famille des Saltimbanques*. In Rilke's description, the figures of the painting are forever frozen in space and time. Their poses may suggest movement, but the motion is never more than a suggestion. Poetry, on the other hand, can capture the motion of the acrobats. Rilke's acrobats "twist and catapult," arranging themselves in particular shapes, only to fall out of those shapes and reform in others an instant later.[110] The most beautiful moments of their art may be the most impressive feats of their tumbling, such as the highest leap or the fastest swing. Judith Ryan reminds us, however, that these instances are fleeting, and most of the performance shows the audience that the glimpses of seeming transcendence they offer are granted only due to the acrobats' constant falling back to earth.[111] In this sense, the acrobats are excellent subjects for Rilke's poetry, and for two reasons. In the first place, their activity reveals that the power of poetry derives, in part, from its capacity to capture change, a quality that eludes painting and the other static arts. In the second, the acrobat's repeated return to earth brings them back to their origins, forcing a confrontation with a sort of humble stability. While Rilke will ultimately dismiss the acrobats as a model for the poet—their motivations are the cheap ones of applause and lucre—they remain a powerful symbol of Rilke's recognition in the fifth elegy that change and stasis are components of both the mundane and the beautiful, and that neither transience nor transcendence alone is the whole story of poetic art, a lesson to which Hunter's "Sentinel" also attests by confirming that a flower must "root in what / is less than beautiful."

HUNTER, RILKE, AND THE TASK OF TRANSFORMATION

The preceding remarks on "Warmup," "A Clatter Like Fine Mist," and "Sentinel" are guided, in large part, by one of the strongest dynamics that governs the development of the *Duino Elegies*: the poet's slow turn away from appeals to the transcendent and toward a different sense of the poetic work. This different sense has several components, but they all depend on a reorientation in the direction of openness and transformation. Komar writes of this stage of Rilke's poetics that "the poetic task is the creation of an aesthetic space in which the image takes on meaning far beyond what the self alone can provide."[112] The evocation of "meaning far beyond what the self alone can provide" echoes that channeling of the generative energies to which the Romantic fragment directs its readers. In the *Duino Elegies*, the mechanism of creation is one of internalization—the engagement of consciousness with an object or situation which is taken in by the poet and then altered fundamentally into an image that imbues that everyday object or situation with persistent duration. In this way, that which is subject to the fluctuating changes of the mortal world can be preserved, given a place in eternity, while the artist's role in the process carries her out of any solipsism by embedding the poetic consciousness in a deep engagement with reality. The seventh elegy offers a key passage pointing to the power, and poetic necessity, of this engagement:

> Each of you had her hour,
> or if not an hour,
> an instant, at least,
> between two moments when
> life burst into flower.
> Every blessed petal.
> Your veins throbbed with it.
> . . . .
> but even the most visible
> of joys cannot be seen
> until transformed—within.[113]

Some lines later, he continues:

> Yes, if one thing survives
> before which we genuflected,
> which we served or worshiped,
> it passes intact into the invisible.[114]

As Rilke here describes it, the result of the engagement of the poet with the world is a reciprocal process—the imagination extends itself, reaching from the poet out into the world, and then affirms the value of that part of the world by internalizing and transforming it, preserving it in the space of the poetic image. In this way, the poem recognizes that transcendence is not needed for joy, and that poetic power comes not from escape from the world but from the power of the word.

A consideration of those aspects of Hunter's poetics that are indebted to Rilke must therefore treat his use of this Rilkean variety of poetic image, and to explore this point, this chapter turns to a poem of Hunter's that offers his most direct and extensive poetic comment on the Grateful Dead, "An American Adventure." "An American Adventure" was conceived as the first piece in a sequence called *The Bride of Entropy*, which was also to include "Silver Marbles" and "The Bride of Entropy," and was due for publication by Penguin.[115] However, that book did not appear. Instead, "An American Adventure" was collected in *Sentinel*, and "Silver Marbles" and "The Bride of Entropy" later appeared, alongside a poem presented as the sequence's fourth section, "Number and None," on Hunter's website. Like Rilke's *Duino Elegies*, *The Bride of Entropy* series is, in part, devoted to an interrogation of the validity of the artistic process and the power of the artist, and it returns repeatedly to Rilkean subject matter, images, and movement, particularly in the case of the poem's concern with the action of the poetic mind and the work of poetic language in relation to the world.

"An American Adventure" opens with the establishment of two elements. The first offers a comment on the nature of poetic saying, and the second presents an image that encapsulates the project of the early Grateful Dead. Central to its definition of poetic speech is a relation between immediacy and poetic validity:

> If what was seen is to be spoken of,
> it must be said all in a breath or
> it becomes something else: a glyph,
> a gloss, a reflection of a vase bearing
> an artificial flower on a living stem.[116]

In these lines, Hunter asserts, truth is embodied—if it emerges, it must do so via the poet's breath. There is something here of the situational immediacy of musical improvisation, and also of a more general resistance to calcification—the false flower, the mirror, and the glyph are all images familiar from Rilke's verse, and each of them characterizes varieties of pseudopoetic speech that genuine poetry supersedes. So, while Hunter's presentation of poetic speech here sounds to some degree more like Ginsberg than Rilke, it shares with the latter poet belief in the importance of inspiration and concern with the distinction between more and less authentic modes of expression.

Having advanced a controlling formulation of the poetic, Hunter proffers the poem's first image:

> Behold a city half visible along
> the cloud line, studded with
> faraway spires, domes, turrets
> and other paraphernalia with
> which deep-seated yearning
> tends to outfit a horizon.
>
> A beckoning beam glimmers
> across furlongs of pale grain
> waving between us and what seems
> our individual and collective destiny.[117]

The fantastic city, with its echoes of Samuel Taylor Coleridge's "Kubla Khan," John Winthrop's "city upon a hill," Katharine Lee Bates's "America the Beautiful," and the "white wheat / Wavin' in the wind" of "Mountains of the Moon" is an image of the ambitions of Hunter, the Grateful Dead, and their community. Too, much like the statue of Rilke's "Archaic Torso of Apollo," the fabulous city calls to the poet, demanding action rather than mere detached observation. Despite its brilliance, the vision as formulated in this passage at first sounds too naive to be maintained, and the poem immediately begins to interrogate its validity, much as Ken Kesey interrogates the legacy of Neal Cassady in *The Further Inquiry*. On one hand, archival documentation of the 1960s contradicts the glory of the vision:

> snapshots
> from the era indicate that it
> might have been otherwise

with "no evidence of spires" and "unadorned city concrete" that is "not all that clean," rather than the beauty initially set forth.[118] On the other hand, Hunter remains suspicious of the historical record's disenchantment with the image, asserting, "Time is the great counterfeiter—/ it was not like that. I know."[119] The opening of the poem constructs a test case through a Rilkean lens, posing three central questions: Were the ambitions of the Grateful Dead false? Or were they an impractical pursuit of the transcendent—the sort of option to which Rilke is first drawn but from which he later turns? Or were they true and directed toward something more immediate, less otherworldly?

While much of the remainder of the first part of "An American Adventure" investigates assaults on the visionary image, even asserting its total collapse at points, the second part returns the reader to a reformulation of it, here carried into the post-Garcia-coma days of the late 1980s:

> The spires of another day are
> finally visible again, still set
> firmly on the horizon, though
> the beckoning beam no longer
> seems to operate . . .
> could it be that we've arrived?
> Then why are the spires still
> at a distance? Because that's
> what they are—they're the
> *faraway* spires. That's all.[120]

The simplicity and colloquial verbal shrug of that closing "That's all" pulls the spires out of the realm of the transcendent, making of them a component of Hunter's vision of San Francisco. Too, the distant spires proffer themselves as emblems of the poetic spirit reaching outward, entering foreign spaces rather than remaining isolated from them. This clarification of the image's nature certifies its provenance and arbitrates between different interpretations of it. The fabulous city is neither an unattainable or transcendent alternative to the world, nor merely the bare facts of the documented past against which Hunter first tested the image. Instead, it is a presentation of the world as encountered and transformed by the poetic imagination. "An American Adventure" closes by conjoining that conclusion with a return to the poem's opening assertions regarding inspiration and breath:

>   should the thing
> that wants saying not be said
> in a breath, so that it steps forth
> and *stays* said
>
> . . . .
>
> it might just as well never be said at all.[121]

With this "*stays* said," Hunter acknowledges that the articulation of the vision of the everyday world transformed into poetic image proffers a means to escape both transcendence and impermanence, showing a path that overcomes the transient without unresolvable devotion to something outside the world.

As it "steps forth" and "*stays* said," the central image of "An American Adventure" answers to the permanency Rilke described as the heart of the transformative power of the poetic imagination. To assert that *The Bride of Entropy* as a whole is a Rilkean poem would be to misrepresent the piece. Yet, taken together with the other Rilkean elements of Hunter's poetry, the image of the fabulous city illustrates just how convincingly Rilke's example modeled for Hunter a means to conceive of the poetic voice, to delineate the power and authenticity of his art, and to find space for that poetic power to assert itself while negotiating the difficult terrain between the ephemeral and the eternal. In these ways, the writings that emerged after Hunter's translations of Rilke's works were published suggest that those translations were not just a temporary preoccupation, but an ongoing source of inspiration, which observation contributes much to an understanding of why Hunter's publication record changed so dramatically in the early 1990s. More broadly, Hunter's periodic use of poetic strategies and perspectives modeled by Rilke earns the Austrian poet a place alongside Joyce, Eliot, and those other Modernist writers on whose works Hunter would draw when composing both poems and songs.

The cases of the Modernist forebears to Hunter's artistic sensibilities are by no means the only ones for which listeners and readers must account; if nothing else, the earlier chapters of this book hopefully reveal something of the band's broad engagement with literary predecessors. In discussing his poetry, too, Hunter explains that his net was cast wide. In an interview, for example, he mentions that his initial work as a poet was rather old-fashioned, that it "harkened back about a century," but also that he was awakened to contemporary verse by encountering Lew Welch's *On Out*, and had since followed the poems of such major late twentieth-century American writers as James Merrill and John Ashbery, as well as being fascinated by the work of the Language poets, who were at the cutting edge of contemporary American poetry at the time of his remarks.[122] So, while Hunter's poetry signals his close reading of Modernism in general and Rilke in particular, the work of understanding his poetry in relation to the tradition must be an ongoing scholarly effort. Ultimately, like images of a world transformed by the poetic imagination in Rilke's poetry, Hunter's poetic spirit continued developing, honing its sensibilities, expanding its reach, and drawing on an ever-wider set of models as it grappled with central preoccupations of the Grateful Dead.

Conclusion
ALL THAT'S STILL UNSUNG

The preceding chapters have argued that the Grateful Dead's songs engage various forms of literary fragmentation, from the grotesque recombination of dead flesh in the construction of Frankenstein's creature to the disoriented estrangement of the self that is central to Rimbaud's figure of the poet. These presences, written under the sign of incompletion, dramatize the philosophical difficulties discussed in this volume's introduction in relation particularly to Jean-Luc Nancy's engagements with the German Romantics. Such difficulties include, but are by no means restricted to, the notion that the completion of philosophy lies beyond philosophy, claims that the poetic fragment is especially amenable to the expression of the perpetually incomplete process of becoming that defines genuine poetry, and conceptions of the self-presentation of art as staging an endless dance between form and chaos, characterized by an open freedom from which emerge both aesthetic objects and philosophical thought. This conception of the fragment as more powerful due to its productive incompletion sits well with those remarks by Jerry Garcia and Robert Hunter about the degree to which the members of the Grateful Dead are drawn as both listeners and composers to the kinds of songs they first encountered in the folk tradition, which stage evocative ambiguities that leave audiences pondering open questions rather than sated by truisms and platitudes.

Recognizing the degree to which the Grateful Dead's songs work as fragments that exist in intertextual relation not only to such popular sources as the American and British folk traditions or the works of the band's musical contemporaries, but also to materials that are generally regarded as exemplary instances of canonical literary works, allows for a much richer sense of their achievement. Rather than being only a successful psychedelic rock and roll band, the Grateful Dead proved an inclination toward repeated engagement with the primal openness that offers the space through which song can emerge. Intertextual conversation with poems and fictions by Rimbaud, Mary Shelley, Allen Ginsberg, Arthur Conan Doyle, Robert Burns, Rainer Maria Rilke, James Joyce, William Shakespeare, William Carlos Williams, Bob Dylan, Johann Wolfgang von Goethe, T. S. Eliot, Walt Whitman, Lord Tennyson, Jack Kerouac, and others marked that engagement, which inspired the band's songwriting in direct and indirect ways. Indeed, one path that this book hopefully indicates would lead the curious in the direction of other literary figures and works that are important to the band. Ken Kesey and Kurt Vonnegut, while mentioned here and there in the preceding pages, did not receive the attention that a different version of this text may have given them and are exceptionally promising choices for extended consideration. The place of biblical texts, nursery rhymes, and folk and fairy tales in the lyrics could likewise bear substantial attention. Furthermore, the connections between the Grateful Dead and the Beats could justify one or more additional studies equal in length to this one. In addition, many in the Grateful Dead's circle produced writings that may be seen as complements or supplements to the work of the song lyrics: Alan Trist and Brigid Meier are published poets and essayists; Maureen Hunter's art skates the line between the visual, the written, and the sung on album covers, around liner notes, and in book illustrations; and numerous near and distant relations have published memoirs, autobiographies, reflective essays, and reminiscences, such as Rhoney Stanley's *Owsley and Me* and Paul Perry's *On the Bus*. Furthermore, the poetry and other texts by the band's lyricists, including works by Robert Hunter not dealt with herein, as well as the many published and unpublished pieces by Robert M. Petersen, are essential companions to the lyrics. Each of these, and other texts from the pens of the band's friends and coconspirators, would serve admirably as an entrance into the Grateful Dead's work, world, and literary identity.

While the preceding chapters direct their attention to the matters described above, this conclusion reverses the terms of the argument. Rather than considering the Grateful Dead in relation to texts by literary authors and philosophers whose careers preceded or coincided with that of the band, it instead considers what is gained when we think about the band's songwriting as evidence of participation in a current of literary exercise that passes the aesthetic values and conceptual preoccupations of select earlier texts forward to other, future writers. Aspects of this consideration were indirectly engaged in the earlier chapter on the Grateful Dead and Dylan. For the next few pages, this book will look at the band in terms of three broad areas of inquiry: texts that treat the Grateful Dead as a subject in its own right; texts that employ the Grateful Dead as an icon of a particular incarnation of late twentieth-century American counterculture; and, finally, works that employ the Grateful Dead's lyrics as structural or stylistic intertexts for later literary expression. The lines between these categories are porous, but still provide a useful shape for what follows.

The first of these areas, the band treated in propria persona, includes what are likely the most familiar texts of those considered in this conclusion, and the most significant among them were written by the late twentieth century's best-regarded journalists and essayists. Perhaps the most famous example is Tom Wolfe's *The Electric Kool-Aid Acid Test*. That book was discussed in chapter 1, and it remains, in many ways, a high-water mark for writing about the band's early scene. Scholars of the Grateful Dead may balk at this assertion, as there are definitely problems with Wolfe's reportage. One complaint may simply be a matter of focus. Figures like Dennis McNally and Blair Jackson have produced books devoted to the band and its members, while Wolfe makes them supporting characters in a work that focuses much more on Kesey and the other Merry Pranksters. A second complaint may be that Wolfe was not present for some of the earlier and wilder gatherings described in the text, a point that makes his information secondhand at best, or even dubiously sourced in some cases—qualities that ultimately undercut the authenticity that participatory journalism can allow.

Despite such reservations, Wolfe's book does more than almost any other contemporary document to capture the spirit of the Acid Tests and the band's participation in them. For the Grateful Dead scholar, his best passages provide a glimpse of the freedom regarding playing that Garcia often identified as the defining feature of the experience: "Those who were . . . not on the bus . . . would come to the realization that there was no schedule. The Grateful Dead did not play in *sets*; no eight numbers to a set, then a twenty-five-minute break, and so on, four or five sets and then the close-out. The Dead might play one number for five minutes or thirty minutes. Who kept time? Who *could* keep time. . . . The Dead could get just as stoned as anyone else."[1] Wolfe also offers arguments for the centrality of the Grateful Dead to the development of a new idiom. He writes, "Through the Dead's experience with the Pranksters was born the sound known as 'acid rock.'"[2] More elaborate is the following: "'Mixed Media' entertainment—this came straight out of the Acid Tests' combination of light and movie projections, strobes, tapes, rock 'n' roll, black light. 'Acid rock'—the sound of the Beatles' *Sergeant Pepper* album and the high-vibrato electronic sounds of the Jefferson Airplane, the Mothers of Invention, and many other groups—the mothers of it all were the Grateful Dead at the Acid Tests."[3] One may argue whether these claims are right or wrong, but they are now familiar and have become, for many readers, authoritative, and it is worth remembering that Wolfe's book was published in 1968. There has been, in other words, a journalistic recognition, almost from the first, that the Grateful Dead was a central node for some of the key changes in popular music and American culture in the latter part of the twentieth century.

Of a piece with Wolfe, but more enthusiastic in his celebrations of the Grateful Dead, and just about everything else for that matter, was Hunter S. Thompson. Thompson had been present for many of the earliest Merry Prankster events, but his turn to appreciation of the Grateful Dead was somewhat delayed. In a 1967 letter to John Grabree at *Playboy*, for example, Thompson writes that "Denson and Country Joe (McDonald) are flaming intellectuals, compared to ... Jerry Garcia of the Grateful Dead."[4] A few years on the scene made a tremendous difference, and by 1970, Thompson was writing to Carey McWilliams at *The Nation*, "At the moment my writing room is full of 'New Speedway Boogie' by the Grateful Dead. It says more than anything I've read in five years."[5] A letter written about a month later, to John Lombardi at *Rolling Stone*, increases the stakes: "If the Grateful Dead came to town, I'd beat my way in with a fucking tire iron, if necessary. I think *Workingman's Dead* is the heaviest thing since *Highway 61* and 'Mr. Tambourine Man' (with the ... exception of Herbie Mann's *Memphis Underground*)."[6] Later in the same letter, he offers a top-ten list of recent records, with *Workingman's Dead* in fourth place, behind only Mann and two entries from Dylan.

Thompson surprises a bit by attributing *Workingman's Dead* to "Warlocks et al."[7] Lombardi and others hip to the early San Francisco scene may have remembered that the Grateful Dead had been the Warlocks, but Thompson's use of the name is revealing. The statement is a referential one, but it is also inflected by a rhetorically valuable deictic component, effectively the declaration "I was there at the start." This part of Thompson's missive thus treats the Grateful Dead as a marker of social belonging, shared experience, and common cause. These qualities are valuable not only in courting publishers, but also in terms of defining the sort of political cohort desirable in the context of Thompson's run for sheriff of Aspen, Colorado, in 1970 and his career as political commentator. Readers of later volumes from Thompson would encounter references to the band sprinkled throughout. These moments serve much as the mention of the Warlocks did in the letter to Lombardi—there is a common cultural store that implies values and social orientations that appeal to the cognoscenti.

To the list of premiere journalism that engaged the band and its scene in the early years must be added Joan Didion's *Slouching Towards Bethlehem*, which appraises the Haight in part through interactions with the Grateful Dead. Her take on the San Francisco scene is almost entirely negative, beginning with the suspicion of an "uneasy apprehension" defining the national mood and the declaration of the Bay Area as the most apparent site of "social hemorrhaging." The band appears briefly in the profile of an anonymous teenager Didion meets in the Psychedelic Shop, whom she later encounters in Golden Gate Park, "when the Grateful Dead are playing."[8] A few pages later, Didion is in Sausalito, at the band's rehearsal space. Neither the band members nor the music receives much attention, as Didion focuses on the "little girls" hanging out while the band practices. The only quote is attributed to Garcia, in a comment about playing the Cheetah in Los Angeles: "We were up there drinking beer where Lawrence Welk used to sit."[9] The remark seems detached from not only the context, as was presumably the point in an essay about how the Haight lacks any moral or political center, but also, and more frustratingly, the history and personalities of the band. For Didion, the hippies are finally resistant to facility with and responsibility for language. She generalizes about the people she meets, "They feed back exactly what is given them. Because they do not believe in words . . . their only proficient vocabulary is society's platitudes."[10] From the feminists to the most lost runaway, for Didion, the Haight is little more than an accumulation of vapid clichés.

Didion is, of course, an outstanding stylist, and this essay is one of her great early successes, but one notes several points of concern about it, in terms of its status as reliable reportage on both the Grateful Dead and the Haight in general. Thompson's take on the same scene in the same year is an instructive point of comparison. The election of Ronald Reagan was a moment of disenchantment for the Haight, Thompson explains, and the "scene developed very suddenly in the winter of 1966–1967 from the quiet, neo-Bohemian enclave that it had been for four or five years to the crowded defiant dope fortress that it is today."[11] Members of the Grateful Dead and their immediate circle often acknowledged as much, and their journeys away from and eventual abandonment of the Haight in 1966 and 1967—for Los Angeles, for New Mexico, for Olompali, for Lagunitas, and for territory beyond the peninsula generally—were their response. As Sue Swanson succinctly explained, in remarking on changes in 1967, "The next thing we knew, there were tour buses coming down Haight Street. Then we were out of there."[12] That the band and its circle recognized exactly the problem Thompson thoughtfully diagnosed and Didion presented with confusion, detachment, and published dismissal may leave the informed reader of Didion more than a little frustrated. There is an opportunity missed here, and it is to some degree a victim of Didion's reportorial method, which Kathleen Vandenberg claims operates "ironically, dismissively, condescendingly." Rather than fully assessing the Haight and acknowledging that even some of the people she interviewed there share her concerns about it, she frames the countercultural ground zero in terms of a vacuous anti-intellectualism on the cusp of total social and spiritual disaster.[13] The Grateful Dead fan reading Didion's piece feels the loss of a chance for an extended first-person account of an underdocumented space important to the band's early history, while readers in general will find it hard to appreciate what the Haight had been and, by contrast, was becoming. Intriguingly, Didion remained cognizant of the band long after this essay was composed. In addition to writing nonfiction about the Haight, she includes characters named Garcia and Weir in her novel *The Last Thing He Wanted*.

Didion's synecdochic treatment of the Grateful Dead as an emblem of the Haight is similar to mentions of the band in poetry and fiction by a wide variety of authors. In most cases, these instances are primarily a matter of fleshing out characters or establishing tone. In Philip K. Dick's *VALIS*, for example, a character named Gloria is situated via her attitude to the band. Here, she is conversation with the novel's protagonist, Horselover Fat:

> "My favorite Dead album is *Workingman's Dead*," Gloria said at one point. "But I don't think they should advocate taking cocaine. A lot of kids listen to rock."
>
> "They don't advocate it. The song's just about someone taking it. And it killed him, indirectly; he smashed up his train."[14]

The fact that Fat has listened closely enough to identify the song "Casey Jones" as antidrug sets the stage for the novel's disenchantment with chemical intoxication, but Dick's passage also illustrates that he, like some of his characters, has listened to the Grateful Dead enough to offer informed comments on its lyrics. This inference is supported by the appearance of the phrase "rat in a drain ditch"—a line from the Grateful Dead's "He's Gone"— in Dick's *The Transmigration of Timothy Archer*, the final book in the trilogy that begins with *VALIS*.[15]

A similar sort of shorthand characterization is evident in David Foster Wallace's novel *Infinite Jest*, in which appreciation of the Grateful Dead distinguishes a character who is among the many figures on the fringe of the text's central narratives—Dr. Robert "Sixties Bob" Monroe. Sixties Bob first appears only briefly, as an unknowing link in the criminal distribution of the experimental film that is at the heart of the novel, but he later wins a descriptive passage of greater length due to his connection to a fence named Kite, an underworld associate of one of the novel's protagonists, Don Gately.[16] In this later instance, Sixties Bob is described as a "septuagenarian pink-sunglasses-and-Nehru-jacket-wearing" treatment specialist who had "in yore days interned at Sandoz and was one of T. Leary's original circle ... at T. Leary's now legendary house in West Newton MA, and is now ... the intimate acquaintance of Kite, because Sixties Bob is an even bigger Grateful Dead fanatic maybe even than Kite, and sometimes got together with Kite and several other Dead devotees ... and argued about which Dead shows and bootlegs of Dead shows were the greatest of all time in different regards, and just basically had a hell of a time."[17] Sixties Bob is clearly a type, and his minibiography a good example of the proliferation of briefly glimpsed peripheral storylines that support the primary action of Wallace's maximalist fiction. He is also, intriguingly, an example of the degree to which Grateful Dead fans have remained a strong presence, even in texts from which the band and its music are largely absent.

Dick and Wallace offer fictions in which the name of the band and the enthusiasm of its fans serve as a sort of shorthand to sketch character and mood. Contemporary poets deploy the moniker to similar purpose. Adrian C. Louis's "The Boy Distinctly Remembers" is one example. Another comes from James Merrill, whose *The Changing Light at Sandover* was praised by Hunter in his 1992 conversation with Steve Silberman.[18] In his "Self-Portrait in Tyvek™ Windbreaker," a sort of oblique engagement with John Ashbery's "Self-Portrait in a Convex Mirror" (another poem Hunter praises), Merrill describes his preparations for the gym, one part of which is the selection of a soundtrack for his workout.[19] He settles on the songs of Roberto Murolo, explaining, "I picked his tape in lieu of something grosser / Or loftier, say the Dead or Arvo Pärt."[20] Merrill's erudition and passion for composed music would incline us to think that the Estonian contemporary classical composer Pärt would be an obvious choice, but while he does label the band "grosser" in comparison, the reader might note with appreciation that Merrill at least considers the Grateful Dead fair competition for the rarefied musical company the poem offers. I was fortunate enough to visit Merrill's house in 2008 as a guest of Piotr Gwiazda, then the writer in residence, and again for a conference on Merrill and his work in 2009. On both occasions, I leafed through some of the several shelves' worth of 33 and 78 rpm records that remained in Merrill's Stonington, Connecticut, home, even several years after his death. Although I am sorry to say I did not uncover any Grateful Dead albums hiding in the enviably extensive collection of operas, it is nevertheless charming to know that this VW-driving poet once had a Grateful Dead tape or two in the collection.

While the essayists, novelists, and poets discussed in the preceding paragraphs invoke the Grateful Dead and its fans for a variety of purposes, it is not generally the case that their writing engages the band and its music. This situation does not, however, always obtain. Robert Cooperman's poetry provides indispensable examples of the latter, collected in books like his *Not Too Old to Rock and Roll* and *A Tale of the Grateful Dead*. Steven Brust's *Brokedown Palace* and Allen Steele's *Orbital Decay* were published by Ace, an essential publisher of speculative fiction. Both books wear the influence of the Grateful Dead on their sleeve, as do several by George R. R. Martin, including those in his hugely popular *A Song of Ice and Fire* series.[21] Mainstream publishing houses have supported Grateful Dead–adjacent fictions such as William J. Craddock's *Be Not Content* (Doubleday), Daniel Jones's *After Lucy* (William Morrow), and Mitch Myers's *The Boy Who Cried Freebird* (Harper), and smaller but well-respected presses with outstanding lists have also supported literary fiction related to the Grateful Dead. Examples of the latter include Dave Housley's *If I Knew the Way, I Would Take You Home* (Dzanc) and Dean Budnick's *Might as Well* (Rare Bird).

One example of a more robust engagement with the band's aesthetic is Richard Brautigan's 1968 poem "The Day They Busted the Grateful Dead," which was inspired by the October 1967 arrest of Bob Weir, Ron McKernan, and several friends and colleagues on charges of marijuana possession following a raid on the band's house at 710 Ashbury. The poem concludes with the following stanza:

> The day they busted the Grateful Dead
> turned like the wet breath of alligators
> blowing up balloons the size of the
> Hall of Justice.[22]

The appearance of the alligators in this closing stanza echoes their presence in each of the earlier ones. They collectively nod to the band's song "Alligator," which entered setlists in early 1967, but also lend the whole a sense of menace.

At the same time, the absurd balloons have a touch of the Prankster in them, and the surreal image of alligators inflating balloons on a scale comparable to the center of San Francisco's legal authority is more risible than otherwise. Doubly deflating is the ambiguity that resides in the "blowing up" of the balloons. The pun allows one to consider that the Hall of Justice is itself nothing more than a plastic shell full of hot air, one that may be "blown up" in the sense of its self-inflating importance or, alternatively, "blown up" in the sense of being exploded as an emblem of authority by the absurdity of bringing legal pressure to bear on the Grateful Dead's possession of marijuana.

Brautigan's piece strikes the perfect note in the sense that it presents the bust at 710 Ashbury in the appropriate tonal register. The event was an attempt at political theater on the part of San Francisco law enforcement, but the fallout offered an invaluable opportunity for the band to stage a critical response. The news media were, of course, on board, eager for a scoop, and the bust promised a salacious perspective on the (il)legality of Haight-Ashbury mores. However, as Grateful Dead historians such as Dennis McNally and Nicholas Meriwether have explained, the band's management recognized the opportunity for both satisfying moral outrage and publicity. Manager Danny Rifkin and friend Harry Shearer penned a speech, read at a press conference following the bust, that was effectively the band's first publicity statement.[23] That this statement struck out boldly at the persecution of, and draconian punishments imposed on, marijuana users in 1967 was a risk, but a calculated one, as few gestures could more effectively cement the band's underground credibility than its outspoken rejection of the principles behind, and the media circus that surrounded, the bust, even as the trial and sentencing for those arrested still hung in the air. Such countercultural credibility would earn more than a little attention, with portions of the statement being reprinted as a broadside circulated in the Haight and reproduced in a variety of periodicals, including the inaugural issue of *Rolling Stone*.[24] Brautigan's poem echoes these facets of the day the Grateful Dead were busted—the event was not just an arrest, but an opportunity to win hearts, minds, and ears.

Among other pieces inspired by the Grateful Dead and the scene that surrounds them are those Douglas Coupland collects in his *Polaroids from the Dead*. The book pairs Polaroid photographs with prose sketches that straddle the line between documentary essay and fiction. The first section of the text, titled "Polaroids from the Dead," presents prose snapshots of Grateful Dead concert scenes. The second offers essays on topics in popular culture, and the final, the "Brentwood Notebook," is an extended essay on that Los Angeles zip code—and Grateful Dead fans might speculate about the significance of that neighborhood's name in relation to keyboardist Brent Mydland. The first section's texts, Coupland explains in his introduction, were inspired by what he "'experienced' at a series of Grateful Dead concerts at the Oakland–Alameda County Coliseum the weekend before" he "turned thirty, in 1991."[25] As Coupland's birthday is December 30, these would be the shows of December 27 and 28, 1991. Throughout the book, Coupland explores what he calls a moment in the early 1990s during which "American society seemed to be living in a 1980s hangover and was unclear in its direction."[26] This lack of direction pervades the portraits of concertgoers, whose conversations circle around matters of corporatization, consumer culture, intoxication, and the collapse of intergenerational values. Despite the emptiness that characterizes the text's portraits of fans and the scene writ large, the final chapter of "Polaroids from the Dead," "How Clear Is Your Vision of Heaven?," offers a tonic—a vision of "a core truth, a germ that refuses to die, an essence of purity and love" that allows at least one character, Columbia, to "live her own life peacefully."[27]

On its surface, Columbia's conviction regarding the "core truth" is ambiguous. It could be an ennobling vision, one that offers potential spiritual rejuvenation to the more clueless among those Coupland describes. Alternately, the "core truth" may be an example of the most banal sort of useful fiction, a self-deception that is more attractive but no more valid than the platitudes and non sequiturs that plague the words and shape the actions of the book's less insightful characters. A few factors encourage a reading of the "core truth" in the former, more positive, sense, and they emerge via the book's most engaging presentations of narrative. One of these is a story that Columbia tells her children, as they drift off to sleep in a van in the Coliseum's parking lot. Here, she narrates a variation on the Fisher King legends in which the ruler of a land suffering extreme drought is visited repeatedly by a living skeleton, who explains that the populace's desire for rain is an emblem of their culture's spiritual deficiency. After repeated failures to heed the skeleton's words, the king capitulates, accepting the fact that he and the people of the kingdom suffer because they refuse to accept their own mortality. Once the king consents to the skeleton's wisdom, rain falls on the parched kingdom. By the time Columbia finishes, her children have drifted off to sleep, and rain begins to fall on the roof of the van in which they rest. Their dreams are of the skeleton, who dances.[28]

Storytelling does more in this narrative than merely carrying children off to bed. It provides generational continuity, and not only for Columbia and her children. Readers learn that she used to ask her mother about "the sixties," only to be told, "You just had to be there."[29] At the same time, her mother would "regale" her "with endless tales of that long-gone era."[30] These stories are those from which Columbia's "core truth" emerges, and there is within them, as well as within that truth, something that lies beyond representation. As her mother asserts, "It was like a friend you loved very much who died. . . . While you might make new friends in your life, the new friends can never truly appreciate your old, dead friend because no matter how much you try to describe that dead friend, your new friends never knew the old friends when the old friends were alive."[31] Columbia's mother has it both ways—she asserts that the past is beyond description while simultaneously offering "endless tales" describing it. To put that otherwise, she registers memory as a measure of loss, even as she builds bulwarks against loss via narration of the past.

Coupland thus ends the section of *Polaroids from the Dead* given over to the Grateful Dead with a fascinating glimpse of a set of productive narrative fragments. Columbia finds in her mother's storytelling a connection to her ancestors, and she thinks of herself in this regard as "a conduit through which has flowed an entity older and larger than herself."[32] That is, the mother's narratives are fragments that do not so much conclude as serve as a path that leads into the past, even as they stage the past as a route to the future. Columbia's bedtime story likewise narrates an opportunity for redemption, but the fact that this redemption unfolds most vividly in the dreaming heads of her young children means it may need to wait for its fulfillment in their future. Her stories, like those of her mother, will form the basis of her own children's tales, which will come to fruition only when her own present has become the past of memory. The conjunction of loss and completion here acknowledges their incompatibility, but simultaneously, even if paradoxically and hesitantly, suggests continuities between them. This collapsing of the distinction between the memory of paradise lost and the hope for paradise regained is the salvific message Columbia puts in the mouth of her fictional skeleton-prophet: "As we live, we are also dead."[33] The narrative's irresolution allows readers to recognize that Columbia's story offers a glimpse of a whole but does not, indeed cannot, entirely determine it. The narrative play between unification and extension, on the one hand, and resistance to final resolution, on the other, along with fluctuations between creation and destruction, suggest that key elements of the Romantic fragment flourish in this postmodern setting.

That Coupland's collection resists closure and foregrounds the fragmentary as suggestive but not totalizing recalls the remarks on the fragment that opened this book. This understanding of the fragment finds it among the most profound of forms, where its incompletion is not a fault but rather an evocative openness suggestive of a source that is both enriching and dangerous, one that is variable and inexhaustible, an indeterminate space from which music, poetry, and thought alike emerge. Jerry Garcia once explained regarding performance, "You can't repeat things because each time is different. The universe has changed. Everything has changed. And so each time you go out with this idea, you have to learn it all over again from the ground up because it's a new time, it's a new experience, and consequently, everything you know about it, you have to disallow. It's new."[34] This sense of performance, like the band's sense of songwriting, is one of ongoing invention, relishing fragments of ideas, melodies, inheritances, and, especially, those contexts that proffer openness to what is yet to emerge. Coupland's *Polaroids from the Dead* is among the texts that not only draws on the words and music of the Grateful Dead and the culture that surrounds them, but foregrounds the structural terms of that world, finding in the constellation of fragments they engaged, tested, and performed a model for its own narrative form.

Each of the literary texts discussed in the five preceding chapters is presented as context for the Grateful Dead's engagement with permutations of the literary-philosophical fragment. Coupland's text and the others mentioned in this conclusion provide a glimpse of what the Grateful Dead offer the literary in return. From their acknowledgment of the band's role as an emblem of the conundrums of late twentieth-century popular culture and as an inspirational embodiment of countercultural iconoclasm, to the band's modeling of a path of artistic openness and invention that courts its own mysterious origins, these literary texts show how the band members' activities reciprocated all they gained from the traditions that inspired them throughout their career. The moments of openness are the expression of a means to—and a model of—the sort of generative potential found when one disallows what one knows, favoring the emergence of the new.

In "Attics of My Life," the Grateful Dead describes a task that one might regard as a statement about the band's artistic intent. The speaker of the song declares the need for "Seeking all that's still unsung," envisioning a related space

> Where . . .
> . . . the secrets all are told
> And the petals all unfold

"The truth of love," "Reuben and Cérise" likewise proposes, is something that "an unsung song must tell." Garcia's remarks about every performance being different due to the principle of universal mutability remind us that this unfolding of the petals is more than elusive—something that transpires only in "the secret space of dreams" toward which any given performance directs our attention. Nevertheless, in repeatedly turning to that space—in seeking to sing those unsung songs that one must tell—the Grateful Dead's lyrics and music draw our attention not only to the moment of performance, but also to the fluid and free indeterminacy that is the precondition of poetic and philosophical production, as well as to the foundational openness of art.

Acknowledgments

I have often asserted that listening to the Grateful Dead teaches one how to listen to the Grateful Dead. Writing this book has repeatedly reminded me that the process is by no means one that unfolds in a closed system.

I want to thank the participants in and organizers of the meetings of the Grateful Dead Scholars Caucus and the Grateful Dead Studies Association. Many of you have provided constructive feedback, and even more have been a source of inspiration as I worked on this book. G. Ganter, Jesse Jarnow, Peter Richardson, Nathaniel Racine, and Jay Williams have been especially kind and helpful.

Likewise essential in terms of feedback and guidance are everyone involved with the Studies in the Grateful Dead series and at Duke University Press. In the case of the latter, Lisa Lawley, Alejandra Mejía, and Dean Smith deserve special mention for their patient support. Thank you, all—it has been great to work with you. The press also arranged for manuscript reviewers who offered very helpful feedback and for my wonderful copy editor, Nicholas Taylor. This book is better because of their advice, and I remain tremendously appreciative of the insights they shared. Special mention is absolutely due to Nicholas Meriwether. Nick, you are a superlative and inspiring example of just how much careful attention, sharp insights, and a steady hand can achieve.

Thanks are due as well to my colleagues at Boston University. My dean, Natalie McKnight, has been consistently supportive, as have my chairs, Thomas Finan, Kevin Stoehr, and Adam Sweeting. Extra appreciation is extended to the two research assistants who helped at points: Alexander Batt and Stephanie Stone.

I acknowledge, with thanks, the support of the editors of *Literary Matters*. An earlier version of this book's third chapter was published as an article in that journal, and I am grateful to its editors for giving the piece its first home and for granting me permission to reproduce much of that article's text in this volume. Ernest Suarez was especially helpful in both the case of original publication and that of republication permissions.

Finally, and most importantly, I would like to offer my thanks on a number of personal fronts. My father helped me get to my first Grateful Dead show, several decades ago. That I was able to bring him to events that included performances by Bill Kreutzmann, Phil Lesh, Bob Weir, and Mickey Hart many years later is a point of some satisfaction. My wife, Kathleen, has probably listened to more Grateful Dead music than anyone who is not much of a fan should reasonably have to hear. Kathleen, your support and the example of your own achievements as a scholar are responsible for any measure of success that these pages may achieve. And, most of all, thanks to my sons, who keep me grounded, remind me of the virtues of play, and do not roll their eyes too often when I take charge of our home and car playlists. I could not do it without you.

Notes

INTRODUCTION. BEYOND DESCRIPTION

1. Garcia, "Jerry Garcia Interview."
2. Garcia, "Peter Simon Interviews Jerry Garcia, 1975," 50:20.
3. See, for example, Garcia, "Grateful Dead Revisited"; Hunter, "Fractures of Unfamiliarity and Circumvention in Pursuit of a Nice Time"; Hunter, "Song Goes On," 117–21; Hunter and Garcia, "Hunter/Garcia; Words/Music," 209–10.
4. Shenk and Silberman, *Skeleton Key*, 51.
5. See, for example, Shan C. Sutton's "The Deadhead Community." The band also acknowledged the power of the music to change its audience. Drummer Mickey Hart asserted, "We're in the transportation business. We move minds" (McNally, *Long Strange Trip*, 538). Grateful Dead bassist Phil Lesh formulated the same point in a similar fashion: "The Grateful Dead group mind was in essence an engine of transformation. . . . As long as the only things we cared about were exploration and ecstasy, that's how long it remained pure" (Lesh, *Searching for the Sound*, 333).
6. Garcia, "Jerry Garcia Interview."
7. Trist and Dodd, *Complete Annotated Grateful Dead Lyrics*, 52.
8. Heching, "Grateful Dead Bassist and Founding Member Phil Lesh Has Died at 84."
9. Lesh, *Searching for the Sound*, 56n. Sturgeon is a descendent of Ralph Waldo Emerson (Williams, "Theodore Sturgeon, Storyteller," 330). One definition of "bleshing" in *More Than Human* reads, "Everyone all together being something, even if they all did different things. Two arms, two legs, one body, one head, all working together, although a head can't walk and arms can't think. . . . Maybe it was a mixture of 'blending' and 'meshing,' but . . . it was a lot more than that" (Sturgeon, *More Than*

Human, 148). In terms of the relation between this science-fictional concept and the music of the Grateful Dead, it is interesting that one of the characters has a hard time explaining bleshing and resorts to the metaphor of "a band," with "everyone playing different instruments with different techniques and different notes, to make a single thing move along together" (210). As another character puts it more succinctly elsewhere, *"Multiplicity is our first characteristic; unity our second"* (358). Sturgeon served as a model for Kurt Vonnegut's recurrent character Kilgore Trout; Vonnegut remarked of Trout in an interview, "He was modeled after Theodore Sturgeon, a really swell science fiction writer.... I think it's funny when someone is named after a fish" (Vonnegut, interview). Vonnegut's books were long a fascination of the Grateful Dead, and Garcia in particular.

10   Garcia, "Jerry Garcia Reflects."
11   Walker, "Anthem," 24.
12   Shenk and Silberman, *Skeleton Key*, 333, 336.
13   In traditional philosophical discourse, the "subject" is the mental construct that unifies our perceptions and thoughts into a self-identifying whole. One might think of it as that version of ourselves that we think of as "I."
14   Kant, *Critique of Pure Reason*, 152; Kant, *Kritik der reinen Vernunft*, A 13, B 27.
15   Kant, *Critique of Pure Reason*, 276; Kant, *Kritik der reinen Vernunft*, A 145–46, B 185.
16   Kant, *Critique of Pure Reason*, 347; Kant, *Kritik der reinen Vernunft*, A 249, B 306.
17   Lacoue-Labarthe and Nancy, *Literary Absolute*, 32.
18   Fichte, *Early Philosophical Writings*, 65; Fichte, *Johann Gottlieb Fichtes sämmtliche Werke*, 10.
19   Hegel, *Logic*, 536.
20   Lacoue-Labarthe and Nancy, *Literary Absolute*, 40.
21   Lacoue-Labarthe and Nancy, *Literary Absolute*, 41–42.
22   Lacoue-Labarthe and Nancy, *Literary Absolute*, 48.
23   Nancy, *Logodaedalus*, 90–94.
24   *Friedrich Schlegel's "Lucinde,"* 157.
25   Lacoue-Labarthe and Nancy, *Literary Absolute*, 12.
26   *Friedrich Schlegel's "Lucinde,"* 175.
27   Lacoue-Labarthe and Nancy, *Literary Absolute*, 48.
28   Lacoue-Labarthe and Nancy, *Literary Absolute*, 12.
29   Blanchot, *"Athenaeum,"* 166.
30   Blanchot, *"Athenaeum,"* 172.
31   Schlegel, *Kritische Ausgabe*, 283; translation mine.
32   Schlegel, *On the Study of Greek Poetry*, 21.
33   Lacoue-Labarthe and Nancy, *Literary Absolute*, 52.
34   Lacoue-Labarthe and Nancy, *Literary Absolute*, 73.

35 Bakunin, *Bakunin on Anarchism*, 57.
36 *Friedrich Schlegel's "Lucinde,"* 253.
37 Lacoue-Labarthe and Nancy, *Literary Absolute*, 56–57.
38 Lacoue-Labarthe and Nancy, *Literary Absolute*, 16.
39 *Kant's Critique of Aesthetic Judgment*, 86.
40 Hegel, *Logic*, 162.
41 Nancy, *Experience of Freedom*, 54.
42 Blackman, "'Betty and Dupree.'"
43 Hughes, *Hanging the Peachtree Bandit*, 9–14, 102–5 passim.
44 Meriwether, "12/1/66," 120–21.
45 A diegetic narrator is one in the world of the story. An extradiegetic voice comes from outside the story world(s) inhabited by characters.
46 Odum and Johnson, *Negro Workaday Songs*, 55–56.
47 Odum and Johnson, *Negro Workaday Songs*, 57–59.
48 The delay in naming the subject of an action, in this case, a speaker, creates an ambiguity that has a variety of effects on the audience. Stylisticians recognize this as a traditional literary figure: cataphora.
49 Hill and Bithell, "Introduction to Music Revival," 20.
50 Feintuch, "Revivals on the Edge," 9.
51 Garcia, "Hunter/Garcia; Words/Music," 210; Jackson, *Garcia*, 158.
52 Virgil, *Georgics*, 5–7.
53 Frost, *Selected Letters*, 133.
54 Hesiod, *Hesiod* 1:87. See esp. line 11.
55 Eliot, *Collected Poems*, 68–69, 75; Nikhilananda, *Upanishads*, 239–40.
56 Exod. 3:13–14, *Scofield Reference Bible*.
57 *Romeo and Juliet*, 1.2.90–107, 2.1.156. Here and in all following quotations, I rely on Shakespeare, *Riverside Shakespeare*.
58 Bernardo, "Sex and Salvation," 306.
59 Alighieri, *Inferno*, 5.28–30.
60 Alighieri, *Purgatorio*, 34.139.
61 Homer, *Iliad*, 455.
62 Homer, *Odyssey*, 451.
63 Alighieri, *Purgatorio*, 31.42–45.
64 Plotinus, *Enneads*, 54.
65 Fumagalli, "Derek Walcott's *Omeros*," 21.

CHAPTER 1. THAT'S WHEN IT ALL BEGAN

1 Weinreich, "Locating a Beat Aesthetic," 51.
2 Garcia, "Jerry Garcia Reflects."
3 *Portable Jack Kerouac*, 566, 568; Foye, introduction to *Herbert Huncke Reader*, xvii.
4 Charters, introduction to *Portable Beat Reader*, xix–xxii.
5 Pöhlmann, *Future-Founding Poetry*, 1–3.
6 Lesh, *Searching for the Sound*, 252.

7   McNally, *Desolate Angel*, 124.
8   Ginsberg, *Collected Poems*, 126, 131.
9   The most powerful and eloquent delineations of this despair to be found in Beat texts may be those of William S. Burroughs. As Rob Turner explains, characters such as Pantopon Rose in *Naked Lunch*, among many others across Burroughs's career, confront "existential self-annihilation" as a version of the Cold War–era shadow of "mutually assured extinction" (Turner, *Counterfeit Culture*, 104–5).
10 Ginsberg, *Collected Poems*, 131.
11 Ginsberg, *Deliberate Prose*, 232.
12 Ginsberg, *Deliberate Prose*, 232.
13 Garcia, "Conversation with Jerry Garcia," 21.
14 Teichman, "Night the Grateful Dead Inspired a 'Cast-of-Thousands Orgy.'"
15 As Gregory Stephenson argues, the clearest Beat expression of the attitude might be that found in Gregory Corso's poem "Power," which reads, in part, "A thirst for Power is drinking sand" (Stephenson, *Daybreak Boys*, 82; Corso, *Mindfield*, 90). The Beat alternative to power, David Stephen Calonne explains, is a view of and action in the world that seeks to liberate rather than to control (Calonne, *Spiritual Imagination of the Beats*, 11).
16 *Conversations with Jack Kerouac*, 54.
17 Hedrick, "Oral History Interview with Wally Hedrick"; McNally, *Long Strange Trip*, 14.
18 Kerouac, *Dharma Bums*, 13–16.
19 Davidson, *San Francisco Renaissance*, 3–4.
20 McNally, *Long Strange Trip*, 14.
21 McNally, *Long Strange Trip*, 14–15.
22 McNally, *Long Strange Trip*, 15.
23 Richardson, *No Simple Highway*, 25.
24 McNally, *Long Strange Trip*, 14.
25 Garcia et al., *Garcia*, 24.
26 Garcia, "Music Never Stops."
27 "Project MK-Ultra."
28 Wolfe, *Electric Kool-Aid Acid Test*, 210.
29 McNally, *Long Strange Trip*, 82.
30 Hassett, *How the Beats Begat the Pranksters*, 6.
31 McNally, *Long Strange Trip*, 124, 161.
32 McNally, *Long Strange Trip*, 177; Johnson, "Three Generations of Beat Poetics," 82.
33 Mortenson, "Allen Ginsberg and Beat Poetry," 87.
34 Gleason, "On the Town," 42.
35 Greenfield, *Dark Star*, 100.

36 Intriguingly, Kerouac discusses Cassady using similar terms in *Big Sur* (134–35).
37 Garcia and Weir, "Interview with Jerry Garcia and Bob Weir."
38 Barlow, "Cassidy's Tale."
39 Hunter and Garcia, "Hunter/Garcia; Words/Music," 214.
40 Kerouac, *Portable Jack Kerouac*, 565–66; Calonne, *Spiritual Imagination of the Beats*, 1; Vogel, "Dream and the Dystopia," 400.
41 McNally, *Long Strange Trip*, 250.
42 Hunter and Garcia, "Hunter/Garcia; Words/Music," 223.
43 Kozlovsky, "Beat Literature," 38.
44 Kerouac, *On the Road*, 17.
45 Kozlovsky, "Beat Literature," 38.
46 Kerouac, *On the Road*, 38.
47 Rimbaud, *Complete Works, Selected Letters*, 304.
48 Kerouac, *On the Road*, 17.
49 Williams, *Collected Poems*, 1:217.
50 Williams, *Collected Poems*, 1:217; Ginsberg, *Collected Poems*, 126; Kerouac, *On the Road*, 8.
51 Corso, *Mindfield*, 105; Ginsberg, *Collected Poems*, 126; Welch, *Ring of Bone*, 64.
52 Kerouac, *Portable Jack Kerouac*, 483; Kerouac, *Visions of Cody*, 351.
53 Tytell, *Naked Angels*, 21–22.
54 Gelpi, *American Poetry After Modernism*, 95.
55 Williams, *Collected Poems*, 1:263.
56 Holsapple, *Birth of the Imagination*, 148, 293–99.
57 Williams, *Collected Poems*, 1:224.
58 Williams, *Collected Poems*, 2:314.
59 Ginsberg et al., *Book of Martyrdom and Artifice*, 383; Williams, "Introduction," 811–12.
60 Ginsberg, *Howl*, 12–13.
61 Ginsberg, *Collected Poems*, 126.
62 Ginsberg, *Deliberate Prose*, 320.
63 Johnson, *Three Generations of Beat Poetics*, 84.
64 Heine, *Poetics of Breathing*, 49–50.
65 Costello, "Poetry of Walt Whitman and Allen Ginsberg."
66 Whitman, *Leaves of Grass*, 202.
67 Freedman, "Whitman, Crane, and the Beats," 232.
68 Ginsberg, *Collected Poems*, 128.
69 Ginsberg, *Collected Poems*, 394.
70 Garcia, interview by Blair Jackson and David Gans, 49.
71 Jackson and Gans, *This Is All a Dream*, 161–62.
72 Dodd, "Other One."
73 Whitman is explicitly mentioned in Robert Hunter's story "The One with the Rabbit," in which a character weighs Whitman's work against

that of Keats, particularly the latter's "Ode on a Grecian Urn." Keats intrigues the Grateful Dead fan because, among other reasons, Hunter's novel *The Silver Snarling Trumpet* takes its name from Keats's "The Eve of St. Agnes." "The One with the Rabbit" is one of those stories Hunter originally distributed via email under the collective heading of *Red Sky Fishing*. While these texts still circulate informally among fans, the original publication information is difficult to uncover. In a journal entry of February 16, 2007, Hunter writes about *Red Sky Fishing* as an "eighth-month experiment in publishing via email," and M. Luke Myers mentions in an online fan forum post of March 12, 2007, that the stories were being sent every Thursday (Hunter, "Journal 2006–2007"; Myers, "Robert Hunter's Bio"). This suggests that "The One with the Rabbit" would have been distributed by Hunter in late 2006 or early 2007.

CHAPTER 2. JUST LIKE MARY SHELLEY

1. Jackson, "Chapter 17 Additions."
2. Scully and Dalton, *Living with the Dead*, 270.
3. McNally, *Long Strange Trip*, 551.
4. Hunter, *Box of Rain*, 180. Sources for Hunter's *Armageddon Rag* materials remain scattered. He included lyrics for one piece, "Resurrection Rag," in *A Box of Rain*, noting that it was of a pair with a song that was not included in the book, "Armageddon Rag." "Resurrection Rag" was recorded with and released on the first album by the Dinosaurs. Recordings of Hunter's July 28, 1984, show include some comments from the stage about the Nazgûl, in which he explains that two songs he played that night, "Blood on the Sheets" and "Raging," were also composed for the project. Recordings of an unofficially circulating studio session attributed to the Nazgûl, dated June 13, 1985, include Hunter among the performers. The track list for the session includes both "Armageddon Rag" and "Resurrection Rag," as well as a piece titled "Raise Your Arms Clap Your Hands."
5. Garcia, introduction to *Grateful Dead Comix*, v.
6. King, "My Pretty Pony."
7. Rollins, "Twilight Zone," 38.
8. Fiedler, *Love and Death in the American Novel*, 108–9.
9. Fiedler, *Love and Death in the American Novel*, 109.
10. Fiedler, *Love and Death in the American Novel*, 115.
11. Campbell, "'All You Need Is Love,'" 114–15; Doorman, "Revolution or Repetition," 147–48.
12. Perry, "New Life for the Dead," 51.
13. Sanders, *Short Oxford History of English Literature*, 356.
14. Tolley, "Preromanticism," 16.
15. Michaels, "Bob Dylan"; Burns, *Complete Works*, 264.
16. Burns, *Complete Works*, 173.

17   Burns, *Complete Works*, 174.
18   Shelley, *Frankenstein*, 147.
19   Garcia, "Movie That Changed My Life."
20   Jackson, *Grateful Dead Gear*, 34–35.
21   Jackson, *Grateful Dead Gear*, 39.
22   Jarnow, *Heads*, 17.
23   Richardson, *No Simple Highway*, 40.
24   McNally, *Long Strange Trip*, 311.
25   McNally, *Long Strange Trip*, 312.
26   McNally, *Long Strange Trip*, 312; Gissen-Stanley and Davis, *Owsley and Me*, 191–97.
27   Richardson, *No Simple Highway*, 35.
28   Hunter, "Song Goes On," 114–16.
29   Richardson, *No Simple Highway*, 153.
30   Shelley, *Frankenstein*, 33.
31   Poole, *Workingman's Dead*, 1–2.
32   Hunter and Garcia, "Hunter/Garcia; Words/Music," 226.
33   Hunter and Garcia, "Hunter/Garcia; Words/Music," 226.
34   Garcia, "Jerry Garcia"; Hunter, "Song Goes On," 123; McNally, *Long Strange Trip*, 288, 318.
35   Wood, *Tragic Odes of Jerry Garcia*, 4. The attribution of this quote to Garcia serves the point, but as the preceding chapter indicates, Lesh also used it. The spirit of the expression was thus clearly a component of the band's general sensibilities.
36   Jackson, *Grateful Dead*, 108–9.
37   "*Workingman's Dead* 50, Episode 3: 'Dire Wolf.'"
38   Sharp and Campbell, *English Folk Songs*, 2:59.
39   Krassner, *Confessions*, 294.
40   McNally, *Long Strange Trip*, 611; Poole, *Workingman's Dead*, 60.
41   McNally, *Long Strange Trip*, 316.
42   Hunter, journal entry for July 29, 1996.
43   "*Workingman's Dead* 50, Episode 3: 'Dire Wolf.'"
44   A fen is a type of mire. The discursive field of the song's geographic features thus finds here an additional connection between Arthur Conan Doyle's novel and the folk tradition via the setting of Fennario.
45   Brown, "Black Dog," 175. The Grateful Dead was not alone in finding inspiration in folklore's demonic dogs. Nick Drake's "Black Eyed Dog" is another example.
46   Doyle, *Hound of the Baskervilles*, 110.
47   Clausson, "Degeneration, 'Fin-de-Siècle' Gothic," 67–68.
48   Clausson, "Degeneration, 'Fin-de-Siècle' Gothic," 78.
49   Jackson, *Grateful Dead*, 109.
50   McNally, *Long Strange Trip*, 317.
51   Jackson, *Grateful Dead*, 109.

52 Miller, *Raven and the Whale*, 82–83.
53 Hunter, interview, 18.
54 Massey, *Gaping Pig*, 126.
55 Massey, *Gaping Pig*, 126–27.
56 Massey, *Gaping Pig*, 131.
57 Poole, *Workingman's Dead*, 18.
58 Guttzeit, "Authoring Monsters," 283–84.
59 Massey, *Gaping Pig*, 128.
60 Massey, *Gaping Pig*, 136.
61 Guttzeit, "Authoring Monsters," 281–82.
62 Jackson, *Grateful Dead*, 109.
63 Massey, *Gaping Pig*, 128.
64 Thompson, *Fear and Loathing*, 68.
65 Thompson, *Fear and Loathing*, 68.
66 McNally, *Long Strange Trip*, 345.
67 McNally, *Long Strange Trip*, 352.
68 McNally, *Long Strange Trip*, 360–62.
69 McNally, *Long Strange Trip*, 377.
70 McNally, *Long Strange Trip*, 317.
71 Twain, *Mark Twain*, 282; Fiedler, *Love and Death*, 127.
72 Jackson, *Grateful Dead Gear*, 26. The band would invoke Edgar Allan Poe directly on April 19, 1982, when members—mostly Lesh—offered remarks during "Space" that included several references to, and some quotations from, Poe's poem "The Raven."
73 Hunter, "Man Behind the Words," 25.
74 Fiedler, *Love and Death*, 127.
75 Hunter, "Standing in the Soul," 7.
76 Brown and Brown, "*Faust* and the Gothic Novel," 69.
77 Brown and Brown, "*Faust* and the Gothic Novel," 69.
78 Trist and Dodd, *Complete Annotated Grateful Dead Lyrics*, 112.
79 Goethe, *Sämtliche Werke*, 7/1:1150–1323.
80 Brown and Brown, "*Faust* and the Gothic Novel," 74.
81 Trist and Dodd, *Complete Annotated Grateful Dead Lyrics*, 111–12.
82 In Goethe's text, Gretchen sings a song, while jailed for infanticide, which derives from the "Juniper Tree," a fairy tale collected by the Brothers Grimm. The lyrics describe the situation of the tale's victim, concluding with two lines that anticipate key lyrics in the Grateful Dead's "Wharf Rat": "Then I became a beautiful bird of the forest; / fly away, fly away!" (Goethe, *Sämtliche Werke*, 7/1:4419–20; translation mine).
83 Brown and Brown, "*Faust* and the Gothic Novel," 74.
84 Anchor, "Motherhood and Family," 40.
85 Anchor, "Motherhood and Family," 40.
86 Goethe, *Sämtliche Werke*, 7/1:6287–88; translation mine.

87	Goddu, *Gothic America*, 9–10.
88	Gallego, "Gothic in North American 'Subcultures,'" 175.
89	Redding, *Haints*, 7.
90	Hunter and Garcia, "Hunter/Garcia; Words/Music," 220–21.
91	Gallego, "Gothic in North American 'Subcultures,'" 181.
92	Fiedler, *Love and Death*, 127.
93	Tantillo, "Damned to Heaven," 454; Goethe, *Sämtliche Werke*, 7/1:317, 342–49.
94	Aguirre, "Gothic Fiction and Folk-Narrative," 10–12.

CHAPTER 3. PERCHANCE TO DREAM

An earlier version of this chapter appeared as Christopher Coffman, "Clowns in the Burying Ground: Ovid, William Shakespeare, and the Grateful Dead," *Literary Matters* 15, no. 3 (Spring 2023), https://www.literarymatters.org/15-3-clowns/.

1	Shakespeare, *Hamlet*, 4.5.50.
2	Romeo, Juliet, and Shakespeare are also mentioned in another song that the Grateful Dead performed, albeit only once. The instance in question was a rainforest benefit concert on September 24, 1988, during which numerous musicians performed on their own and in various combinations. At one point, the Grateful Dead was joined by Suzanne Vega for a few songs, including Robyn Hitchcock's "Chinese Bones." This piece opens with the words, "Watching Romeo dissolve"; the second verse begins, "Watching Juliet unrobe"; and the third verse includes a line that starts, "Something Shakespeare never said."
3	Shakespeare, *Tempest*, 1.2.397–98; Shakespeare, *King John*, 4.2.11–16.
4	Thomas and Faircloth, *Shakespeare's Plants and Gardens*, 297–98.
5	Seng, *Vocal Songs*, 131–62 passim.
6	Shakespeare, *Hamlet*, 4.5.48–55.
7	Shakespeare, *Hamlet*, 4.5.175–77.
8	Shakespeare, *Hamlet*, 4.5.184–85.
9	*Poems of Tennyson*, 355.
10	*Poems of Tennyson*, 357n.
11	Shakespeare, *King Lear*, 3.2.74–77.
12	Shakespeare, *King Lear*, 3.4.115–19.
13	Azarian, "Another Musical Walk."
14	McNally, *Long Strange Trip*, 27; Azarian, "Another Musical Walk."
15	Greenberg, "Tom Azarian CD Looks Back"; Baron, "Thrill Lives On."
16	Shakespeare, *King Lear*, 3.6.108–10.
17	Shakespeare, *King Lear*, 3.4.102; 3.4.109.
18	Sharp and Campbell, *English Folk Songs*, 2:324; 1:28, 31, 34.
19	Shakespeare, *King Lear*, 4.6.86–92.
20	Shakespeare, *King Lear*, 4.6.164.

21   Shakespeare, *King Lear*, 4.6.40–41.
22   Shakespeare, *Richard III*, 1.3.352.
23   See, for instance, Bell, *Shakespeare's Great Stage of Fools*, 107; and Goldsmith, *Wise Fools in Shakespeare*, 41.
24   Shakespeare, *Hamlet*, 5.1.184–95.
25   Shakespeare, *Hamlet*, 3.1.59–67.
26   Hunter and Garcia, "Hunter/Garcia; Words/Music," 233.
27   My summary of the Althaea myth is based on the version found in the Loeb edition of Ovid's *Metamorphoses*.
28   The 1567 translation of Ovid's *Metamorphoses* preferred by Shakespeare is available in *Shakespeare's Ovid, Being Arthur Golding's Translation of the Metamorphoses*.
29   Shakespeare, *2 Henry VI*, 1.1.232–35.
30   Shakespeare, *2 Henry IV*, 2.2.147, 2.4.231.
31   Jackson, *Garcia*, 39. I am grateful to Jesse Jarnow for reminding me, during conversation on February 20, 2019, of this pre–Grateful Dead performance space. The Boar's Head coffeehouse moved to the Peninsula Jewish Community Center in San Carlos in 1962, which in turn moved to a Belmont Hills location in 1963—about a year before the coffeehouse closed permanently in 1964 (Angus, "Boar's Head #1"; Angus, "Boar's Head #2").
32   Shakespeare, *2 Henry IV*, 2.2.87–93.
33   Bate, *Shakespeare and Ovid*, 21.
34   Shakespeare, *2 Henry IV*, 5.5.41, 5.5.47–56.
35   Garcia, interview by Blair Jackson and David Gans, 85–86.
36   Eliot, *Collected Poems*, 59; Shakespeare, *Hamlet*, 4.5.72–73.
37   I am indebted for this insight to the song chart on the scroll included with the Grateful Dead's *30 Trips Around the Sun*, the text of which is attributed to Jesse Jarnow.
38   Trist and Dodd, *Complete Annotated Grateful Dead Lyrics*, 52.
39   See, for an example of such conclusions by a historian, Wood, *1549 Rebellions*, 10, 226, 239–40.
40   For arguments regarding the place of this play in the literary history of historical drama, consult Ribner, *English History Play*, 71–76. The traditional reading of the text in relation to Shakespeare's work was established by Tillyard, *Shakespeare's History Plays*.

CHAPTER 4. ON THE HEELS OF RIMBAUD

1   Hunter and Garcia, "Hunter/Garcia; Words/Music," 220.
2   Constanten, *Between Rock and Hard Places*, 76.
3   "Random Notes," 4.
4   Glatt, *Live at the Fillmore East*, 343–44.
5   Helm and Davis, *This Wheel's on Fire*, 228.
6   Carr, "By the Chicken Wire," 64.

7   Greenfield, *Dark Star*, 239–40.
8   Jerry Garcia Family, "1980–11–16 The Warfield, San Francisco CA."
9   Sounes, *Down the Highway*, 380, 433.
10 McNally, *Long Strange Trip*, 50; Jackson, *Garcia*, 58.
11 McNally, *Long Strange Trip*, 50.
12 Garcia, "Jerry Garcia, the Guru," 35.
13 Garcia et al., *Garcia*, 14.
14 Garcia et al., *Garcia*, 13.
15 Jackson, *Garcia*, 134.
16 Shenk and Silberman, *Skeleton Key*, 76.
17 Jackson, *Garcia*, 344.
18 Sounes, *Down the Highway*, 298.
19 Dylan, *Chronicles*, 148.
20 Heylin, *Bob Dylan*, 613.
21 Dylan, *Chronicles*, 150.
22 Dylan, *Chronicles*, 151.
23 Heylin, *Bob Dylan*, 613.
24 Williams, *Bob Dylan*, x.
25 Dylan, "Dylan Now."
26 Garcia, "Jerry Garcia Raps," 28.
27 McNally, *Long Strange Trip*, 587–88.
28 Dylan, tribute, 31.
29 Junod, "Who Is This Bob Dylan?"
30 Greenfield, *Dark Star*, 338.
31 Hunter, "February 25, 1988," 275.
32 Brinkley, "Bob Dylan's America."
33 Lethem, "Genius of Bob Dylan."
34 Dylan, interview, 59.
35 Dylan, interview, 59.
36 Doyle, "Life with Dylan," 22.
37 Sounes, *Down the Highway*, 417.
38 Dylan, *Philosophy of Modern Song*, 137.
39 Dylan, *Philosophy of Modern Song*, 137–38.
40 Dylan, *Philosophy of Modern Song*, 138.
41 Dylan, *Philosophy of Modern Song*, 138.
42 Dylan, *Philosophy of Modern Song*, 138.
43 Dylan, *Philosophy of Modern Song*, 139.
44 Dylan, *Philosophy of Modern Song*, 139.
45 Dylan, *Philosophy of Modern Song*, 139.
46 Dylan, "*Rolling Stone* Interview," 13.
47 Dylan, liner notes to *Desire*.
48 Shelton, *Bob Dylan*, 83.
49 Hunter, foreword to *Alleys of the Heart*, v.
50 Rimbaud, *Complete Works, Selected Letters*, 306.

51	Translation mine.
52	Mai, *Bob Dylan the Poet*, 47.
53	Rimbaud, *Season in Hell*, 95.
54	Rimbaud, *Season in Hell*, 95.
55	Rimbaud, *Complete Works, Selected Letters*, 304.
56	Hampton, *Bob Dylan*, 106.
57	Hampton, *Bob Dylan*, 110.
58	Rimbaud, *Season in Hell*, 101.
59	That "Black-Throated Wind" offers some particularly vexing interpretive ambiguities is suggested by its unusual performance history. It premiered on March 2, 1972, but disappeared from the repertoire during the band's mid-1970s hiatus. It only returned in early 1990. That year saw Barlow and Weir experimenting with alternate lyrics, although none seemed to satisfy, and performances settled back into the original version.
60	Fowlie, *Age of Surrealism*, 59–60.
61	Rimbaud, *Season in Hell*, 101.
62	Hunter, *Box of Rain*, 35.
63	Hunter, *Sentinel*, 77.

CHAPTER 5. LIKE AN ANGEL

1	McNally, *Long Strange Trip*, 574; Jackson, *Garcia*, 385.
2	McNally, *Long Strange Trip*, 582–84, 592, 610–12; Richardson, *No Simple Highway*, 291–94; Jackson, *Garcia*, 448–49; Greenfield, *Dark Star*, 222–34 passim.
3	McNally, *Long Strange Trip*, 611–12; Greenfield, *Dark Star*, 313.
4	Jackson, *Garcia*, 427; Jarnow, liner notes to *Ready or Not*.
5	Huyssen, "Paris/Childhood," 113.
6	Junyk, "'Fragment from Another Context,'" 262–63; Baudelaire, *"Painter of Modern Life,"* 12.
7	Parry, *Interventions into Modernist Cultures*, 2.
8	Parry, *Interventions into Modernist Cultures*, 2–3.
9	Eliot, *Collected Poems*, 69.
10	O'Donnell, "Bobby, Béla, and Borrowing."
11	Lesh, *Searching for the Sound*, 119–20.
12	Weir, "Art of Jerry Garcia."
13	Kreutzmann and Eisen, *Deal*, 24.
14	Meriwether, "Robert Hunter, William Faulkner," 56–57.
15	Yeats, *Collected Works*, 56.
16	Hunter, "Songs of Innocence, Songs of Experience," 12, 18.
17	Ginsberg, *Journals*, 3; *Conversations with Allen Ginsberg*, 82; Morgan, *I Celebrate Myself*, 86, 131, 155, 195, 206, 445.
18	Eliot, *Collected Poems*, 3.
19	Eliot, *Collected Poems*, 3.

20 McNally, *Long Strange Trip*, 27; Hunter, "Songs of Innocence, Songs of Experience," 12; Meriwether, "Robert Hunter, William Faulkner," 54; Jackson, *Garcia*, 25.
21 Hunter, "Standing in the Soul," 6–7.
22 Constanten, *Between Rock and Hard Places*, 73.
23 "Grateful Dead's Phil Lesh and the CSM Jazz Band."
24 Osmond-Smith, *Playing on Words*, 4, 9, 53.
25 Brightman, *Sweet Chaos*, 85; Jackson, *Garcia*, 349.
26 McNally, *Long Strange Trip*, 387.
27 Hunter, *Box of Rain*, 94n.
28 Jackson, *Garcia*, 10; McNally, *Long Strange Trip*, 26.
29 Ellmann, *James Joyce*, 21, 136, 143.
30 Kenner, *Ulysses*, 10.
31 Joyce, *Ulysses*, 320.
32 Joyce, *Ulysses*, 323.
33 Joyce, *Ulysses*, 323.
34 McNally, *Long Strange Trip*, 27.
35 Joyce, *Finnegans Wake*, 628, 3.
36 Joyce, *Finnegans Wake*, 207, 232.
37 Joyce, *Finnegans Wake*, 3.
38 Joyce, *Finnegans Wake*, 3.
39 Joyce, *Finnegans Wake*, 32.
40 von Phul, "Who Sleeps at *Finnegans Wake*?," 28.
41 von Phul, "Who Sleeps at *Finnegans Wake*?," 28.
42 Joyce, *Finnegans Wake*, 193.
43 Joyce, *Finnegans Wake*, 287.
44 Joyce, *Finnegans Wake*, 47.
45 Morse, "Cain, Abel, and Joyce," 4.
46 Campbell and Robinson, *Skeleton Key to Finnegans Wake*, 21.
47 Campbell and Robinson, *Skeleton Key to Finnegans Wake*, 14.
48 Cazden et al., *Folk Songs of the Catskills*, 458.
49 Garcia et al., *Signpost to New Space*, 100–101; Hart and Lieberman, *Planet Drum*, 119, 121; Tuedio and Spector, "Preface," 8–9; Trudeau, "Super-Metacantric Analysis," 97–98.
50 Hunter, "Standing in the Soul," 7; Hunter, "Rose Grows from the Shadows," 25; Hunter and Garcia, "Hunter/Garcia; Words/Music," 222–23.
51 *Poetry of Rilke*, 222–23.
52 Freedman, *Life of a Poet*, 129.
53 Gass, *Reading Rilke*, 23.
54 *Poetry of Rilke*, 217–19.
55 Ryan, "*Neue Gedichte/New Poems*," 133.
56 Hirsch, *Poet's Glossary*, 196.
57 Hirsch, *Poet's Glossary*, 196–97.
58 *Works of Henry Wadsworth Longfellow*, 275.

59	Sacks, *English Elegy*, 20.	
60	Hunter, "Standing in the Soul," 7.	
61	Hunter, *Idiot's Delight*, 69.	
62	Hunter, *Idiot's Delight*, 70.	
63	Eliot, *Collected Poems*, 57.	
64	"Le printemps m'a apporté l'affreux rire de l'idiot." Rimbaud, *Season in Hell*, 4; translation mine.	
65	Hunter, *Idiot's Delight*, 115.	
66	Ramazani, *Poetry of Mourning*, xi.	
67	Ramazani, *Poetry of Mourning*, 3.	
68	Gilbert, "'Rats' Alley,'" 184–85.	
69	Rae, "Introduction," 28.	
70	Komar, "*Duino Elegies*," 84–92 passim.	
71	Ryan, *Rilke, Modernism and Poetic Tradition*, 219.	
72	Rilke, *Werke*, 2:201.	
73	Rilke, *Duino Elegies; Sonnets to Orpheus*, 3.	
74	Rilke, *Duino Elegies; Sonnets to Orpheus*, 3.	
75	Komar, "*Duino Elegies*," 82.	
76	Hunter, *Night Cadre*, 1.	
77	Huyssen, "Paris/Childhood," 117.	
78	Rilke, *Duino Elegies; Sonnets to Orpheus*, 73.	
79	Hunter, *Night Cadre*, 51.	
80	Hunter, *Night Cadre*, 51.	
81	Hunter, *Night Cadre*, 51.	
82	Hunter, *Night Cadre*, 51.	
83	Ryan, *Rilke, Modernism and Poetic Tradition*, 180.	
84	Ryan, *Rilke, Modernism and Poetic Tradition*, 180–81.	
85	Rilke, *Duino Elegies; Sonnets to Orpheus*, 77.	
86	Hunter, *Night Cadre*, 93.	
87	Hunter, *Night Cadre*, 93.	
88	Hunter, *Sentinel*, 34.	
89	Rilke, *Duino Elegies; Sonnets to Orpheus*, 3.	
90	Rilke, *Duino Elegies; Sonnets to Orpheus*, 36–37.	
91	Komar, "Rethinking Rilke's *Duineser Elegien*," 194–95.	
92	Hunter, *Night Cadre*, 29.	
93	Hunter, *Night Cadre*, 29.	
94	Hunter, *Night Cadre*, 29.	
95	Hunter, *Night Cadre*, 29.	
96	Komar, "Rethinking Rilke's *Duineser Elegien*," 197.	
97	Hunter, *Night Cadre*, 80.	
98	Hunter, *Night Cadre*, 80.	
99	Hunter, *Night Cadre*, 80.	
100	Hunter, *Night Cadre*, 80.	
101	Hunter, *Sentinel*, 43.	

102	Hunter, *Sentinel*, 54.
103	Hunter, *Sentinel*, 54.
104	Hunter, *Sentinel*, 55.
105	Hunter, *Sentinel*, 60.
106	Hunter, *Sentinel*, 44–45.
107	Rilke, *Duino Elegies; Sonnets to Orpheus*, 35.
108	Ryan, *Rilke, Modernism and Poetic Tradition*, 194.
109	Hunter, *Sentinel*, 61.
110	Rilke, *Duino Elegies; Sonnets to Orpheus*, 35.
111	Ryan, *Rilke, Modernism and Poetic Tradition*, 190.
112	Komar, "Rethinking Rilke's *Duineser Elegien*," 198.
113	Rilke, *Duino Elegies; Sonnets to Orpheus*, 51.
114	Rilke, *Duino Elegies; Sonnets to Orpheus*, 51.
115	Hunter, "Standing in the Soul," 1.
116	Hunter, *Sentinel*, 121.
117	Hunter, *Sentinel*, 122.
118	Hunter, *Sentinel*, 123.
119	Hunter, *Sentinel*, 123.
120	Hunter, *Sentinel*, 138–39.
121	Hunter, *Sentinel*, 148.
122	Hunter, "Standing in the Soul," 6, 8.

CONCLUSION. ALL THAT'S STILL UNSUNG

1	Wolfe, *Electric Kool-Aid Acid Test*, 218.
2	Wolfe, *Electric Kool-Aid Acid Test*, 189.
3	Wolfe, *Electric Kool-Aid Acid Test*, 223.
4	Thompson, *Proud Highway*, 639.
5	Thompson, *Fear and Loathing in America*, 336.
6	Thompson, *Fear and Loathing in America*, 343.
7	Thompson, *Fear and Loathing in America*, 344.
8	Didion, *We Tell Ourselves Stories*, 69.
9	Didion, *We Tell Ourselves Stories*, 71.
10	Didion, *We Tell Ourselves Stories*, 93.
11	Thompson, *Great Shark Hunt*, 456.
12	Greenfield, *Dark Star*, 105.
13	Vandenberg, *Joan Didion*, 17.
14	Dick, *VALIS*, 14.
15	Dick, *Transmigration of Timothy Archer*, 180.
16	Wallace, *Infinite Jest*, 481, 721–23, 927.
17	Wallace, *Infinite Jest*, 927.
18	Hunter, "Standing in the Soul," 8.
19	Hunter, "Standing in the Soul," 8.
20	Merrill, *Collected Poems*, 670.
21	*Guardian*, "George R. R. Martin."

22	Brautigan, "Day They Busted," 39.
23	Meriwether, "Note on the Textual History," 96; McNally, *Long Strange Trip*, 226.
24	Meriwether, "Note on the Textual History," 96.
25	Coupland, *Polaroids from the Dead*, 2.
26	Coupland, *Polaroids from the Dead*, 1.
27	Coupland, *Polaroids from the Dead*, 62.
28	Coupland, *Polaroids from the Dead*, 57–61, 63.
29	Coupland, *Polaroids from the Dead*, 62.
30	Coupland, *Polaroids from the Dead*, 62.
31	Coupland, *Polaroids from the Dead*, 62.
32	Coupland, *Polaroids from the Dead*, 62.
33	Coupland, *Polaroids from the Dead*, 61.
34	Garcia and Weir, "Interview with Jerry Garcia and Bob Weir."

Bibliography

Aguirre, Manuel. "Gothic Fiction and Folk-Narrative Structure: The Case of Mary Shelley's *Frankenstein*." *Gothic Studies* 15, no. 2 (2013): 1–18.

Alighieri, Dante. *Inferno*. Translated by Robert M. Durling. New York: Oxford University Press, 1996.

Alighieri, Dante. *Purgatorio*. Translated by W. S. Merwin. New York: Knopf, 2001.

Anchor, Robert. "Motherhood and Family in Goethe's *Faust*: Gretchen's Mother and the Gretchen Tragedy." *Historical Reflections/Réflexions Historiques* 23, no. 1 (1997): 29–48.

Angus, Harry G. "Boar's Head #1, 1101 or 1107 San Carlos Avenue, San Carlos, CA." *Jerry's Brokendown Palaces*, March 29, 2015. http://jerrygarciasbrokendownpalaces.blogspot.com/2015/03/boars-head-1-1101-or-1107-san-carlos.html.

Angus, Harry G. "Boar's Head #2, Jewish Community Center (3), Holly Street? or Cherry Street?, San Carlos, CA." *Jerry's Brokendown Palaces*, July 13, 2012. http://jerrygarciasbrokendownpalaces.blogspot.com/2012/06/boars-head-carlos-bookstalls-loft-san.html.

Azarian, Tom. "Another Musical Walk Down Memory Lane." *The Bridge*, February 17, 2021. https://montpelierbridge.org/2021/02/another-musical-walk-down-memory-lane/.

Bakunin, Mikhail. *Bakunin on Anarchism*. Translated by Sam Dolgoff. Montreal: Black Rose Books, 2002.

Barlow, John Perry. "Cassidy's Tale." *Literary Kicks*. Last modified November 3, 1994. https://litkicks.com/barlowonneal/.

Baron, Josh. "The Thrill Lives On: David Grisman Reflects on Jerry Garcia." *Relix*, August 1, 2012. https://relix.com/articles/detail/the-thrill-lives-on-david-grisman-reflects-on-jerry-garcia/.

Bate, Jonathan. *Shakespeare and Ovid*. Oxford: Oxford University Press; Clarendon, 1994.

Baudelaire, Charles. *"The Painter of Modern Life" and Other Essays*. Translated by Jonathan Mayne. New York: Phaidon Press, 1995.

Bell, Robert H. *Shakespeare's Great Stage of Fools*. New York: Palgrave Macmillan, 2011.

Bernardo, Aldo S. "Sex and Salvation in the Middle Ages: From the *Romance of the Rose* to the *Divine Comedy*." *Italica* 67, no. 3 (1990): 305–18.

Blackman, Patrick. "'Betty and Dupree'—A Digital Compendium, Part 2—The Classics." *SingOut!*, October 27, 2014. https://singout.org/betty-and-dupree-a-digital-compendium-part-2-the-classics/.

Blanchot, Maurice. "*The Athenaeum*." *Studies in Romanticism* 22, no. 2 (1983): 163–72.

Brautigan, Richard. "The Day They Busted the Grateful Dead." In *The Grateful Dead Reader*, edited by David G. Dodd and Diana Spaulding, 39. New York: Oxford University Press, 2000.

Brightman, Carol. *Sweet Chaos: The Grateful Dead's American Adventure*. New York: Simon and Schuster; Pocket, 1998.

Brinkley, Douglas. "Bob Dylan's America." *Rolling Stone*, no. 1078 (May 14, 2009).

Brown, Jane K., and Marshall Brown. "*Faust* and the Gothic Novel." In *Interpreting Goethe's "Faust" Today*, edited by Jane K. Brown, Meredith Lee, and Thomas P. Saine, in collaboration with Paul Hernadi and Cyrus Hamlin, 68–80. Columbia, SC: Camden House, 1994.

Brown, Theo. "The Black Dog." *Folklore* 69, no. 3 (1958): 175–92.

Burns, Robert. *The Complete Works of Robert Burns*. New York: Appleton, 1852.

Calonne, David Stephen. *The Spiritual Imagination of the Beats*. Cambridge: Cambridge University Press, 2017.

Campbell, Colin. "'All You Need Is Love': From Romance to Romanticism: The Beatles, Romantic Love and Cultural Change." *Etnofoor* 19, no. 1 (2006): 111–23.

Campbell, Joseph, and Henry Morton Robinson. *A Skeleton Key to Finnegans Wake*. New York: Buccaneer, 1976.

Carr, Patrick. "By the Chicken Wire, Dylan Stalks the Dead." *Village Voice* 17, no. 39 (September 28, 1972): 64–65.

Cazden, Norman, Herbert Haufrecht, and Norman Studer. *Folk Songs of the Catskills*. Albany: State University of New York Press, 1983.

Charters, Ann. Introduction to *The Portable Beat Reader*, edited by Ann Charters, xv–xxxvi. New York: Viking, 1992.

Clausson, Nils. "Degeneration, 'Fin-de-Siècle' Gothic, and the Science of Detection: Arthur Conan Doyle's *The Hound of the Baskervilles* and the Emergence of the Modern Detective Story." *Journal of Narrative Theory* 35, no. 1 (2005): 60–87.

Coffman, Christopher. "Clowns in the Burying Ground: Ovid, William Shakespeare, and the Grateful Dead." *Literary Matters* 15, no. 3 (Spring 2023). https://www.literarymatters.org/15-3-clowns/.

Constanten, Tom. *Between Rock and Hard Places: A Musical Autobiodyssey*. Eugene, OR: Hulogosi, 1992.

Corso, Gregory. *Mindfield: New and Selected Poems*. New York: Thunder's Mouth Press, 1989.
Costello, Bonnie. "The Poetry of Walt Whitman and Allen Ginsberg." *American Academy of Arts and Sciences Bulletin*, Summer 2016. https://www.amacad.org/news/poetry-walt-whitman-and-allen-ginsberg.
Coupland, Douglas. *Polaroids from the Dead*. New York: Harper, 1996.
Davidson, Michael. *The San Francisco Renaissance: Poetics and Community at Mid-Century*. Cambridge: Cambridge University Press, 1989.
Dick, Philip K. *The Transmigration of Timothy Archer*. New York: Vintage, 1982.
Dick, Philip K. *VALIS*. London: Gollancz, 1981.
Didion, Joan. *We Tell Ourselves Stories in Order to Live: Collected Nonfiction*. New York: Knopf, 2006.
Dodd, David. "The Other One." *Greatest Stories Ever Told*. Last modified June 27, 2013. https://www.dead.net/features/greatest-stories-ever-told/greatest-stories-ever-told-other-one.
Doorman, Maarten. "Revolution or Repetition: Woodstock's Romanticism." *Bulletin of the German Historical Institute* 14 (2019): 131–48.
Doyle, Arthur Conan. *The Hound of the Baskervilles*. New York: McClure, 1902.
Doyle, Patrick. "Life with Dylan." *Rolling Stone*, no. 1242 (August 27, 2015).
Dylan, Bob. "Bob Dylan Songs." *Bob Dylan*. Accessed May 8, 2025. https://www.bobdylan.com/songs/.
Dylan, Bob. *Chronicles*. Vol. 1. New York: Simon and Schuster, 2004.
Dylan, Bob. "Dylan Now." Interview by Robert Hilburn. *Los Angeles Times*, September 16, 1991. https://www.latimes.com/entertainment/la-et-bob-dylan-hilburn-1992-story.html.
Dylan, Bob. Interview by Serge Kaganski. *Mojo*, no. 51 (February 1998).
Dylan, Bob. Liner notes to *Desire*. Columbia, CK33893, 1975, compact disc.
Dylan, Bob. *The Philosophy of Modern Song*. New York: Simon and Schuster, 2022.
Dylan, Bob. "The *Rolling Stone* Interview." Part 1. Edited by Ralph J. Gleason. *Rolling Stone* 1, no. 3 (December 14, 1967): 12–14. Transcription of Bob Dylan press conference, moderated by Ralph J. Gleason, KQED, San Francisco, December 3, 1965.
Dylan, Bob. Tribute to Jerry Garcia. *Rolling Stone*, no. 717 (September 21, 1995).
Eliot, T. S. *Collected Poems, 1909–1962*. New York: Harcourt Brace, 1991.
Ellmann, Richard. *James Joyce*. New York: Oxford University Press, 1982.
Feintuch, Burt. "Revivals on the Edge: Northumberland and Cape Breton—A Keynote." *Yearbook for Traditional Music* 38 (2006): 1–17.
Fichte, Johann Gottlieb. *Early Philosophical Writings*. Edited and translated by Daniel Breazeale. Ithaca, NY: Cornell University Press, 1988.
Fichte, Johann Gottlieb. *Johann Gottlieb Fichtes sämmtliche Werke*. Vol. 1. Edited by I. H. Fichte. Berlin: Veit, 1845.
Fiedler, Leslie. *Love and Death in the American Novel*. New York: Criterion, 1960.
Fowlie, Wallace. *Age of Surrealism*. Bloomington: Indiana University Press, 1960.
Foye, Raymond. Introduction to *The Herbert Huncke Reader*, edited by Benjamin G. Schafer, xv–xviii. New York: William Morrow, 1997.

Freedman, Linda. "Whitman, Crane, and the Beats." In *William Blake in Context*, edited by Sarah Haggarty, 227–34. Cambridge: Cambridge University Press, 2019.

Freedman, Ralph. *Life of a Poet: Rainer Maria Rilke*. New York: Farrar, Straus and Giroux, 1995.

Frost, Robert. *Selected Letters*. Edited by Lawrance Thompson. New York: Holt, Rinehart, and Winston, 1964.

Fumagalli, Maria Cristina. "Derek Walcott's *Omeros* and Dante's *Commedia*: Epics of the Self and Journeys into Language." *Cambridge Quarterly* 29, no. 1 (2000): 17–36.

Gallego, Carlos. "The Gothic in North American 'Subcultures.'" In *The Cambridge Companion to the Modern Gothic*, edited by Jerrold E. Hogle, 174–90. Cambridge: Cambridge University Press, 2014.

Gans, David, ed. *Conversations with the Dead: The Grateful Dead Interview Book*. Cambridge, MA: Da Capo Press, 2002.

Garcia, Jerry. "A Conversation with Jerry Garcia." Interview with Jon Carroll. *Playboy Guide: Electronic Entertainment*, Spring/Summer 1982, 19–25.

Garcia, Jerry. "The Grateful Dead Revisited: A 1976 Interview with Jerry Garcia." Interview by Steve Weitzman. *Relix*, August 1, 2013. https://relix.com/articles/detail/the_grateful_dead_revisited_a_1976_interview_with_jerry_garcia/.

Garcia, Jerry. Interview by Blair Jackson and David Gans, April 28, 1981. In Gans, *Conversations with the Dead*, 31–88.

Garcia, Jerry. Introduction to *Grateful Dead Comix*, edited by Jeff Tamarkin and David Scheiner, v–vi. New York: Hyperion, 1992.

Garcia, Jerry. "Jerry Garcia: The Complete 1985 *Frets* Interview." Interview by Jas Obrecht. *Jas Obrecht Music Archive*, September 1, 2010. Archived December 9, 2011. https://web.archive.org/web/20111209230442/http://jasobrecht.com/jerry-garcia-the-complete-1985-interview/.

Garcia, Jerry. "Jerry Garcia Interview: November 12, 1987." Interview by Mary Eisenhart. Accessed February 2, 2025. http://www.yoyow.com/marye/garcia.html.

Garcia, Jerry. "Jerry Garcia Raps." *San Francisco Oracle of the Spiritual Revolution* 1, no. 4 (n.d.): 27–28.

Garcia, Jerry. "Jerry Garcia Reflects on the Grateful Dead's Relentless Success and Ever-Growing Catalog." Interview by James Henke. *Rolling Stone*, no. 616 (October 31, 1991). https://www.rollingstone.com/feature/jerry-garcia-grateful-dead-1991-interview-99993/.

Garcia, Jerry. "Jerry Garcia, the Guru." Interview by Ralph J. Gleason. In *The Grateful Dead Reader*, edited by David G. Dodd and Diana Spaulding, 20–38. New York: Oxford University Press, 2000.

Garcia, Jerry. "The Movie That Changed My Life." AMC, 1995. Video, 2:15. https://www.facebook.com/jerrygarciaofficial/videos/just-like-mary-shelleyjust-like-frankensteinclank-your-chains-and-count-your-cha/1051991039340296/.

Garcia, Jerry. "The Music Never Stops: *The Rolling Stone* Interview with Jerry Garcia." Interview by Anthony DeCurtis. *Rolling Stone*, no. 664 (September 2, 1993).

Garcia, Jerry. "Peter Simon Interviews Jerry Garcia, 1975." Interview by Peter Simon. *SoundCloud*, MVY Radio, 1975. Audio, 58:52. https://soundcloud.com/mvyradio/peter-simon-interviews.

Garcia, Jerry, Charles Reich, and Jann Wenner. *Garcia: A Signpost to New Space.* Cambridge, MA: Da Capo Press, 1972.
Garcia, Jerry, and Bob Weir. "Interview with Jerry Garcia and Bob Weir April 16, 1991." Interview by Howard Rheingold. Last modified October 14, 2016. https://hrheingold.medium.com/interview-with-jerry-garcia-bob-weir-april-16-1991-dff48d26foaf.
Gass, William H. *Reading Rilke: Reflections on the Problems of Translation.* New York: Knopf, 1999.
Gelpi, Albert. *American Poetry After Modernism: The Power of the Word.* Cambridge: Cambridge University Press, 2015.
Gilbert, Sandra M. "'Rats' Alley': The Great War, Modernism, and the (Anti) Pastoral Elegy." *New Literary History* 30, no. 1 (1999): 179–201.
Ginsberg, Allen. *Collected Poems, 1947–1980.* New York: Harper and Row, 1984.
Ginsberg, Allen. *Conversations with Allen Ginsberg.* Edited by David Stephen Calonne. Jackson: University Press of Mississippi, 2019.
Ginsberg, Allen. *Deliberate Prose: Selected Essays, 1952–1995.* New York: Harper, 2000.
Ginsberg, Allen. *Howl: Original Draft Facsimile, Transcript, and Variant Versions, Fully Annotated by Author, with Contemporaneous Correspondence, Account of First Public Reading, Legal Skirmishes, Precursor Texts, and Bibliography.* Edited by Barry Miles. New York: Harper Perennial Modern Classics, 2006.
Ginsberg, Allen. *Journals: Early Fifties, Early Sixties.* New York: Grove, 1977.
Ginsberg, Allen, Juanita Lieberman-Plimpton, and Bill Morgan. *The Book of Martyrdom and Artifice: First Journals and Poems, 1937–1952.* Cambridge, MA: Da Capo Press, 2006.
Gissen-Stanley, Rhoney, and Tom Davis. *Owsley and Me: My LSD Family.* Rhinebeck, NY: Monkfish Book Publishing, 2012.
Glatt, John. *Live at the Fillmore East and West: Getting Backstage and Personal with Rock's Greatest Legends.* Guilford, CT: Lyons Press, 2016.
Gleason, Ralph. "On The Town: A Big Rock Party for the Cameras." *San Francisco Chronicle*, February 6, 1970, 42.
Goddu, Teresa A. *Gothic America: Narrative, History, and Nation.* New York: Columbia University Press, 1997.
Goethe, Johann Wolfgang von. *Sämtliche Werke.* Vol. 7/1, *Faust, Texte.* Frankfurt am Main: Deutscher Klassiker, 1999.
Goldsmith, Robert Hillis. *Wise Fools in Shakespeare.* East Lansing: Michigan State University Press, 1963.
"The Grateful Dead's Phil Lesh and the CSM Jazz Band." *College of San Mateo.* Last updated December 8, 2017. https://news.collegeofsanmateo.edu/2017/12/the-grateful-deads-phil-lesh-and-the-csm-jazz-band/.
Greenberg, Mark. "Tom Azarian CD Looks Back to Depression-Era South." *Barre-Montpelier* [VT] *Times Argus*, October 17, 2018. https://www.timesargus.com/news/tom-azarian-cd-looks-back-to-depression-era-south/article_99062415-5bcb-528d-a198-2b1d8b5e8d94.html.

Greenfield, Robert. *Dark Star: An Oral Biography of Jerry Garcia*. New York: Broadway Books, 1996.
Guardian, The. "George R. R. Martin Says Grateful Dead Inspired Previous Work." *Guardian Music*, May 5, 2015. https://www.theguardian.com/music/2015/may/05/grateful-dead-inspired-george-rr-martin.
Guttzeit, Gero. "Authoring Monsters: Mary Shelley, Edgar Allan Poe and Early Nineteenth-Century Figures of Gothic Authorship." *Forum for Modern Language Studies* 54, no. 3 (2018): 279–92.
Hampton, Timothy. *Bob Dylan: How the Songs Work*. New York: Zone Books, 2019.
Hart, Mickey, and Fredric Lieberman. *Planet Drum: A Celebration of Percussion and Rhythm*. New York: HarperCollins, 1991.
Hassett, Brian. *How the Beats Begat the Pranksters and Other Adventure Tales*. N.p.: Gets Things Done Publishing, 2017.
Heching, Dan. "Grateful Dead Bassist and Founding Member Phil Lesh Has Died at 84." CNN *Entertainment*, October 27, 2024. https://www.cnn.com/2024/10/25/entertainment/phil-lesh-death/.
Hedrick, Wally. "Oral History Interview with Wally Hedrick, 1974 June 10–24." Interview by Paul Karlstrom and Julia Hedrick. *Smithsonian*. Accessed April 4, 2025. https://www.aaa.si.edu/collections/interviews/oral-history-interview-wally-hedrick-12869.
Hegel, G. W. F. *The Logic of Hegel*. Translated by William Wallace. Oxford: Clarendon Press, 1968.
Heine, Stefanie. *Poetics of Breathing: Modern Literature's Syncope*. Albany: State University of New York Press, 2021.
Helm, Levon, with Stephen Davis. *This Wheel's on Fire: Levon Helm and the Story of the Band*. Chicago: Chicago Review Press, 2000.
Hesiod. *Hesiod*. Vol. 1. Edited and translated by Glenn W. Most. Loeb Classical Library 57. Cambridge, MA: Harvard University Press, 2006.
Heylin, Clinton. *Bob Dylan: Behind the Shades*. New York: HarperCollins, 2000.
Hill, Juniper, and Caroline Bithell. "An Introduction to Music Revival as Concept, Cultural Process, and Medium of Change." In *The Oxford Handbook of Music Revival*, edited by Caroline Bithell and Juniper Hill, 3–42. New York: Oxford University Press, 2014.
Hirsch, Edward. *A Poet's Glossary*. Boston: Houghton Mifflin Harcourt, 2014.
Holsapple, Bruce. *The Birth of the Imagination: William Carlos Williams on Form*. Albuquerque: University of New Mexico Press, 2016.
Homer. *Iliad*. Vol. 2, *Books 13–24*. Translated by A. T. Murray, revised by William F. Wyatt. Loeb Classical Library 171. Cambridge, MA: Harvard University Press, 1925.
Homer. *Odyssey*. Vol. 1, *Books 1–12*. Translated by A. T. Murray, revised by George E. Dimock. Cambridge, MA: Harvard University Press, 1919.
Hughes, Tom. *Hanging the Peachtree Bandit: The True Tale of Atlanta's Infamous Frank DuPre*. Charleston, SC: History Press, 2014.
Hunter, Robert. *Box of Rain: Lyrics, 1965–1993*. New York: Viking Penguin, 1993.

Hunter, Robert. "February 25, 1988; San Rafael, California." Interview by David Gans. In Gans, *Conversations with the Dead*, 266–89.

Hunter, Robert. Foreword to *Alleys of the Heart: The Collected Poems of Robert M. Petersen*, by Robert M. Petersen, v–vi. Eugene, OR: Hulogosi, 1988.

Hunter, Robert. "Fractures of Unfamiliarity and Circumvention in Pursuit of a Nice Time." *Robert Hunter Archive*, March 4, 1996. Archived November 1, 1996. https://web.archive.org/web/19961101220511/http://www.dead.net/RobertHunterArchive.html/files/Essays/fauthreply.html.

Hunter, Robert. *Idiot's Delight*. New York: Hanuman, 1992.

Hunter, Robert. Interview by Robert O'Brian. *Relix* 13, no. 5 (1986): 18–19.

Hunter, Robert. Journal entry for July 29, 1996. In "Journal 8.06.96," *Robert Hunter Archive*. Archived November 1, 1996. https://web.archive.org/web/19961101214618/http://www.dead.net/RobertHunterArchive.html/files/journal/15journal_8.06.96.html.

Hunter, Robert. "Journal 2006–2007." *Robert Hunter Archive*, February 2, 2006–August 6, 2007. Archived August 4, 2024. https://web.archive.org/web/20240804102714/http://www.hunterarchive.com/files/newjournal/56journal_2006.html.

Hunter, Robert. "The Man Behind the Words (Part 2)." Interview by Monte Dym and Bob Alson. *Relix* 5, no. 2 (May–June 1978): 21–28.

Hunter, Robert. *Night Cadre*. New York: Viking, 1991.

Hunter, Robert. "A Rose Grows from the Shadows: The Grateful Dead's Lyricist Speaks About His Life and His Art." In Gans, *Conversations with the Dead*, 22–30.

Hunter, Robert. *Sentinel*. New York: Penguin, 1993.

Hunter, Robert. "The Song Goes On: An Interview: February 23, 1988." Interview by Blair Jackson. In *Goin' Down the Road: A Grateful Dead Traveling Companion*, edited by Blair Jackson, 106–24. New York: Harmony Books, 1992.

Hunter, Robert. "Songs of Innocence, Songs of Experience." Interview by Mary Eisenhart. *Golden Road*, no. 4 (Fall 1984): 12–19.

Hunter, Robert. "Standing in the Soul." Interview by Steve Silberman. *Poetry Flash*, no. 237 (December 1992): 1, 6–9, 11.

Hunter, Robert, and Jerry Garcia. "Hunter/Garcia; Words/Music: An Interview About Songwriting and Inspiration." Interview by Blair Jackson. In *Goin' Down the Road: A Grateful Dead Traveling Companion*, edited by Blair Jackson, 205–34. New York: Harmony Books, 1992.

Huyssen, Andreas. "Paris/Childhood: The Fragmented Body in Rilke's *Notebooks of Malte Laurids Brigge*." In *Modernity and the Text: Revisions of German Modernism*, edited by Andreas Huyssen and David Bathrick, 113–41. New York: Columbia University Press, 1989.

Jackson, Blair. "Chapter 17 Additions." Archived November 27, 2021. https://web.archive.org/web/20211127021304/http://www.blairjackson.com/chapter_seventeen_additions.htm.

Jackson, Blair. *Garcia: An American Life*. New York: Viking Penguin, 1999.

Jackson, Blair. *Grateful Dead Gear: The Band's Instruments, Sound Systems, and Recording Sessions from 1965 to 1995*. San Francisco: Backbeat Books, 2006.

Jackson, Blair. *Grateful Dead: The Music Never Stopped*. New York: Delilah, 1983. Distributed by Putnam.

Jackson, Blair, and David Gans. *This Is All a Dream We Dreamed: An Oral History of the Grateful Dead*. New York: Flatiron Books, 2015.

Jarnow, Jesse. *Heads: A Biography of Psychedelic America*. Philadelphia: Da Capo Press, 2015.

Jarnow, Jesse. Liner notes to *Ready or Not*, by the Grateful Dead. Rhino R2 596008, 2019, compact disc.

Jarnow, Jesse. Liner notes to *30 Trips Around the Sun*, by the Grateful Dead. Rhino R7 547369, 2015, 80 compact discs and 7-inch 45 RPM vinyl.

Jerry Garcia Family. "1980–11–16 The Warfield, San Francisco CA—Jerry Garcia." 2014. https://jerrygarcia.com/show/1980-11-16-the-warfield-san-francisco-ca/.

Johnson, Ronna C. "Three Generations of Beat Poetics." In *The Cambridge Companion to American Poetry Since 1945*, edited by Jennifer Ashton, 80–93. Cambridge: Cambridge University Press, 2013.

Joyce, James. *Finnegans Wake*. 1939. Reprint, New York: Viking Penguin, 1967.

Joyce, James. *Ulysses*. 1922. Reprint, New York: Random House; Vintage, 1986.

Junod, Tom. "Who Is This Bob Dylan?" *Esquire* 161, no. 2 (February 1, 2014). https://classic.esquire.com/article/2014/2/1/who-is-this-bob-dylan.

Junyk, Ihor. "'A Fragment from Another Context': Modernist Classicism and the Urban Uncanny in Rainer Maria Rilke." *Comparative Literature* 62, no. 3 (Summer 2010): 262–82.

Kant, Immanuel. *Critique of Pure Reason*. Translated by Paul Guyer and Allen W. Wood. Cambridge: Cambridge University Press, 1998.

Kant, Immanuel. *Kant's Critique of Aesthetic Judgment*. Translated by James Creed Meredith. Oxford: Clarendon Press, 1911.

Kant, Immanuel. *Kritik der reinen Vernunft*. 2 vols. 1781, 1787. London: Routledge, 1994.

Kenner, Hugh. *Ulysses*. Revised ed. Baltimore: Johns Hopkins University Press, 1987.

Kerouac, Jack. *Big Sur*. New York: Penguin, 1962.

Kerouac, Jack. *Conversations with Jack Kerouac*. Jackson: University Press of Mississippi, 2005.

Kerouac, Jack. *The Dharma Bums*. 1958. Reprint, New York: Penguin, 1976.

Kerouac, Jack. *On the Road*. New York: Penguin, 1957.

Kerouac, Jack. *The Portable Jack Kerouac*. Edited by Ann Charters. New York: Penguin, 1995.

Kerouac, Jack. *Visions of Cody*. New York: Penguin, 1972.

King, Stephen. "My Pretty Pony." Read by Jerry Garcia. In *Nightmares and Dreamscapes*. Vol. 2. Audio, 53:55. New York: Penguin HighBridge Audio, 1994.

Komar, Kathleen L. "The *Duino Elegies*." In *The Cambridge Companion to Rilke*, edited by Karen Leeder and Robert Vilain, 80–94. Cambridge: Cambridge University Press, 2010.

Komar, Kathleen L. "Rethinking Rilke's *Duineser Elegien* at the End of the Milennium." In *A Companion to the Works of Rainer Maria Rilke*, edited by Erika A. Metzger and Michael M. Metzger, 188–208. Rochester, NY: Camden House, 2001.

Kozlovsky, Roy. "Beat Literature and the Domestication of American Space." *AA Files* 51 (Winter 2005): 36–47.

Krassner, Paul. *Confessions of a Raving, Unconfined Nut: Misadventures in the Counterculture*. New York: Simon and Schuster, 1993.

Kreutzmann, Bill, and Benjy Eisen. *Deal: My Three Decades of Drumming, Dreams, and Drugs with the Grateful Dead*. New York: St. Martin's Press, 2015.

Lacoue-Labarthe, Philippe, and Jean-Luc Nancy. *The Literary Absolute: The Theory of Literature in German Romanticism*. Translated by Philip Barnard and Cheryl Lester. Albany: State University of New York Press, 1988.

Lesh, Phil. *Searching for the Sound: My Life with the Grateful Dead*. New York: Little, Brown, 2005.

Lethem, Jonathan. "The Genius of Bob Dylan." *Rolling Stone*, no. 1008 (September 7, 2006).

Longfellow, Henry Wadsworth. *The Works of Henry Wadsworth Longfellow; Poems*. Vol. 3. Boston: Houghton Mifflin, 1910.

Mai, Anne-Marie. *Bob Dylan the Poet*. Odense: University Press of Southern Denmark, 2018.

Massey, Irving. *The Gaping Pig: Literature and Metamorphosis*. Berkeley: University of California Press, 1976.

McNally, Dennis. *Desolate Angel: Jack Kerouac, the Beat Generation, and America*. New York: McGraw-Hill, 1979.

McNally, Dennis. *A Long Strange Trip: The Inside History of the Grateful Dead*. New York: Broadway Books, 2002.

Meriwether, Nicholas G. "A Note on the Textual History of the Dead's 1967 Statement." *Proceedings of the Grateful Dead Studies Association* 3 (2023): 95–98.

Meriwether, Nicholas G. "Robert Hunter, William Faulkner, and 'It Must Have Been the Roses.'" In *All Graceful Instruments: The Contexts of the Grateful Dead Phenomenon*, edited by Nicholas G. Meriwether, 52–71. Newcastle: Cambridge Scholars, 2007.

Meriwether, Nick. "12/1/66." Concert review. In *The Deadhead's Taping Compendium*. Vol. 1, *1959–1974*, edited by Michael M. Getz and John Dwork, 120–24. New York: Henry Holt, 1998.

Merrill, James. *Collected Poems*. New York: Knopf, 2001.

Michaels, Sean. "Bob Dylan: Robert Burns Is My Biggest Inspiration." *The Guardian*, October 6, 2008. https://www.theguardian.com/music/2008/oct/06/bob.dylan.robert.burns.inspiration.

Miller, Perry. *The Raven and the Whale: The War of Words and Wits in the Era of Poe and Melville*. New York: Greenwood Press, 1956.

Morgan, Bill. *I Celebrate Myself: The Somewhat Private Life of Allen Ginsberg*. New York: Penguin, 2007.

Morse, J. Mitchell. "Cain, Abel, and Joyce." *ELH* 22, no. 1 (March 1955): 48–60.

Mortenson, Erik. "Allen Ginsberg and Beat Poetry." In *The Cambridge Companion to the Beats*, edited by Steven Belletto, 77–91. Cambridge: Cambridge University Press, 2017.

Myers, M. Luke [confusions_prince]. "Robert Hunter's Bio." *RUKIND*, March 12, 2007. https://www.rukind.com/viewtopic.php?t=2113.

Nancy, Jean-Luc. *The Experience of Freedom*. Translated by Bridget McDonald. Stanford CA: Stanford University Press, 1993.

Nancy, Jean-Luc. *Logodaedalus: Le Discours de la syncope*. Paris: Aubier-Flammarion, 1976.

Nikhilananda, Swami, ed. and trans. *The Upanishads*. London: George Allen and Unwin, 1963.

O'Donnell, Shaugn. "Bobby, Béla, and Borrowing in 'Victim or the Crime.'" In *All Graceful Instruments: The Contexts of the Grateful Dead Phenomenon*, edited by Nicholas G. Meriwether, 38–51. Newcastle: Cambridge Scholars, 2007.

Odum, Howard W., and Guy B. Johnson. *Negro Workaday Songs*. Chapel Hill: University of North Carolina Press, 1926.

Osmond-Smith, David. *Playing on Words: A Guide to Luciano Berio's "Sinfonia."* London: Royal Musical Association, 1985.

Ovid. *Metamorphoses*, Books 1–8. 3rd ed. Translated by Frank Justus Miller. Loeb Classical Library 42. Cambridge, MA: Harvard University Press, 1984.

Ovid. *Shakespeare's Ovid, Being Arthur Golding's Translation of the Metamorphoses*. Carbondale: Southern Illinois University Press, 1961.

Parry, Amie Elizabeth. *Interventions into Modernist Cultures: Poetry from Beyond the Empty Screen*. Durham, NC: Duke University Press, 2007.

Perry, Charles. "A New Life for the Dead: Grateful Dead Handle Their Business." *Rolling Stone*, no. 148 (November 22, 1973).

Plotinus. *The Enneads*. Translated by Stephen MacKenna. London: Penguin, 1991.

Pöhlmann, Sascha. *Future-Founding Poetry: Topographies of Beginnings from Whitman to the Twenty-First Century*. Rochester, NY: Camden House, 2015.

Poole, Buzz. *Workingman's Dead*. New York: Bloomsbury, 2016.

"Project MK-Ultra." *Freedom of Information Act Electronic Reading Room*, April 3, 2018. https://www.cia.gov/readingroom/document/06760269.

Rae, Patricia. "Introduction: Modernist Mourning." In *Modernism and Mourning*, edited by Patricia Rae, 13–49. Lewisburg, PA: Bucknell University Press, 2007.

Ramazani, Jahan. *Poetry of Mourning: The Modern Elegy from Hardy to Heaney*. Chicago: University of Chicago Press, 1994.

"Random Notes." *Rolling Stone*, no. 83 (May 27, 1971).

Redding, Arthur. *Haints: American Ghosts, Millennial Passions, and Contemporary Gothic Fictions*. Tuscaloosa: University of Alabama Press, 2011.

Ribner, Irving. *The English History Play in the Age of Shakespeare*. London: Routledge, 1965.

Richardson, Peter. *No Simple Highway: A Cultural History of the Grateful Dead*. New York: St. Martin's Griffin, 2014.

Rilke, Rainer Maria. *Duino Elegies; The Sonnets to Orpheus*. Translated by Robert Hunter. Eugene, OR: Hulogosi, 1993.
Rilke, Rainer Maria. *The Poetry of Rilke*. Translated by Edward Snow. New York: Farrar, Straus and Giroux; North Point Press, 2009.
Rilke, Rainer Maria. *Werke: Kommentierte Ausgabe in vier Bänden mit einem Supplementband*. 4 vols. Edited by Manfred Engel, Ulrich Fülleborn, Dorothea Lauterbach, Horst Nalewski, and August Stahl. Frankfurt am Main: Insel, 1996.
Rimbaud, Arthur. *Complete Works, Selected Letters*. Translated by Wallace Fowlie. Chicago: University of Chicago Press, 1966.
Rimbaud, Arthur. *A Season in Hell*. Translated by Louise Varèse. New York: New Directions, 1961.
Rollins, Elizabeth. "The Twilight Zone." *The Mix* 9, no. 12 (December 1985): 32–33, 38, 40, 42.
Ryan, Judith. *Rilke, Modernism and Poetic Tradition*. Cambridge: Cambridge University Press, 1999.
Ryan, Lawrence. "*Neue Gedichte / New Poems*." In *A Companion to the Works of Rainer Maria Rilke*, edited by Erika A. Metzger and Michael M. Metzger, 128–53. Rochester, NY: Camden House, 2001.
Sacks, Peter M. *The English Elegy: Studies in the Genre from Spenser to Yeats*. Baltimore: Johns Hopkins University Press, 1987.
Sanders, Andrew. *The Short Oxford History of English Literature*. Rev. ed. Oxford: Clarendon Press, 1996.
Schlegel, Friedrich. *Friedrich Schlegel's "Lucinde" and the Fragments*. Translated by Peter Firchow. Minneapolis: University of Minnesota Press, 1971.
Schlegel, Friedrich. *Kritische Ausgabe*. Vol. 18. Paderborn: Ferdinand Schöningh, 1963.
Schlegel, Friedrich. *On the Study of Greek Poetry*. Translated by Stuart Barnett. Albany: State University of New York Press, 2001.
Scofield Reference Bible. Edited by C. I. Scofield. New York: Oxford University Press, 1945.
Scott, John W., Stu Nixon, and Mike Dolgushkin, eds. *DeadBase 50*. N.p.: Watermark Press, 2015.
Scully, Rock, and David Dalton. *Living with the Dead*. Boston: Little, Brown, 1996.
Seng, Peter J. *The Vocal Songs in the Plays of Shakespeare: A Critical History*. Cambridge, MA: Harvard University Press, 1967.
Shakespeare, William. *The Riverside Shakespeare*. 2nd ed. Boston: Houghton Mifflin, 1997.
Sharp, Cecil J., and Olive Dame Campbell. *English Folk Songs from the Southern Appalachians*. 2 vols. London: Oxford University Press, 1932.
Shelley, Mary. *Frankenstein*. 1831. Reprint, New York: Dover, 1994.
Shelton, Robert. *Bob Dylan: No Direction Home*. London: Palazzo Editions, 2021.
Shenk, David, and Steve Silberman. *Skeleton Key: A Dictionary for Deadheads*. New York: Doubleday, 1994.

Sounes, Howard. *Down the Highway: The Life of Bob Dylan*. New York: Grove Press, 2021.
Stephenson, Gregory. *The Daybreak Boys: Essays on the Literature of the Beat Generation*. Carbondale: Southern Illinois University Press, 1990.
Sturgeon, Theodore. *More Than Human*. Thorndike, ME: Thorndike Press, 1953.
Sutton, Shan C. "The Deadhead Community: Popular Religion in Contemporary American Culture." In *Deadhead Social Science: You Ain't Gonna Learn What You Don't Want to Know*, edited by Rebecca G. Adams and Robert Sardiello, 109–28. Walnut Creek, CA: AltaMira Press, 2000.
Tantillo, Astrida Orle. "Damned to Heaven: The Tragedy of *Faust* Revisited." *Monatshefte* 99, no. 4 (2007): 454–68.
Teichman, Mimi. "The Night the Grateful Dead Inspired a 'Cast-of-Thousands Orgy' at the Mississippi River Festival." *St. Louis Post-Dispatch*, July 8, 2022. https://www.stltoday.com/news/archives/the-night-the-grateful-dead-inspired-a-cast-of-thousands-orgy-at-the-mississippi-river/article_eaa9d3d8-febd-11ec-9795-b3d28e9c5224.html.
Tennyson, Alfred. *The Poems of Tennyson*. Edited by Christopher Ricks. London: Longmans, 1969.
Thomas, Vivian, and Nicki Faircloth. *Shakespeare's Plants and Gardens: A Dictionary*. London: Bloomsbury, 2014.
Thompson, Hunter S. *Fear and Loathing in America: The Brutal Odyssey of an Outlaw Journalist*. New York: Simon and Schuster, 2000.
Thompson, Hunter S. *Fear and Loathing in Las Vegas: A Savage Journey into the Heart of the American Dream*. New York: Random House, 1972.
Thompson, Hunter S. *The Great Shark Hunt: Strange Tales from a Strange Time*. New York: Warner Books, 1979.
Thompson, Hunter S. *The Proud Highway: Saga of a Desperate Southern Gentleman, 1955–1967*. New York: Villard, 1997.
Tillyard, E. M. W. *Shakespeare's History Plays*. New York: Macmillan, 1947.
Tolley, Michael J. "Preromanticism." In *A Companion to Romanticism*, edited by Duncan Wu, 12–22. Oxford: Blackwell, 1998.
Trist, Alan, and David Dodd, eds. *The Complete Annotated Grateful Dead Lyrics*. New York: Free Press, 2005.
Trudeau, Robert H. "A Super-Metacantric Analysis of 'Playing in the Band.'" In *Reading the Grateful Dead: A Critical Survey*, edited by Nicholas C. Meriwether, 93–108. Lanham, MD: Scarecrow Press, 2012.
Tuedio, Jim, and Stan Spector. "Preface: Kaleidoscopic Entry to the Show." In *The Grateful Dead in Concert*, edited by Jim Tuedio and Stan Spector, 7–9. Jefferson, NC: McFarland, 2010.
Turner, Rob. *Counterfeit Culture: Truth and Authenticity in the American Prose Epic Since 1960*. Cambridge: Cambridge University Press, 2019.
Twain, Mark. *Mark Twain*. New York: Crown; Greenwich, 1982.
Tytell, John. *Naked Angels*. New York: Grove Weidenfeld, 1976.
Vandenberg, Kathleen. *Joan Didion: Substance and Style*. Albany: State University of New York Press, 2021.

Virgil. *The Georgics*. Bilingual ed. Translated by David Ferry. New York: Farrar, Straus and Giroux, 2005.

Vogel, Andrew. "The Dream and the Dystopia: Bathetic Humor, the Beats, and Walt Whitman's Idealism." *Amerikastudien / American Studies* 58, no. 3 (2013): 389–407.

Vonnegut, Kurt. Interview by Jesse Kornbluth and Robert Weide, hosted by Marlene T. *The Book Report*, November 22, 1996. Archived January 15, 1998. https://web.archive.org/web/19980115150204/http://www.flf.com/mnight/aol_qa.htm.

von Phul, Ruth. "Who Sleeps at *Finnegans Wake*?" *James Joyce Review* 1 (1957): 27–38.

Walker, Bill. "Anthem: A Walkers Guide." Accessed February 4, 2025. https://static1.squarespace.com/static/5cb8cbbbcc78540001d0eb7a/t/5cc34e0b15fcc0ce99ffe30c/1556303373000/AnthemGuide.pdf.

Wallace, David Foster. *Infinite Jest*. Boston: Back Bay Books, 1996.

Weinreich, Regina. "Locating a Beat Aesthetic." In *The Cambridge Companion to the Beats*, edited by Steven Belletto, 51–61. Cambridge: Cambridge University Press, 2017.

Weir, Roberta. "The Art of Jerry Garcia: 'A Line on Paper Is Like a Note in the Air.'" *Garcia Weir Gallery*, 2019. Accessed January 23, 2020. http://www.garciaweirgallery.com/jerry-garcia.html.

Welch, Lew. *Ring of Bone: Collected Poems*. San Francisco: City Lights, 2012.

Whitman, Walt. *Leaves of Grass*. 1855. Reprint, New York: Vintage; Library of America, 1992.

Williams, Paul. *Bob Dylan: Performing Artist, 1986–1990 and Beyond, Mind Out of Time*. London: Omnibus Press, 2004.

Williams, Paul. "Theodore Sturgeon, Storyteller." Afterword to *Case and the Dreamer: The Complete Stories of Theodore Sturgeon*, vol. 13, edited by Noel Sturgeon 327–54. Berkeley, CA: North Atlantic Books, 2010.

Williams, William Carlos. "Introduction by William Carlos Williams to *Howl*." In *Collected Poems, 1947–1980*, by Allen Ginsberg, 811–12. New York: Harper and Row, 1984.

Williams, William Carlos. *The Collected Poems of William Carlos Williams*. Vol. 1, *1909–1939*. New York: New Directions, 1986.

Williams, William Carlos. *The Collected Poems of William Carlos Williams*. Vol. 2, *1939–1962*. New York: New Directions, 1988.

Wolfe, Tom. *The Electric Kool-Aid Acid Test*. 1968. Reprint, New York: Bantam, 1981.

Wood, Andy. *The 1549 Rebellions and the Making of Early Modern England*. New York: Cambridge University Press, 2007.

Wood, Brent. *The Tragic Odes of Jerry Garcia and the Grateful Dead: Mystery Dances in the Magic Theater*. London: Routledge, 2020.

"*Workingman's Dead* 50, Episode 3: 'Dire Wolf.'" *Good Ol' Grateful Deadcast*, December 9, 2021. Audio, 48:54. https://www.dead.net/deadcast/workingmans-dead-50-episode-3-dire-wolf.

Yeats, W. B. *The Collected Works of W. B. Yeats*. Vol. 1, *The Poems*. 2nd ed. New York: Scribner, 1997.

Index

Acid Tests, 44–48, 199–200
Aeschylus: *Libation Bearers*, 113; *Oresteia*, 105
Ahlers, Ozzie, 65
"Alabama Getaway" (Grateful Dead), 119, 125, 133
Albin, Peter, 115
Albin, Rodney, 115
Alembic, 71
Alighieri, Dante, 183; *Commedia*, 25–28, 175; *Inferno*, 26–27; *Purgatorio*, 27; *Vita Nuova*, 28
"All Along the Watchtower" (Dylan), 125, 128, 136
Alleys of the Heart (Petersen), 138, 175; foreword to (Hunter), 138, 175
"Alligator" (Grateful Dead), 55, 204
Altamont Speedway Free Festival, 41, 85–86
"Althea" (Grateful Dead), 31, 40, 97–98, 109–14, 116–20, 181
Amagamalin Street (Hunter), 157
"American Adventure, An" (Hunter), 192–95
American Beauty (Grateful Dead), 30, 73–75, 85, 90, 107
Andersen, Eric, 156
Andersen, Hans Christian: "The Marsh King," 104
Andrews, Betty, 14
Anthem of the Sun (Grateful Dead), 4, 49, 51, 73, 161
Aoxomoxoa (Grateful Dead), 15, 73–74, 104
"Armageddon Rag" (Hunter), 218n4
Ashbery, John: "Self-Portrait in a Convex Mirror," 196, 203
Athenaeum (periodical), 7, 10
"Attics of My Life" (Grateful Dead), 208
Auden, W. H., 160; "In Memory of W. B. Yeats," 175
Avalon Ballroom, 15, 47, 55

avant-garde classical music, 160–61, 203
Azarian, Tom ("Tom Banjo"), 106

Bakunin, Mikhail, 11
"Ballad of a Thin Man" (Dylan), 142
Bama (W. D. Stewart): "Stackerlee," 15
Band, The, 123, 129; *Before the Flood* (*see* Bob Dylan); *Music from Big Pink*, 75; "The Night They Drove Old Dixie Down," 94
Baraka, Amiri, 48
Barlow, John Perry, 26–27, 138, 156, 225n59; Bob Weir and Neal Cassady, 49. *See also* Grateful Dead (songs)
Bartók, Béla, 160
Barton, Charles: *Abbott and Costello Meet Frankenstein*, 30, 70
Bates, Katharine Lee: "America the Beautiful," 193
Baum, L. Frank, 25, 28
Beach Boys, 123
Bear. *See* Stanley, Augustus Owsley, III,
Beat Generation, 35, 51, 58, 60, 63, 135, 198; American voice of, 38, 52–53, 56, 62; contemporary voice of, 41–43; future-founding poetry and, 30, 39, 41, 49, 62, 216n9; Jerry Garcia on, 36; Wally Hedrick and, 43–44; Modernism and, 160; name of movement, 37, 50, 55; politics of, 40, 216n15; post-Beat culture and, 43, 45–48, 51; Walt Whitman and, 59; William Carlos Williams and, 54
"Beat It on Down the Line" (Grateful Dead), 144
Beckett, Samuel, 161
Before the Flood (Dylan), 137
Belafonte, Harry, 14
Berio, Luciano, 161

Berkeley Poetry Conference, 48
Berlin Alexanderplatz (Döblin), 181
"Bertha" (Grateful Dead), 74
Bierce, Ambrose: "An Occurrence at Owl Creek Bridge," 87
Big Brother and the Holding Company, 115
"Bird Song" (Grateful Dead), 86
Black Mountain Boys, 13
"Black Muddy River" (Grateful Dead), 31, 109, 133
"Black Peter" (Grateful Dead), 72, 85, 176
"Black-Throated Wind" (Grateful Dead), 87, 144–45, 147–49, 224n59
Blanchot, Maurice, 9–11
Blonde on Blonde (Dylan), 127, 142–44
"Blood on the Sheets" (Hunter), 218n4
bluegrass, 75
blues, 75, 124, 156
"Blues for Allah" (Grateful Dead), 23
Boar's Head, 115, 222n31
"Bonnie Lass o' Fyvie, The" (traditional), 76. *See also* "Peggy-O" (Grateful Dead); "Pretty Peggy-O" (Dylan)
Boston University, 72
Bourne, Christie, 72
"Box of Rain" (Grateful Dead), 86
Box of Rain (Hunter), 157
"Boys in the Barroom" (Hunter), 184
Bralove, Bob, 40
Brautigan, Richard: "The Day They Busted the Grateful Dead," 33, 204–5
"Bride of Entropy, The" (Hunter), 192
Bride of Entropy, The (Hunter), 192, 195
Brihadaranyaka Upanishad, 23
"Brokedown Palace" (Grateful Dead), 68, 86, 133
Brown, Charles Brockden, 87
"Brown-Eyed Women" (Grateful Dead), 40, 74, 87, 185
Browning, Page, 46
Brust, Steven: *Brokedown Palace*, 204
Budnick, Dean: *Might as Well*, 204
Buena Vista Studio, 87
Burke, Edmund, 67
Burns, Robert, 31, 67–69, 135, 198; "Auld Lang Syne," 68; "Halloween," 68; "A Red, Red Rose," 68; "Tam O'Shanter," 68
Burroughs, William S., 43, 47, 216n9; *Junkie*, 43; *Naked Lunch*, 43, 216n9

Cade, Jack, 120
California School of Fine Arts, 44
Campbell, Joseph, 5, 169–70; *A Skeleton Key to Finnegans Wake*, 161
Campbell, Larry, 133
"Candyman" (Grateful Dead), 86
"Can't Come Down" (Grateful Dead), 39, 55
card games, 80, 83, 89, 173

Cargill, Melissa, 71
"Carrion Crow, The" (nursery rhyme), 104–8
"Casey Jones" (Grateful Dead), 72, 85, 202
Cassady, Neal, 30, 44, 46–47, 49, 193, 217n36; Jerry Garcia and Bob Weir on, 45, 48; *Joan Anderson Letter*, 41–43; "The Other One" and, 50–53, 55, 62
"Cassidy" (Grateful Dead), 51, 68, 74, 125
Charles, Andrew, 156
Chelsea Hotel, 37
"China Cat Sunflower" (Grateful Dead), 23, 152
"China Doll" (Grateful Dead), 166
"Chinatown Shuffle" (Grateful Dead), 74
Christian, Charlie, 134
City Lights, 43
"Clatter Like Fine Mist, A" (Hunter), 187, 191
"Cold Rain and Snow" (Grateful Dead), 51
Cold War, 30, 39, 53, 216n9
Coleridge, Samuel Taylor: "Kubla Khan," 193
"Comes a Time" (Grateful Dead), 74–75
comics, 30, 65, 152
Conrad, Joseph: *Heart of Darkness*, 25
Constanten, Tom, 5, 74, 104, 122, 157, 160–61; "Dark Star," 3, 119
Cooperman, Robert, 204
Corso, Gregory, 55, 216n15
"Cosmic Charlie" (Grateful Dead), 60
counterculture, 41, 47, 67, 71, 75, 129, 199; Neal Cassady and, 46
Coupland, Douglas: *Polaroids from the Dead*, 33, 205–8
Craddock, William J.: *Be Not Content*, 204
"Cream Puff War" (Grateful Dead), 40, 143
Creeley, Robert, 48
"Cryptical Envelopment" (Grateful Dead), 49–50, 53

"Dark Star" (Grateful Dead), 3–4, 119, 151–52, 160, 319
David Nelson Band, 161
Dead Heads (periodical), 84, 156
"Deal" (Grateful Dead), 87
Desire (Dylan), 136
"Desolation Row" (Dylan), 98–100, 103–4, 112, 118, 124, 150, 152
Desperado (periodical), 156
Dick, Philip K.: *The Transmigration of Timothy Archer*, 202; *VALIS*, 33, 202
Didion, Joan: *The Last Thing He Wanted*, 202; *Slouching Towards Bethlehem*, 33, 201–2
Di Prima, Diane, 58
"Dire Wolf" (Grateful Dead), 31, 74, 76–84, 86, 88–91, 95–96, 125
Dixon, Willie, 156
Dog Moon (Hunter), 157
"Doin' that Rag" (Grateful Dead), 101

Donne, John, 25
"Don't Think Twice, It's All Right" (Dylan), 124
"Door to the Sea, The" (Hunter), 181–85
Dostoevsky, Fyodor, 42
Down in the Groove (Dylan), 130, 132
Doyle, Arthur Conan: *The Hound of the Baskervilles*, 31, 77–78, 89
Dracula, 70
Drake, Nick: "Black Eyed Dog," 219n45
Duino Elegies. See Rainer Maria Rilke
Duncan, Robert, 48
DuPre, Frank, 14–19
"Dupree's Diamond Blues" (Grateful Dead), 14–20, 29, 73–74
"Duquesne Whistle" (Dylan), 132
Dylan, Bob, 76, 136, 138–39, 141, 198–99; Robert Burns and, 68; collaborations with, 31–32, 123–26, 133; as composer, 121–22, 151; Jerry Garcia and, 40, 116–17, 129–31, 134; influence of Grateful Dead on, 31–32, 122–23, 128–30, 132–33; Never Ending Tour, 130; Nobel Prize and, 122, 126, 153; performances by, 126–27; *The Philosophy of Modern Song*, 133–35; recordings of Grateful Dead songs, 132; William Shakespeare and, 98–101, 103, 112, 118; Hunter S. Thompson on, 200
Dylan, Bob (albums): *Before the Flood*, 137; *Blonde on Blonde*, 127, 142–44; *Desire*, 136; *Down in the Groove*, 130, 132; *Dylan and the Dead (see* Grateful Dead: albums; *Good as I Been to You*, 130; *Highway 61 Revisited*, 142; *John Wesley Harding*, 75; *Oh Mercy*, 130; *Tempest*, 132; *Time Out of Mind*, 130; *Together Through Life*, 132; *Under a Red Sky*, 130; *World Gone Wrong*, 130
Dylan, Bob (songs): "All Along the Watchtower," 125, 128, 136; "Ballad of a Thin Man," 142; "Desolation Row," 98–100, 103–4, 112, 118, 124, 150, 152; "Don't Think Twice, It's All Right," 124; "Duquesne Whistle," 132; "It Takes a Lot to Laugh, It Takes a Train to Cry," 123; "It's All Over Now, Baby Blue," 123–25, 127, 136, 143; "It's Alright, Ma (I'm Only Bleeding)," 151; "Mr. Tambourine Man," 140–41; "Positively 4th Street," 40, 143; "Pretty Peggy-O," 76; "Queen Jane Approximately," 136, 151; "Rainy Day Women #12 & 35," 125; "She Belongs to Me," 99, 123, 127; "Silvio," 132; "Stuck Inside of Mobile with the Memphis Blues Again," 98; "Ugliest Girl in the World," 132; "Visions of Johanna," 144–45, 148; "When I Paint My Masterpiece," 125, 128, 136; "You're Gonna Make Me Lonesome When You Go," 136
Dylan and the Dead. See Grateful Dead (albums)

Electra, 104–5
elegies, 174–75, 177–78, 180

"Eleven, The" (Grateful Dead), 61, 101
Eliot, T. S., 32, 36, 161, 195, 198; "The Love Song of J. Alfred Prufrock," 160; *The Waste Land*, 23, 118, 159–60, 176, 181
"Empty Pages" (Grateful Dead), 74, 87
ephemerality, 92, 104, 111, 195
Ernst, Max, 160
Euripides: *Hecuba*, 115; *The Trojan Women*, 115
Europe '72 (Grateful Dead), 73
Exodus, 23
"Eyes of the World" (Grateful Dead), 166

"Faster We Go, the Rounder We Get, The" (Grateful Dead), 50, 53, 62
Faulkner, William, 87, 160; "A Rose for Emily," 160
Fennario, 76–78, 80, 89–91, 219n44
Ferlinghetti, Lawrence, 43–44
Fichte, Johann Gottlieb, 7, 67
"Finnegan's Wake" (traditional), 170
"Fire on the Mountain" (Grateful Dead), 51
Fisher, Terence, 78
Flight of the Marie Helena (Hunter), 157
folk tradition, 80, 87, 101, 118, 127, 151, 170; "Dire Wolf" and, 83; "Dupree's Diamond Blues" and, 15–16, 19–20; Faust and, 88–89; literary fragment and, 197; "Mountains of the Moon" and, 104–5. *See also* Fennario
Foster, Stephen, 134
fragment, 29, 32, 37, 45, 138, 207–8; "Black-Throated Wind" and, 149; Bob Dylan's William Shakespeare and, 100; folk songs and, 2; future-founding poetry and, 38, 41, 56; gothic and, 67, 69; Grateful Dead music and, 4, 13–14, 98, 104, 107, 122; Robert Hunter's poetry and, 184; James Joyce and, 165; limit of philosophy and, 5–6, 8–9, 11–2, 24, 197; Modernism and, 158–59; "Mountains of the Moon" and, 104, 107; Rainer Maria Rilke and, 172, 191; productive power of, 16, 30, 92, 111, 119, 139, 142; "Visions of Johanna" and, 144
"Franklin's Tower" (Grateful Dead), 141–42
"Friend of the Devil" (Grateful Dead), 31, 40, 85, 88–96, 132–33
Front Street, 129
Frost, Robert, 20, 22
Further Inquiry, The (Kesey), 46–48, 52–53
future-founding poetry, 37–39, 41, 53, 63, 149; "That's It for the Other One" and, 49, 62

Garcia, Jerry, 38, 40, 50, 52, 70, 94, 118–19; Beats and, 44–48; Joan Didion and, 201–2; "Dire Wolf" and, 77, 83–85; Bob Dylan and, 117, 121–22, 126–27, 129–35, 153; Frankenstein and, 70; *Garcia Plays Dylan*, 132; Grateful Dead and, 4, 60, 74, 199; David Grisman and, 107; James Joyce and, 161–63, 168, 170; literary and

INDEX   245

Garcia, Jerry (continued)
  musical traditions and, 14, 19, 36, 75, 78; lyric fragments and, 2–3, 197, 208; sharing stage with Bob Dylan, 123–24; speculative fiction and, 65
Garcia, Joe, 163
Gass, William, 173
Georgia Straight (periodical), 156
German Expressionism, 70
German Romanticism, 92–93, 102, 119, 139–40, 175, 197; "Black-Throated Wind" and, 149; "China Cat Sunflower" and, 152; fragment, 8, 32; James Joyce and, 165; literary absolute, 93, 109, 114; Rainer Maria Rilke and, 158–59, 183; "Saint of Circumstance" and, 28–29. See also *Athenaeum* (periodical)
Giant's Harp, The (Hunter), 157
Ginsberg, Allen: "Howl," 39–40, 43, 55, 57, 59; *Howl and Other Poems*, 43, 57; "Wichita Vortex Sutra," 60
Gissen-Stanley, Rhoney, 71, 198
Glass Lunch (Hunter), 157
Godchaux, Donna Jean, 119, 123
Godchaux, Keith, 119
Goethe, Johann Wolfgang von, 42, 118, 198; "Euphrosyne," 183; *Faust*, 31, 90–95; the *Faustbuch* (*Historia von D. Johann Faustus*) and, 88–89
"Goin' Down the Road Feeling Bad" (traditional) 144
"Golden Road (to Unlimited Devotion), The" (Grateful Dead), 55
Good as I Been to You (Dylan), 130
Gothic literature, 66–67, 73, 87, 93–95; American, 31, 87; Robert Burns and, 68–69; "Dire Wolf" and, 76, 80, 82–84; English, 66–67; "Friend of the Devil" and, 88–89; Sherlock Holmes and, 79; "Ramble on Rose" and, 75
Go to Heaven (Grateful Dead), 24, 109
Graham, Gerrit, 156
Grateful Dead (Grateful Dead), 73
Grateful Dead (albums): *American Beauty*, 30, 73–75, 85, 90, 107; *Anthem of the Sun*, 4, 49, 51, 73, 161; *Aoxomoxoa*, 15, 73–74, 104; *Dylan and the Dead*, 32, 122; *Europe '72*, 73; *Go to Heaven*, 24, 109; *Grateful Dead*, 73; *The History of the Grateful Dead, Vol. 1 (Bear's Choice)*, 73; *In the Dark*, 32, 131, 155; *Live/Dead*, 73; *Postcards from the Hanging*, 132; *Wake of the Flood*, 74, 137, 162, 167, 169–71; *Workingman's Dead*, 30, 73–75, 77, 82, 84–85, 200
Grateful Dead (songs): "Alabama Getaway," 119, 125, 133; "Alligator," 55, 204; "Althea," 31, 40, 97–98, 109–14, 116–20, 181; "Attics of My Life," 208; "Bertha," 74; "Bird Song," 86; "Black Muddy River," 31, 109, 133; "Black Peter," 72, 85, 176; "Black-Throated Wind," 87, 144–45, 147–49, 224n59; "Blues for Allah," 23; "Box of Rain," 86; "Brokedown Palace," 68, 86, 133; "Brown-Eyed Women," 40, 74, 87, 185; "Candyman," 86; "Can't Come Down," 39, 55; "Casey Jones," 72, 85, 202; "Cassidy," 51, 68, 74, 125; "China Cat Sunflower," 23, 152; "China Doll," 166; "Chinatown Shuffle," 74; "Comes a Time," 74–75; "Cosmic Charlie," 60; "Cream Puff War," 40, 143; "Cryptical Envelopment," 49–50, 53; "Dark Star," 3–4, 119, 151–52, 160, 319; "Deal," 87; "Dire Wolf," 31, 74, 76–84, 86, 88–91, 95–96, 125; "Doin' that Rag," 101; "Dupree's Diamond Blues," 14–20, 29, 73–74; "The Eleven," 61, 101; "Empty Pages," 74, 87; "Eyes of the World," 166; "The Faster We Go, the Rounder We Get," 50, 53, 62; "Fire on the Mountain," 51; "Franklin's Tower," 141–42; "Friend of the Devil," 31, 40, 85, 88–96, 132–33; "The Golden Road (to Unlimited Devotion)," 55; "Here Comes Sunshine," 51, 162–68; "He's Gone," 74, 86, 202; "Jack Straw," 40, 74, 87, 119–20; "Keep Your Day Job," 119; "Let Me Sing Your Blues Away," 166; "Looks Like Rain," 51, 87; "Loose Lucy," 166; "Loser," 87; "Lost Sailor," 24, 40, 141; "Mason's Children," 41, 74, 85, 101; "Mexicali Blues," 86–87; "Mindbender," 40; "Mississippi Half-Step Uptown Toodleloo," 96, 140, 166–68; "Mister Charlie," 60, 74; "Mountains of the Moon," 31, 74, 97, 101, 104–8, 193; "The Music Never Stopped," 141–42; "New Potato Caboose," 138; "New Speedway Boogie," 41, 85; "Operator," 87; "The Other One," 50–51, 53, 55, 60–62, 77, 140; "Picasso Moon," 160; "Playing in the Band," 61, 185; "Pride of Cucamonga," 160; "Ramble on Rose," 30, 69, 74–75, 77; "Reuben and Cérise," 209; "Rosemary," 31, 74, 98, 101–5, 107, 109, 173; "Row Jimmy," 166, 168; "Saint of Circumstance," 14, 24–29; "Silver Apples of the Moon," 160; "So Many Roads," 144; "Space," 220n72; "Standing on the Corner," 39; "Standing on the Moon," 23, 55; "The Stranger (Two Souls in Communion)," 74; "Stella Blue," 74, 133, 160, 166, 169; "Sugar Magnolia," 74; "Sugaree," 87; "Sunshine Daydream," 74; "Tennessee Jed," 74, 87; "Terrapin Station," 2, 13, 19, 118, 140, 171, 181; "That's It for the Other One," 49–50, 53, 62–63, 77, 140; "They Love Each Other," 166; "Till the Morning Comes," 90; "Touch of Grey," 119, 131, 155; "Truckin'," 55, 72, 86, 133–35, 144–45; "Unbroken Chain," 138; "Uncle John's Band," 61, 82; "Victim or the Crime," 160; "Weather Report Suite," 20, 51, 167; "Weather Report Suite, Part 2 (Let It Grow)," 14, 20, 22–24, 29, 160; "West L.A. Fadeaway," 55, 119, 133; "Wharf Rat," 19, 40, 74, 87, 145–48, 220n82; "What's Become of the Baby?," 151–52; "The Wheel," 74

Grateful Dead Movie, The (dir. Garcia and Gast), 38
Gray, Arthur: "Devil's Alphabet," 65
Gray, Thomas: "Elegy Written in a Country Churchyard," 174
Great Gatsby, The (Fitzgerald), 85
Grimm, Jacob and Wilhelm, 220n82
Grisman, David, 107
Grogan, Emmett, 85–86
Gulf War, 157
Guthrie, Woody, 144

Hall, Donald: *Without*, 178
Han-Shan, 104
Hart, Lenny, 86
Hart, Mickey, 5, 65, 86, 133, 170, 212, 213n5
Harvard University, 72
Hawthorne, Nathaniel, 87
Hedrick, Wally, 43–45
Hegel, G. W. F., 7, 12
Hells Angels Motorcycle Club, 44, 86
Hendrix, Jimi, 86
"Here Comes Sunshine" (Grateful Dead), 51, 162–68
"He's Gone" (Grateful Dead), 74, 86, 202
Hesiod, 22, 26, 92
Highway 61 Revisited (Dylan), 142
Hirsch, Edward, 174
History of the Grateful Dead, Vol. 1 (Bear's Choice), The (Grateful Dead), 73
Hitchcock, Robyn: "Chinese Bones," 221n2
Hoffman, John, 43
Hofmann, Albert, 71
Hölderlin, Friedrich, 7; "Brot und Wein," 183
"Holigomena" (Hunter), 181–85
Holmes, John Clellon, 43, 55
Homer: *Iliad*, 26, 115; *Odyssey*, 25, 27
horror fiction, 64–66, 69, 87
Housley, Dave: *If I Knew the Way, I Would Take You Home*, 204
Howell, George, 115
Human Be-In, 47
Hume, David, 7
Huncke, Herbert, 37–38, 55
Hundred Years War, 114
Hunter, Maureen, 198
Hunter, Norman, 161, 164
Hunter, Robert, 74–75, 87, 119, 158, 203; Altamont Speedway Free Festival, 85; *Amagamalin Street* (album), 157; *Box of Rain* (book), 157; Robert Burns and, 67; Neal Cassady and, 47; "Devil's Alphabet" (*see* Arthur Gray); *Duino Elegies* (*see* Rainer Maria Rilke); Bob Dylan and, 31, 121–22, 126–27, 130, 132, 134, 153; Faust, 88; *Flight of the Marie Helena* (album), 157; Frankenstein and, 70, 72; Jerry Garcia on, 2;

MK-Ultra and, 46; Modernism, 160–62; muses, 171, 182; the Nazgûl, 65, 218n4; publications, 156–57; Arthur Rimbaud and, 32, 138–39, 154; William Shakespeare, 111–15; songwriting, 13–15, 18–20, 31, 94, 118, 147, 197; *The Sonnets to Orpheus* (*see* Rainer Maria Rilke); *The Twilight Zone* and, 66; *Visions of the Dead*, 157. *See also* Grateful Dead (songs)
Hunter, Robert (poetry and prose): "An American Adventure," 192–95; "The Bride of Entropy," 192; *The Bride of Entropy*, 192, 195; "A Clatter Like Fine Mist," 187, 191; *Dog Moon*, 157; "The Door to the Sea," 181–85; *The Giant's Harp*, 157; *Glass Lunch*, 157; "Holigomena," 181–85; *Idiot's Delight*, 157, 175–77; *Infinity Minus Eleven*, 157, 181, 185; "Like a Basket," 180; *Night Cadre*, 157, 184, 186; "Number and None," 192; "The One with the Rabbit," 217–18n73; *Red Sky Fishing*, 157, 217–18n73; "Sentinel," 188–89, 191; *Sentinel* (book), 153, 157, 188, 192; *Sentinel* (album), 158; "Silver Marbles," 192; *The Silver Snarling Trumpet*, 217–18n73; *A Strange Music*, 157; "Trapping a Muse," 181, 184–85; "Warmup," 186–91. *See also Alleys of the Heart* (Petersen): foreword to (Hunter)
Hunter, Robert (songs): "Armageddon Rag," 218n4; "Blood on the Sheets," 218n4; "Boys in the Barroom," 184; "Raging," 218n4; "Raise Your Arms Clap Your Hands," 218n4; "Resurrection Rag," 218n4. *See also* "Duquesne Whistle" (Dylan); Grateful Dead (songs); "Silvio" (Dylan); "Ugliest Girl in the World" (Dylan)
Hypnocracy, 157

Idiot's Delight (Hunter), 157, 175–77
improvisation, 3, 36, 45, 49, 94, 119, 193
Infinity Minus Eleven (Hunter), 157, 181, 185
In the Dark (Grateful Dead), 32, 131, 155
"It's All Over Now, Baby Blue" (Dylan), 123–25, 127, 136, 143
"It's Alright, Ma (I'm Only Bleeding)" (Dylan), 151
"It Takes a Lot to Laugh, It Takes a Train to Cry" (Dylan), 123
Ives, Charles, 160

Jackson, Blair, 122, 199
"Jack Straw" (Grateful Dead), 40, 74, 87, 119–20
Jack the Ripper, 69
Jefferson Airplane, 162, 200
Jena, 7–12
Jericho, 69
Jerry Garcia Band, 65, 133
Job, 25
John Wesley Harding (Dylan), 75
Johnson, Robert: "Hellhound on My Trail," 89; "Little Red Rooster," 124

Jones, Daniel: *After Lucy*, 204
Jonson, Ben, 118
Joplin, Janis, 72, 86
Joyce, James, 32, 168–69, 184, 195, 198; father of, 163; *Finnegans Wake*, 161–62, 164–71; *A Portrait of the Artist as a Young Man*, 163; *Ulysses*, 162–64, 167
"Juniper Tree" (Brothers Grimm), 220n82

Kant, Immanuel, 6–9, 11–12
Keats, John, 217–18n73
"Keep Your Day Job" (Grateful Dead), 119
Kerouac, Jack, 37–38, 41, 50, 58, 198; Neal Cassady and, 41–42, 45; *The Dharma Bums*, 43; Jerry Garcia and, 44–45, 48; Robert Hunter and, 134; *On the Road*, 43, 52–53; prose style of, 42, 55; *Visions of Cody*, 55
Kesey, Ken, 44–47, 72, 198–99; *The Further Inquiry*, 193; *Sometimes a Great Notion*, 46
King, Stephen: "My Pretty Pony," 65
Klee, Paul, 160
Kreutzmann, Bill, 133, 156, 160, 212
Kyger, Joanne, 48

Lacoue-Labarthe, Phillippe, 9–10, 12, 28, 41, 45, 109; the fragment, 6, 8, 11, 37–38, 49; subject, 7, 24
"Lady of Carlisle, The" (traditional), 118
Lagin, Ned, 123
Lamantia, Philip, 43
Language Poetry, 196
Leary, Timothy, 72
Lesh, Phil, 3, 46–47, 212, 213n5, 219n35, 220n72; American identify of Grateful Dead, 38; Bob Dylan, 125, 133; *Gormenghast*, 64–65; group mind, 4, 73; James Joyce, 160–62
"Let Me Sing Your Blues Away" (Grateful Dead), 166
Levertov, Denise, 48
Lieberman, Fredric, 170
Life and Death of Jack Straw, The (Peele?), 120
"Like a Basket" (Hunter), 180
Live/Dead (Grateful Dead), 73
Lomax, Alan, 15
Longfellow, Henry Wadsworth, 174
"Looks Like Rain" (Grateful Dead), 51, 87
"Loose Lucy" (Grateful Dead), 166
"Loser" (Grateful Dead), 87
"Lost Sailor" (Grateful Dead), 24, 40, 141
Louis, Adrian C.: "The Boy Distinctly Remembers," 203
Lovecraft, H. P., 79

Machen, Arthur, 79
Mann, Herbie, 200
Mann, Thomas, 160

Margaret of Anjou, 114
Marlowe, Christopher: *The Tragical History of Dr. Faustus*, 88
Martin, George R. R.: *The Armageddon Rag*, 65; *A Song of Ice and Fire*, 204; *Twilight Zone* and, 66
"Mason's Children" (Grateful Dead), 41, 74, 85, 101
Matrix, 15
McClure, Michael, 43, 47, 57–58, 160
McGhee, Brownie, 14
McIntire, Jon, 48
McKernan, Ron ("Pigpen"), 74, 86, 127, 170–71, 204
Meier, Brigid, 198
Melville, Herman, 42, 87
Merrill, James, 196, 204; *The Changing Light at Sandover*, 203; "Self-Portrait in Tyvek™ Windbreaker," 203
Merry Pranksters, 44–48, 52, 199
"Mexicali Blues" (Grateful Dead), 86–87
Millbrook, 72
Milton, John, 56, 174
"Mindbender" (Grateful Dead), 40
Miracle at Marsh Chapel, 72
"Mississippi Half-Step Uptown Toodleloo" (Grateful Dead), 96, 140, 166–68
Mississippi River, 166–67
"Mister Charlie" (Grateful Dead), 60, 74
MK-Ultra, 46, 72
Modernism, 23, 54, 174, 177–78, 180, 195; James Joyce and, 161–62; Modernist fragment, 159; musical compositions, 160; Rainer Maria Rilke and, 32, 158–59, 171, 196
Monk, Peter (Peter Richard Zimels), 156
Monroe, Bill, 107
Monterey Folk Music Festival, 126
Moore, Marianne, 160
Moore, Thomas, 109
"Mountains of the Moon" (Grateful Dead), 31, 74, 97, 101, 104–8, 193
"Mr. Tambourine Man" (Dylan), 140–41
"Music Never Stopped, The" (Grateful Dead), 141–42
Mydland, Brent, 119, 130–31, 155, 206
Myers, Mitch: *The Boy Who Cried Freebird*, 204

Nancy, Jean-Luc, 5, 14, 19, 30, 37, 49, 70, 119; absolute, 119, 187; Johann Gottlieb Fichte and, 7, 67; fragment as productive, 13, 16, 19, 24, 29, 38, 41, 45, 52, 63, 69, 197; freedom and playfulness, 14, 92, 122; German Romantics and, 8, 10–12, 28, 92, 109, 159; Immanuel Kant and, 6–9, 12
Nelson, David, 161
"New Potato Caboose" (Grateful Dead), 138
"New Speedway Boogie" (Grateful Dead), 41, 85
Nietzsche, Friedrich, 9; *The Gay Science*, 170

Night Cadre (Hunter), 157, 184, 186
Novalis (Georg Philipp Friedrich Freiherr von Hardenberg), 7, 12
"Number and None" (Hunter), 192

Oh Mercy (Dylan), 130
Olson, Charles, 48, 59, 60
"One with the Rabbit, The" (Hunter), 217–18n73
"Operator" (Grateful Dead), 87
Orbison, Roy, 125
"Other One, The" (Grateful Dead), 50–51, 53, 55, 60–62, 77, 140
Ovid, 31; *Metamorphoses*, 113, 116

Pacific Recording, 15
Peake, Mervyn, 64–65
"Peggy-O" (Grateful Dead), 76–77, 87, 128
Pentangle, 75
Perry, Paul, *On the Bus*, 198
Peter, Paul, and Mary, 14
Peter Pan, 52
Petersen, Robert M., 139, 156, 198; *Alleys of the Heart*, 138, 175
Petrarch, 25
Petty, Tom. *See* Tom Petty and the Heartbreakers
Philosophy of Modern Song, The (Dylan), 133–35
Picasso, Pablo, 160; *La Famille des Saltimbanques*, 190
"Picasso Moon" (Grateful Dead), 160
Pigpen. *See* McKernan, Ron ("Pigpen")
Plantagenet, Richard, 114
Plath, Sylvia: "Daddy," 178
"Playing in the Band" (Grateful Dead), 61, 185
Plotinus: *Enneads*, 28
Poe, Edgar Allan, 87; "Eldorado," 104; *The Narrative of Arthur Gordon Pym*, 25; "The Raven," 220n72
politics, 11, 38–39, 94, 139, 149, 158; Grateful Dead's resistance to, 40–41; Haight-Ashbury, 201, 205; William Shakespeare, 104, 114; Hunter S. Thompson and, 200
popularity, 31, 119, 131, 156
"Positively 4th Street" (Dylan), 40, 143
Postcards from the Hanging (Grateful Dead), 132
Pound, Ezra, 160; *The Cantos*, 180
"Pretty Peggy-O" (Dylan), 76
"Pride of Cucamonga" (Grateful Dead), 160
Proust, Marcel, 160
Pseudo-Longinus, 67

"Queen Jane Approximately" (Dylan), 136, 151

Radcliffe, Ann, 66
"Raging" (Hunter), 218n4
"Rain," 51
Rainey, Ma, 15

"Rainy Day Women #12 & 35" (Dylan), 125
"Raise Your Arms Clap Your Hands" (Hunter), 218n4
"Ramble on Rose" (Grateful Dead), 30, 69, 74–75, 77
Ram Dass (Richard Alpert), 72
Red Sky Fishing (Hunter), 157, 217–18n73
"Resurrection Rag" (Hunter), 218n4
"Reuben and Cérise" (Grateful Dead), 209
Rexroth, Kenneth, 43–44
Rifkin, Danny, 205
Rilke, Rainer Maria, 32, 48, 134, 159, 188, 191–92, 194, 198; "Archaic Torso of Apollo," 172, 193; "The Bowl of Roses," 172–73; death of, 172; Duino Castle, 171, 180; *Duino Elegies*, 171, 178, 182–83, 186–90; elegiac poetry, 174, 177, 179; fragmentation, 180–81, 184; Robert Hunter's translations of, 157–58; inspiration, 185, 193; Modernism and, 195–96; *The Notebooks of Malte Laurids Brigge*, 158–59; "The Panther," 172; *The Sonnets to Orpheus*, 157–58, 171–72
Rimbaud, Arthur, 53, 122, 143, 150–52, 175, 197–98; "After the Flood," 137; disorientation, 139, 141, 149; "The Drunken Boat," 140, 142, 145, 150; Bob Dylan and, 32, 153; Robert Hunter and, 138, 154; *A Season in Hell*, 176
Rio Grande, 140, 166–67
River Liffey, 165–67
Robbins, Marty: "El Paso," 23
Romanticism, 67, 82, 142, 158, 181, 183; the fragment and, 30, 32, 37–38, 45, 54, 69, 92, 100, 104, 135, 138–39, 149, 165, 184, 191, 207; German philosophy and, 7–12, 28–29, 32, 92–93, 109, 114, 119, 139–40, 149, 152, 159, 165, 175, 197
"Rosemary" (Grateful Dead), 31, 74, 98, 101–5, 107, 109, 173
"Row Jimmy" (Grateful Dead), 166, 168
Russell's paradox, 186

"Saint of Circumstance" (Grateful Dead), 14, 24–29
Sandoz, 71
San Francisco Phoenix (periodical), 156
San Francisco Poetry Renaissance, 43–44
San Mateo College Jazz Band, 161
Saunders, Merl, 65, 123
Schelling, Friedrich Wilhelm Joseph von, 7
Schiller, Friedrich von, 7; "Der Spaziergang," 183
Schlegel, August Wilhelm von, 7
Schlegel, Caroline, 7
Schlegel, Dorothea von, 7
Schlegel, Karl Wilhelm Friedrich von, 7, 9–10; *On the Study of Greek Poetry*, 11
Schleiermacher, Friedrich, 7
science fiction, 64–65, 213–4n9
Scully, Rock, 65
"Sentinel" (Hunter), 188–89, 191

Sentinel (Hunter): book, 153, 157, 188, 192; album, 158
Shakespeare, William, 25, 68, 97, 102, 107, 119–20, 198; *As You Like It*, 110; *Coriolanus*, 115; *Cymbeline*, 115; *Hamlet*, 31, 99–103, 110–12, 116–18; *2 Henry IV*, 113; *2 Henry VI*, 113–4, 120; *King John*, 101; *King Lear*, 98, 101, 104–6, 108, 110, 117; *Much Ado about Nothing*, 100; Ovid and, 31; *Pericles*, 101; *The Rape of Lucrece*, 116; *Richard III*, 109; *Romeo and Juliet*, 25, 99–101, 221n2; *The Tempest*, 101; *Titus Andronicus*, 115; *Troilus and Cressida*, 115; *Twelfth Night*, 110, 115; *Winter's Tale*, 101
Shearer, Harry, 205
"She Belongs to Me" (Dylan), 99, 123, 127
Shelley, Mary, 30, 69, 75, 198; *Frankenstein*, 31, 69, 71–73, 78, 80–83, 94–95, 197
Shelley, Percy Bysshe, 174
Sidney, Sir Philip, 25
"Silver Apples of the Moon" (Grateful Dead), 160
"Silver Marbles" (Hunter), 192
Silver Snarling Trumpet, The (Hunter), 217–18n73
"Silvio" (Dylan), 132
Six Gallery, 43, 59
"Smokestack Lightning" (Grateful Dead), 68
Snyder, Gary, 20, 43, 47, 57
"So Many Roads" (Grateful Dead), 144
Song of Solomon, 25
Sonnets to Orpheus, The. See Rainer Maria Rilke
"Space" (Grateful Dead), 220n72
Spicer, Jack, 43, 48
Spike (periodical), 157
Stagger Lee: example of folk motif, 15–16
"Standing on the Corner" (Grateful Dead), 39
"Standing on the Moon" (Grateful Dead), 23, 55
Stanford University, 46
Stanley, Augustus Owsley, III ("Bear"), 71–72, 86
Steele, Allen: *Orbital Decay*, 204
"Stella Blue" (Grateful Dead), 74, 133, 160, 166, 169
Strange Music, A (Hunter), 157
"Stranger (Two Souls in Communion), The" (Grateful Dead), 74
Straw, Jack, 120
"Stuck Inside of Mobile with the Memphis Blues Again" (Dylan), 98
Sturgeon, Theodore, 213–4n9; *More than Human*, 4, 65–66, 73
"Sugar Magnolia" (Grateful Dead), 74
"Sugaree" (Grateful Dead), 87
Sunday, Billy (William Ashley Sunday), 69
"Sunshine Daydream" (Grateful Dead), 74
Swanson, Sue, 201
Swinburne, Algernon Charles, 175

Tate-LaBianca murders, 77
Tempest (Dylan), 132
Tennyson, Alfred, 104, 198; *In Memoriam A. H. H.*, 174; "The Lady of Shalott," 103, 173
"Terrapin Station" (Grateful Dead), 2, 13, 19, 118, 140, 171, 181
"Tennessee Jed" (Grateful Dead), 74, 87
"That's It for the Other One" (Grateful Dead), 49–50, 53, 62–63, 77, 140
"They Love Each Other" (Grateful Dead), 166
Thomas, Dylan, 36
Thompson, Hunter S., 44, 85, 200–1, 203; *Fear and Loathing on the Campaign Trail '72*, 33
Thurn und Taxis, Marie von, 171
"Till the Morning Comes" (Grateful Dead), 90
Time Out of Mind (Dylan), 130
Together Through Life (Dylan), 132
Tom Petty and the Heartbreakers, 31, 124, 130
"Touch of Grey" (Grateful Dead), 119, 131, 155
transcendence: Robert Hunter and, 195; Rainer Maria Rilke's struggles with, 178–79, 185, 190, 192
"Trapping a Muse" (Hunter), 181, 184–85
Traveling Wilburys, 125
Treaty of Tours, 114
Trips Festival, 47
Trist, Alan, 156, 198
"Truckin'" (Grateful Dead), 55, 72, 86, 133–35, 144–45
Truman, Timothy, 157
Twain, Mark (Samuel Langhorne Clemens), 42, 87
Twilight Zone, The (television series), 65–66
"Two Sisters, The" (traditional), 104, 108

"Ugliest Girl in the World" (Dylan), 132
"Unbroken Chain" (Grateful Dead), 138
"Uncle John's Band" (Grateful Dead), 61, 82
Under a Red Sky (Dylan), 130
University of California, Berkeley, 40, 124

Vancouver Poetry Conference, 48
Van Ronk, Dave, 14
Vega, Suzanne, 221n2
"Victim or the Crime" (Grateful Dead), 160
Virgil (Publius Vergilius Maro): *Aeneid*, 26; *Georgics*, 20–22
"Visions of Johanna" (Dylan) 144–45, 148
Visions of the Dead (Hunter), 157
Vonnegut, Kurt, 65, 198, 213–14n9

Wake of the Flood (Grateful Dead), 74, 137, 162, 167, 169–71
Walker, Bill, 4–5, 73
Wallace, David Foster: *Infinite Jest*, 33, 203
Walpole, Horace: *The Castle of Otranto*, 66
"Warmup" (Hunter), 186–91
War of the Roses, 114

Wasserman, Rob, 156
Watson, Doc, 135
"Weather Report Suite" (Grateful Dead), 20, 51, 167
"Weather Report Suite, Part 2 (Let It Grow)" (Grateful Dead), 14, 20, 22–24, 29, 160
Weir, Bob, 41, 62, 64, 71, 77, 204, 224n59; *Ace*, 74; John Perry Barlow and, 87; Neal Cassady and, 47–49, 51–52; Bob Dylan and, 127–28, 130; "Only a River," 133
Welch, Lew, 48, 55, 57; *On Out*, 195
"West L.A. Fadeaway" (Grateful Dead), 55, 119, 133
Whale, James, 70
Whalen, Philip, 43, 48
"Wharf Rat" (Grateful Dead), 19, 40, 74, 87, 145–48, 220n82
"What's Become of the Baby?" (Grateful Dead), 151–52
"Wheel, The" (Grateful Dead), 74
"When I Paint My Masterpiece" (Dylan), 125, 128, 136
Whitman, Walt, 54, 217–18n73; Ginsberg and, 59–62, 198; "Song of Myself," 58; "When Lilacs Last in the Dooryard Bloom'd," 175

Wildwood Boys, 15, 126
Williams, William Carlos, 198; Beat poets and, 55, 57–59, 62, 160; "For Elsie," 54; *Paterson*, 56; "The Red Wheelbarrow," 56
Willie, The (periodical), 156
Winthrop, John, 193
Wittgenstein, Ludwig, 186
Wolfe, Tom: *The Electric Kool-Aid Acid Test*, 33, 46, 199–200
Wolfman, the, 70
Wolfman Jack (Robert Weston Smith), 69
Workingman's Dead (Grateful Dead), 30, 73–75, 77, 82, 84–85, 200
World Gone Wrong (Dylan), 130

Yeats, W. B.: "The Song of Wandering Aengus," 160
Young, Neil, 123
"You're Gonna Make Me Lonesome When You Go" (Dylan), 136
"You Win Again," 87

Zodiac killer, 77–78, 83, 85–86

www.ingramcontent.com/pod-product-compliance
Lightning Source LLC
Chambersburg PA
CBHW021853230426
43671CB00006B/376